Punishment and Control in Historical Perspective

Also by Helen Johnston

PRISON READINGS
A Critical Introduction to Prison and Imprisonment (*co-edited*)

Punishment and Control in Historical Perspective

Edited By

Helen Johnston
University of Hull, UK

First published 2008 by
PALGRAVE MACMILLAN
Houndmills, Basingstoke, Hampshire RG21 6XS and
175 Fifth Avenue, New York, N.Y. 10010
Companies and representatives throughout the world

PALGRAVE MACMILLAN is the global academic imprint of the Palgrave
Macmillan division of St. Martin's Press, LLC and of Palgrave Macmillan Ltd.
Macmillan® is a registered trademark in the United States, United Kingdom
and other countries. Palgrave is a registered trademark in the European
Union and other countries.

ISBN-13: 978-0-230-54933-3   hardback
ISBN-10: 0-230-54933-0   hardback

This book is printed on paper suitable for recycling and made from fully
managed and sustained forest sources. Logging, pulping and manufacturing
processes are expected to conform to the environmental regulations of the
country of origin.

A catalogue record for this book is available from the British Library.

A catalogue record for this book is available from the Library of Congress.

10   9   8   7   6   5   4   3   2   1
17   16   15   14   13   12   11   10   09   08

Printed and bound in Great Britain by
CPI Antony Rowe, Chippenham and Eastbourne

Contents

Acknowledgements

A huge debt of thanks must go to all of the contributors to this collection, for their energy, enthusiasm, and commitment during this project. I would like to thank John Locker and Bronwyn Morrison for sharing in the initial idea for this collection and Barry Godfrey and Joe Sim for their enthusiasm for historical criminology which has influenced my own interest and development. I would like to thank Gerry Johnstone and Amanda Capern for their helpful comments on the original proposal, and the anonymous reviewers for comments on the proposal and manuscript. I would especially like to thank Yvonne Jewkes and Peter Young for their advice, encouragement and support. Also thanks to Tony Ward, Simon Green, Louise Sturgeon-Adams, and colleagues at the University of Hull. Finally, thanks to Christian for everything else.

Helen Johnston
University of Hull

List of Abbreviations

DPP	Director of Public Prosecutions
HO	Home Office Papers
NA	National Archives, Kew, London
PP	Parliamentary Papers
TNAPSS	Transactions of the National Association for the Promotion of Social Science

Notes on the Contributors

Sarah Anderson completed her PhD in Criminology at Victoria University of Wellington in 2006 and is a policy advisor at the Department of Corrections, New Zealand. Her research interests include the sociology and history of punishment and penal systems, and the relationship between penal governance and popular culture.

Anette Ballinger is Lecturer in Criminology at Keele University, UK. Her research interests include gender and capital punishment in the twentieth century. She is the author of the award-winning book *Dead Woman Walking: Executed Women in England & Wales 1900–1955* (Ashgate: 2000) (Hart Socio-Legal Prize 2001), and has written several book-chapters and journal articles on the subject of gender and punishment in modern history including: 'The Guilt of the Innocent and the Innocence of the Guilty: The Cases of Marie Fahmy and Ruth Ellis' in Myers, A. & Wight, S. (eds) (1996) *No Angels*, London: Pandora; 'Researching and Redefining State Crime: Feminism and the Capital Punishment of Women' in Tombs, S. & Whyte, D. (eds) (2003) *Researching the Crimes of the Powerful: Scrutinising States and Corporations*, New York: Peter Lang Publishing, and 'The Worse of Two Evils? Double Executions and Gender in the 20th Century' in Barton, A., Corteen, K., Scott, D. & Whyte, D. (eds) (2006) *The Criminological Imagination: Readings in Critical Criminologies*, Cullompton: Willan. She is currently working on a book entitled *Capitalising on Punishment: State Power, Gender and Women Who Kill*, to be published by Ashgate, October 2009.

Alyson Brown is Reader in History at Edge Hill University, UK. She has conducted extensive research into the history of crime and punishment and especially on penal history. Her book, *English Society and the Prison* (2003) was well received and widely reviewed. She has also published articles and chapters on this subject, including; 'A History of Experience: Exploring Prisoners' Accounts of Incarceration' in Emsley, C. (ed.) (2005) *The Persistent Prison*, and an article on the 1932 Dartmoor Prison riot in the *British Journal of Criminology* (2007). She has also published a co-authored book with David Barrett (2002) *Knowledge of Evil: Child prostitution and child sexual abuse in twentieth century England*, Cullompton: Willan. Recently her research was used to

name Wil Alsop's 'Creative Prison', an exhibition of which was held at
Winson Green Prison, Birmingham.

Jamie Bennett is a prison manager. He has previously held posts
including Deputy Governor of HMP Whitemoor, a high security
prison, and HMP Gartree, which houses life sentence prisoners. He has
written on a range of criminal justice issues for publications including:
*The Prison Service Journal, Criminal Justice Matters, Journal of Crime,
Conflict & the Media, The Howard Journal* and *Crime, Media, Culture*. He
has also contributed chapters to books including: *Captured by the Media*
edited by Paul Mason (Willan, 2006) and *Handbook on Prisons* edited by
Yvonne Jewkes (Willan, 2007). He is editor of the *Prison Service Journal*
and has edited two books *Understanding Prison Staff* (with Ben Crewe &
Azrini Wahidin) and *Dictionary of Prisons & Punishment* (with Yvonne
Jewkes), both published by Willan in 2008. He is currently undertaking
a PhD with Edinburgh University, researching the working lives of
prison managers.

Michael Fiddler is Lecturer in Criminology at the University of
Greenwich, UK. He completed a doctoral thesis at Keele University in
2006 entitled '*The penal palimpsest: an exploration of prison spatiality*'.
The fieldwork for the PhD was partially conducted in Sing Sing penitentiary, New York. His present research interests include the intersections
of film, architecture and memory in the construction of understandings
of the prison. Recent publications include: 'Panopticon' in Jewkes, Y. &
Bennett, J. (eds) *Dictionary of Prisons and Punishment* (Willan, 2008);
'Projecting the prison: the depiction of the uncanny in The Shawshank
Redemption', *Crime Media Culture*, 3 (2): 192–206; 'Carandiru –
"no home for the truth"', *Prison Service Journal*, 161: 56–8.

Helen Johnston is Lecturer in Criminology at the University of Hull,
UK. She completed her doctoral thesis on the transformations of local
imprisonment in the nineteenth century, at Keele University in 2004.
Publications include: Jewkes, Y. and Johnston, H. (2006) (eds) *Prison
Readings: A critical introduction to prisons and imprisonment*, Cullompton:
Willan; Jewkes, Y. and Johnston, H. (2007) 'The Evolution of Prison
Architecture' in Y. Jewkes (ed.) *Handbook on Prisons*, Cullompton:
Willan; Johnston, H. (2006) '"Buried Alive": Representations of the
Separate System in Victorian England' in P. Mason (ed.) *Captured by the
Media: Prison discourse in popular culture*, Cullompton: Willan.

John P. Locker completed a doctoral thesis at Keele University in 2004 entitled, *'This most pernicious species of crime': embezzlement in its public and private dimensions, c.1850–1930*. Between 2001 and 2005, he worked as a lecturer in Criminology at Keele University. He currently lives in New Zealand, and is a senior researcher with New Zealand Police. Present research interests include policing, and modern and historical aspects of white-collar and workplace crime, on which he has previously published: John P. Locker (2005) 'Quiet thieves, quiet punishment': private responses to the 'respectable' offender, c.1850–1930', *Crime, History & Societies*, 9,1 (winner of the 2004 Herman Diederiks Prize); John P. Locker & Barry Godfrey (2006) 'Ontological Boundaries and Temporal Watersheds in the Development of White-Collar Crime', *British Journal of Criminology*, 46, 6.

Bronwyn Morrison is a Senior Research Advisor for the Research, Evaluation and Modelling Unit at the Ministry of Justice, New Zealand. She completed a PhD in criminology at Keele University in 2005. In addition to her doctoral research on the social and state control of female inebriety, she has previously undertaken research on crime and disorder at tourist destinations, residential burglary, and comparative crime history. Her publications include: 'Practical and philosophical dilemmas in cross-cultural research: the future of comparative crime history', in Godfrey, B., Emsley, C. & Dunstall, G. (eds) (2002) *Comparative Histories of Crime*, and, more recently, *The Conviction and Sentencing of Offenders in New Zealand: 1997 to 2006* (with Soboleva and Chong). At present she is involved in research exploring the operation of discretion in the criminal justice system.

John Pratt is Professor of Criminology at Victoria University of Wellington, New Zealand. John Pratt's books are: *Punishment in a Perfect Society* (Victoria University Press 1992), *Governing the Dangerous* (1997, Federation Press, Sydney), *Punishment and Civilization* (2002, Sage), translated into Spanish in 2006 as *Castigo y Civilizacion* (Editorial Gedisa, Barcelona); *Penal Populism* (2006: Routledge). He has edited or co-edited three books, *Dangerous Offenders* (2000, Routledge), *Crime, Truth and Justice* (2004: Willan), *The New Punitiveness* (2005: Willan). He has also published 70 articles in refereed journals and 35 book chapters. He is on the International Advisory Board of four journals including the British Journal of Criminology. He was Editor of the Australian and New Zealand Journal of Criminology 1997–2005.

Heather Shore is Senior Lecturer in Social and Cultural History at Leeds Metropolitan University, UK. Her main interests are in the history of crime and poverty between the eighteenth and early twentieth centuries. She has published widely on juvenile crime in the nineteenth century. Her well-received monograph, *Artful Dodgers: Youth and Crime in Early Nineteenth Century London*, was published in 1999. She has co-edited two books, with Pamela Cox, *Becoming Delinquent: European Youth, 1660–1960* (Ashgate, 2002), and with Tim Hitchcock, *The Streets of London: From the Great Fire to the Great Stink* (Rivers Oram Press, 2003). She is currently writing a social and cultural history of the underworld from the early eighteenth century to be published by Continuum.

Tony Ward is Reader in Law at the University of Hull, UK. He is co-author with Penny Green of *State Crime: Governments, Violence and Corruption* (London: Pluto Press, 2004) and with Gerry Johnstone of *Law and Crime* (London: Sage, forthcoming), a critical introduction to criminal law and evidence. Apart from state crime, his research interests (and his PhD) centre on the legal issues associated with expert and particularly psychiatric evidence from the nineteenth century to the present. He has published many articles and book chapters on those subjects.

Abigail Wills completed her PhD, entitled 'Juvenile delinquency, residential institutions and the permissive shift, England 1950–1970', at Cambridge University in 2005. She is now a postdoctoral Career Development Fellow in History at Brasenose College, Oxford, UK. Her publications include: 'Delinquency, masculinity and citizenship' *Past and Present*, 187, (2005), and 'Historical myth-making in juvenile justice policy' *History and Policy* (2007). Her current research project explores the history of childhood nutrition and health visiting between 1930 and 1970, continuing her interest in questions of professional expertise, subjectivity, and social policy in twentieth century Britain.

Introduction: Histories of Punishment and Control

Helen Johnston

Recent commentators, in a book series examining the interdisciplinary nature of criminology, and specifically looking at 'history' and 'crime', have discussed the development of historical approaches in criminology and interest in crime history and what might be interpreted as convergence between academic disciplines in this area in recent years (Godfrey *et al.*, 2008). This field has been noted as a particularly buoyant area, and crime history and criminology have 'intertwined' recently, 'come to terms with each other and are now creating their own history of interaction' (Godfrey *et al.*, 2008: 19). Whilst the contributors to this collection have not been questioned as to how they perceive themselves within this debate, it is hoped that this collection also goes some way towards elaborating and demonstrating this 'convergence'. This collection brings together new and established scholars to offer research which takes forward, challenges or develops the existing theoretical perspectives, as well as exploring new territory in historical research, on punishment and social control. This collection is concerned with the delivery of punishment, the experiences of various forms of incarceration, and punishment and control within institutional settings and in wider society between the early nineteenth and the mid twentieth century. Research on punishment and social control has made a significant contribution to criminology and history, and more generally to the social sciences in last 20 to 30 years. They have contributed to our understanding of the emergence of the prison in the nineteenth century, changing penal philosophies and practices, and provided us with a historical understanding of contemporary penal issues. Writers in this field have given us a theoretical framework for understanding punishment, discipline, social control, penal policy and the law not only historically, but also in contemporary Western society. This collection is intended to be read by those in the fields of criminology, sociology and history and to push forward our appreciation of the historical study of punishment and social control since the contributions of theorists in the 1970s and 1980s.

This collection brings together a group of scholars who share a mutual interest in the dynamics of social control, power and punishment in the historical perspective. Predominantly these chapters are case studies of particular aspects of punishment, penal policy, criminal law, and discourses of offenders and subsequently, how they were perceived and treated by the criminal justice system and the public, in the nineteenth and twentieth centuries. The chapters within this collection offer a critical analysis of different types of institutions of punishment and social control; specifically, the local prison, convict prisons, inebriate reformatories, and the relationship between different offenders, the law and the criminal justice system, and experiences of confinement and forms of resistance in different custodial settings. Each chapter offers a detailed methodological case study approach, utilising newspapers, archival sources, parliamentary, official and personal record. The remainder of this chapter will provide an overview of the orthodox and revisionist accounts on prison, punishment and social control and framework for contextualising the following chapter contributions.

Theoretical perspectives on punishment and social control

Research on the history of punishment, imprisonment and social control has been dominated in recent decades by the theoretical work put forward by a number of scholars who were writing in the 1970s and 1980s. These works set out to challenge Whig or orthodox traditional historical accounts which saw the birth of the prison in Western society and changes in punishment, such as the progressive movement away from public and capital punishment, as the march onwards towards a more civilised society. This Whig history, often championed the achievements of individual reformers in the development of such practices, and often through a lens of 'humanitarianism' and benevolence, saw these changes as the movement away from barbaric methods of punishment which triumphed in the orderly institutional focus of punishment in the nineteenth century. Examples of such accounts of the decline in public execution and the rise of the prison in England, include; Cooper (1974); Webbs (1963); Whiting (1975); Stockdale (1977); and Radzinowicz and Hood (1990).

Revisionist scholars, such as Foucault (1977); Ignatieff (1978); Rothman (1971); Melossi and Pavarini (1981); Cohen and Scull (1983) have constructed a competing analysis of changes in punishment, the birth of the prison and social control mechanisms. Broadly these authors share some similarities in their approaches; they argue that the emergence of the modern prison should be seen alongside the development of other institutions which shared similar disciplinary techniques (school, factory, asylum, hospital, for example). Collectively, these authors argue that the prison emerged in a particular relationship with society and developed to control and regulate populations. Separately, they offered more critical and challenging accounts which centred on explanations about power and power relations, economic and philanthropic motives of 'reformers', the interests of the governing class and the operation of state power.

Foucault's influential account, *Discipline and Punish* (1977) opens by contrasting the horrific public torture, mutilation, and execution of regicide Damiens in 1757, with the minutely regulated and ordered timetable for young offenders at Mettray reformatory in 1838. For Foucault, these two contrasting forms of punishment demonstrate two events that occurred during this period; first, the decline in the infliction of, and public displays of torturous punishment and second, the emergence of the prison. For Foucault, there is a shift in the target of punishment, from the body to the mind or the 'soul' of the offender and in the objective of punishment, away from avenging the crime, towards altering the offender. In order to understand or know the criminal, Foucault demonstrates how experts from fields such as psychiatry, criminology and social work are introduced into the criminal justice system to gain knowledge about the offender's character and background and ultimately to try to reform the individual. So, for Foucault, this change is not necessarily a reduction in the severity of punishment, seen in the Whig accounts but a shift in the means and objective of punishment.

Foucault argues that the decline in public punishment did not occur because of a new respect for the individual but rather 'as a tendency towards a more finely tuned justice, towards a close mapping of the social body' (Foucault, 1977: 78). The legal reformers wanted 'not to punish less, but to punish better, to punish with an attenuated severity perhaps, but in order to punish with more universality and necessity; to insert the power to punish deeply into the social body' (Foucault, 1977: 82).

Foucault explains the rise of the prison as the predominant form of punishment in terms of its use of disciplinary techniques. The disciplinary techniques used in the prison were also used by other institutions such as the school, the army, the hospital, the asylum, whose aim was the training of individuals, the formation of 'docile and obedient bodies'. This range of institutions, which surveyed and trained individuals, Foucault located on a 'carceral continuum', as the boundaries between the institutions often blurred. The design, which for Foucault provided the most efficient system of regulation and surveillance, was Jeremy Bentham's Panopticon. In the Panopticon, guards in the central control tower could continuously survey the prison, narrow viewpoints made it impossible for prisoners to see the guard and to know when they were actually being watched (also see Concluding Remarks).

Building on the earlier Marxist interpretation of Rusche and Kirchheimer (1939), that the rise of the prison was linked to the rise of capitalist mode of production, Melossi and Pavarini's, *The Prison and the Factory* (1981), trace the early origins of the houses of correction in the sixteenth century Europe and the use of compulsory labour as a means of teaching inmates 'the discipline of production' (1981: 21). These houses of correction deterred the free labourer through severe conditions, which forced the labourer to accept the conditions of work and life outside, as preferable to that of the prison or the workhouse. Building on these historical origins of the use of labour to instil discipline and obedience, Melossi and Pavarini argue that the 'real dimensions of the penitentiary invention' are seen in the 'prison as a machine' from the early nineteenth century (1981: 144). In periods of high unemployment the conditions in prisons are made more severe and they 'revert to being places for the destruction of the workforce' (*ibid.*). However, when the economy is experiencing low unemployment and rising wages, the prison puts prisoners to useful labour in order to recycle them into the free market, thus the prison 'is like a factory, producing proletarians' (1981: 145). So, for Melossi and Pavarini, the prison is inextricably linked to the capitalist mode of production and similarly, to Foucault, to other social institutions such as the school, workhouse, factory, in disciplining the workforce for the benefit of capitalist production.

David Rothman and Michael Ignatieff's accounts are both concerned with the motives and ideology of the reformers, philanthropy and the consequences of 'reform'. Rothman argues in, *The Discovery of the Asylum*, that we need to be cautious when examining what appears to be progressive change and instead be 'wary about taking reform programs at face value; arrangements designed for the best of motives may have disastrous results. But the difficult problem is to review these events without falling into a deep cynicism' (1971: 295). Platt's earlier account of the juvenile justice system in the US, *The Child Savers* (1969), takes a similar approach. Ignatieff's *A Just Measure of Pain* (1978) also sees a more complicated relationship between the reformers and class interests in the ideological origins of the penitentiary. Reformers had genuine religious and philanthropic views, and this succeeded because it was not just a response to crime, but to social crises at the time and a way to re-establish order (1978: 210). Similarly, to other revisionist accounts, it was no accident that prisons, asylums, work-houses, and schools all looked alike or 'that their charges marched to the same disciplinary cadence' (1978: 215).

David Garland's, *Punishment and Welfare* (1985) argues instead that the period in which the modern 'penal-welfare' complex develops is the end of the nineteenth century, rather than the late eighteenth and early nineteenth century identified by revisionist accounts. He argues that during the period between 1895 and 1914, a more rehabilitative or welfare approach emerges, which is strongly influenced by positivist thought. It is during this period, a number of different offenders are removed from the prison (juveniles, mentally ill, recidivists, inebriates) and special policies are created to deal with these offenders who are seen as needing treatment to 'cure' their behaviour or need to be dealt with differently, for example, the establishment of a separate juvenile justice system and alternatives to custody such as probation and after-care services. Martin Wiener's *Reconstructing the Criminal* (1990) takes a more cultural approach to understanding the development of criminal justice and penal policy in the Victorian and Edwardian period.

The influential work of Norbert Elias, *The Civilizing Process* (1978), has also shaped research in this field, in particularly, Spierenburg's, *The Spectacle of Suffering* (1984) and *The Prison Experience* (1991) argue that changes in punishment and imprisonment evolved over a much longer period of time than identified by revisionist accounts (also see Spieren-burg, 2005). More recently Pratt's *Punishment and Civilisation* (2002), examines changing penal sensibilities and practices over the nine-teenth and twentieth centuries and the ways in which punish-ment became 'recognised as civilised', (despite competing claims), and the consequences of this in light of recent penal developments in the Western world over the last two decades (also see Concluding Remarks).

In terms of capital punishment, influential accounts by Hay (1975), Linebaugh (1975, 1993), and Gatrell (1994) have been concerned with operation of the criminal justice system and the ideology of law which appeared universal, but was deeply class orientated. When considering the end of public execution, recent authors have argued this change was influenced by the need to present a more pleasing image of justice (McGowen, 1983; also see McGowen, 1986, 1994, 2000) and a growing distaste for the carnival of public execution and sympathy for the condemned, reflecting changing sensibilities towards such punishments (Pratt, 2002).

The classic study, *Women's Imprisonment*, by Pat Carlen (1983) had a profound effect on the research of women's imprisonment and punishment in criminology, yet, few historians have attempted to 'redress the gender imbalance which remained after 'the new social histories' of the 1970s revised the story of the nineteenth and early twentieth century prison systems' (Howe, 1994: 133). Over recent decades there have been some significant contributions which have provided a revisionist history of imprisonment which includes women (Freedman, 1981; Rafter, 1983, 1985; O'Brien, 1982; Dobash *et al.*, 1986; Zedner, 1991) and more recently research on England, examining the capital punishment of women in the twentieth century by Ballinger (2000) and the semi-penal institutionalisation of women by Barton (2005) (also see Chapter 2 and Chapter 7).

Introducing the collection

In addressing these themes the collection is divided into three parts, advancing theoretical perspectives; penal policy, prison practice and discourses on offenders; and confinement, discipline and resistance. However, more broadly linkages can be between chapters in a number of different ways. Part I of the book explores theoretical perspectives on punishment and control, seeking to advance our theoretical understanding through case studies of particular aspects of imprisonment and modernity, social control, legal and medical discourses and gender, and operation of the criminal justice and penal system in relation to the treatment of different groups of offenders.

Chapter 1 by Michael Fiddler focuses on the development and evolution of Sing Sing penitentiary, New York. Fiddler argues for a multi-layered approach to the history of Sing Sing, using three overlapping periods of centrality, marginality and adjunct to illuminate this understanding. Fiddler maintains that in the nineteenth century the prison was 'central' to the developing industrial city and the use of labour within the prison was a key feature, not necessarily in terms of production, but in terms of the practice of labour. In the early twentieth century, Sing Sing expanded, developing into a 'Big House' prison. The architecture of Sing Sing became monumental (iconic in cinematic portrayals of the period) yet the prison was marginal, as the offenders were stored away from society, segregated and no longer needed for industry. In concluding, Fiddler discusses the way in which the prison has become adjunct to the contemporary urban environment and how these prisons operate merely to contain a population of 'redundant republic machines'.

Chapter 2 by Anette Ballinger argues for a reconceptualising of gender and social control in explaining the interactions between individuals and the state criminal justice system. Early conceptions of social control were genderised by feminist approaches in the 1970s to embed notions of the social construction of femininity and the specific means by which women were social controlled – reproduction, family, home, work. Within this context, Ballinger maintains that social control and gender conformity have paid little attention to the ways in which *both* men and women are constructed. Ballinger argues that both men who fail to conform to the social construction of 'respectable masculinities' as well as women controlled through 'appropriate femininity' can be perceived as problematic. Through a detailed case study of Ada Allen, accused of murdering her husband in 1945, Ballinger demonstrates how the victim, Donald was constructed as a failure with regard to marriage and work – key components of hegemonic masculinity. Ballinger argues that through reconceptualising social control to address dimensions of both masculinity and female agency allows for a fuller understanding of the ways in which gender relations operate in the social control of women and men before the law.

The importance of the relationship between medical power, punishment and social control has been highlighted by earlier contributions, in relation to prison practices (Sim, 1990), and the ways in which this operates more broadly as a social control mechanism (a number of essays in Cohen and Scull, 1983). Michel Foucault's work on medicine and punishment has been highly influential in this field and it is one area of his work that is taken up by Tony Ward in Chapter 3. Ward illuminates the relationship between medical discourse and punishment in an examination of the English law and psychiatry in the nineteenth and early twentieth centuries. Ward examines Foucault's concept of 'rule of common truth', psychiatric expert evidence and boundaries between responsible and non-responsible subjects and how this operated rather differently in the English adversarial legal system compared to the French inquisitorial system.

One aspect discussed by Ward is, Foucault's view that psychiatric evidence functioned through the 'doubling' of offender and offence. Legal and medical discourses provide a 'switchpoint' in producing similar statements but operating from different discourses; criminal acts are manifestations of pathological traits and the offender is doubled by the delinquent, the bearer of the pathological trait of criminality. This concept of doubling is also illuminated in the treatment of female inebriates in the late nineteenth century (Chapter 7), where habitual drunkenness was increasingly defined as a medical condition or 'disease' especially as regards women. More broadly, the doubling of the legal subject (responsible for a particular act) by the offender or delinquent can also be seen in the treatment of 'good' or 'bad' women and men before the law in Chapter 2. However, in Chapter 6, Locker argues that respectable offenders avoided such doubling by the denial that respectability and criminality could exist together.

Part II of the collection addresses the changes and development in prison policies and penal practices in the nineteenth and early twentieth centuries, and the ways in which particular groups of offenders were discussed in official and public discourses and the consequences of this for treatment of such offenders. Chapter 4 by Helen Johnston examines the role of prison officers in local prisons between 1835 and 1877. She maintains that the role of prison officers in the years before the centralisation of the English prison system exemplifies the paradoxes, not only between policy and practice in the implementation of legislation in local prisons, but also conflicting and competing aims of imprisonment at this time. Despite the interest and commentary on prison regimes and practices during this period, those officers who implemented such practices on a day to day basis, have received little attention in the theoretical approaches of the revisionists and are often overlooked despite the importance of their involvement in the delivery of punishment at this time.

Chapter 5 by Jamie Bennett discusses the direction and development of prison policy and penal practice at the beginning of the twentieth century when Winston Churchill was appointed Home Secretary. Despite the rather short period in office, Churchill has often been regarded as a 'reforming' Home Secretary and this has been linked to Churchill's own experience of imprisonment during the Boer War. Through an examination of prison conditions, prison staff and penal policy, Bennett maintains that Churchill's reforms were often based on amelioration rather than transformation, and despite his ability to bring about some changes, these were not new, but reflecting the liberal welfarist agenda. Churchill's period of office reflected personal tensions, and tensions of the time, during which approaches to crime and the role and use of imprisonment were contested, between discipline and welfare, liberalism and conservatism. This chapter, along with Chapter 2, Chapter 7, Chapter 10 and Chapter 11, also contribute more broadly to the rather neglected period of the first half of the twentieth century, when considering existing research on punishment, penal policy and criminal justice (Emsley, 2005a).

The following three chapters in Part II examine different groups of offenders and the ways in which penal policy and discourses on offending behaviour shaped their treatment by the criminal justice system. The emergence of the 'respectable offender' in the nineteenth century is detailed by John Locker in Chapter 6. Locker explores discourses on white collar crime, the social responses to the respectable offenders, and the impact of this on the punishment of such offenders. Moving beyond a debate about whether this type of offender was treated more leniently or more harshly by the criminal justice system, Locker maintains that respectable offenders bought into question traditional assumptions about crime and offenders. Discourses which operated in court cases and in public opinion resolved the problematic nature of the respectable criminal by rebuilding the symbolic divide between criminal and non-criminal, deviant and normal, and respectable and non-respectable. As such, discourses operated to deconstruct and reconstruct these offenders, through strategies of estrangement and exoneration, as either the 'unrespectable offender', or the 'respectable non-offender' but rarely as respectable and criminal.

The latter part of the nineteenth century saw the removal of particular groups of offenders from the prison, part of a new penal welfare complex (Garland, 1985), and saw the development of other types of institutions, perceived as maintaining less punitive regimes and more rehabilitative practices. The inebriate was one such offender, and the inebriate reformatory was one such institution. Chapter 7 provides a detailed account of inebriate institutions for women by Bronwyn Morrison. She argues that the institutions set up at this time were ones in which women were disproportionately overrepresented, and which extended penal arrangements, rather than departed from them. Morrison maintains that the gendered nature of these institutions was no accident, but based on contemporary discourses of the habitual drunkard as female, and concerns over the lack of control over these 'diseased' women. Instead of rehabilitative, treatment or reform, the regimes within these institutions operated to control, segregate and contain women who were often perceived as unmanageable and beyond reform.

Chapter 8 by Heather Shore discusses Victorian and Edwardian responses to the problem of juvenile crime and the evolution of a range of institutions and provision, both state and voluntary, over this period. In the first period, she explores experiments with institutional provision, the first state-run juvenile institution Parkhurst, emigration and transportation, and the Reformatory and Industrial Schools Acts. In the second period, she examines the web of institutions which proliferated for large numbers of working class children, including; schools, reformatories, industrial schools, and training ships. A number of scandals, with regard to excessive punishment and poor treatment, drew attention to the use of training ships in late Victorian and early Edwardian periods. This fed into broader concerns with the punishment and welfare of children in the reformatory and industrial schools system, and culminated in the Children and Young Person's Act 1933.

Part III of the collection explores the experiences of confinement, disciplinary regimes, and various forms of resistance in different institutional settings. The revisionist accounts of the prison in the nineteenth century often leave silent the voices of the confined and the staff (see Chapter 4). The final part of the collection examines the experience and effects of incarceration or institutionalisation on those committed to a range of institutions. In Chapter 9, Sarah Anderson and John Pratt discuss the ways in which prisoner memoirs challenged the legitimacy of official discourses on prison regimes in the late nineteenth century. In a period which saw the centralisation of the local prisons and increased uniformity and severity in prison regimes, they are concerned with the lived experience of punishment and how prisoners' accounts were instrumental in reforms that occurred at the end of the century. In discussing prisoner memoirs, they focus on features of prison life, such as physical deterioration, mental illness, medical care and relations with doctors, which are prevalent in prisoner memoirs and the responses of the prison authorities to widespread criticism during this period.

In Chapter 10, Alyson Brown details the riots at Chatham Convict Prison in 1861 and Dartmoor in 1932, providing a historical approach to our understanding of prison riots. Both riots occurred during significant periods in penal history in England, when there were changing ideas about penal philosophy and changes in the organisation of the prison system. The Chatham riot took place during the end of transportation to Australia and the emergence of the convict system, to house those sentenced to periods of penal servitude. The Dartmoor riot, on the other hand, occurred during a period of more progressive developments in the prison system. Official and public discourses focused on prison conditions and recidivist or habitual offenders, undermining any legitimate or justifiable claims by prisoners, by characterising them as desperate, or having nothing to lose. Yet, in the aftermath of the Dartmoor riot, the administration were able to construct the previous failures of severity and deterrent regimes in the late nineteenth century (see Chapter 9), as a means of protecting their own administration and preserving a more progressive approach.

The final chapter by Abigail Wills examines the experiences of control within institutions and strategies of resistance to authority in residential reform schools, specifically, Approved Schools, Probation Homes and Probations Hostels for young people and children, during the 1950 to 1970 period. Wills presents a more nuanced picture of agency and identity within these institutional settings, and challenges the notion that resistance is ultimately futile, and agency limited in significance. This research demonstrates that various forms of resistance – individual, collective, violent – were a part of daily institutional life and often centred on the inequities of institutionalisation itself, as well as institutional life, relationships with social contacts outside, and personal autonomy, dignity and privacy.

This collection of case studies engages with, criticises and develops more nuanced approaches to the theoretical framework of existing research laid out in this introduction. Together they provide original research and important insights into gaps in our historical knowledge and our understanding of punishment and control in the nineteenth and twentieth centuries.

Part I
Theoretical Perspectives

1

Modernity, The New Republic and Sing Sing: The Creation of a Disciplined Workforce and Citizenry

Michael Fiddler

> ...not only is modern society a cage, but all the people in it are shaped by its bars (Berman, 1982: 27).

Central, marginal and adjunct: three periods of the modern prison

Where do we locate the beginning of modern imprisonment? For Durkheim (1973) and Foucault (1977) modernity and the origin of the prison were synonymous. The early prison arose out of 'the beginnings of the industrialised urban society' (Garland, 1985: 4). Rusche and Kirchheimer (1939), and latterly Melossi and Pavarini (1981), imposed a Marxist reading locating the prison in relation to developing modes of production. Specifically, they made explicit the parallels between the factory and the prison. Alternatively, Cohen (1996) and Mathiesen (1974), envisaged new patterns of imprisonment and penality, typified by the '"hidden discipline" of community corrections' (Garland, 1985: 4). Whereas, for Ignatieff (1978: 62), the prison would not simply stop 'the bacillus of vice', but also the radicalism of the nascent nineteenth century workers' movements. Subsequent writers looked to the post Second World War 'epoch of rehabilitation' (Garland, 1985: 4). In Garland's terms, this saw the move from paternalism and the spiritual to 'a more technical form of social engineering' (1985: 4).

The argument that I elaborate here incorporates these perspectives into a wider whole. I propose that imprisonment, from modernity to late-modernity, can be divided into three over-lapping periods: central, marginal and adjunct. This first period of 'centrality' incorporates Foucauldian notions of discipline, in addition to the work of Rusche and Kirchheimer (1939) and Melossi and Pavarini (1981). The second sees the prison taking on a marginal or 'monumental' aspect that fore-shadows current 'warehousing' discourse. As we shall see, each of these stages had important, but differing implications for prison labour and inmate citizenship more broadly. The scope of this piece looks at Sing Sing across the first two stages before briefly looking to its third contemporary role as an adjunct to the urban.

The 'central' period figuratively, geographically and visually located the prison as central to the developing modern, industrial city. A useful analogy to make is that during this period, ranging from the early to late nineteenth century, the prison was as central to the construction of the modern Western state as the gulag was to Stalinist, Soviet Russia (Piacentini, 2004; Pallot, 2005). As Bosworth and Sparks state, the prison played a special role in the 'great political experiments of modernity – liberal democracy, colonialism, fascism and state social-ism' (2000: 260). This first period of centrality was

...a landscape of steam engines, automatic factories, railroads, vast new industrial zones; of teeming cities that have grown overnight, often with dreadful human consequences... (Berman, 1982: 18–19).

It was a time of immense socio-economic and political change. The prison's function was to produce a citizen capable of the labour neces-sitated by modern, capitalist systems. The prison was a utopic site, a site of ordering that would act as a disciplining beacon for the rest of society. This was to be a 'strange kind of model community' (Evans, 1982: 198) whose effects would radiate throughout the social body.

I contend, following Rusche and Kirchheimer (1939) and Melossi and Pavarini (1981), that the prison was a vehicle by which a modern workforce-cum-citizenry could be moulded and, by extension, assist in the creation of the modern state. The periods following this initial one saw the prison take a trajectory away from societal centre towards, initially at least, the margins and latterly a hybridised space running in parallel to the contemporary urban environment. What I label the 'marginal' period, spanning the early to mid-twentieth century, saw the development of the Big House style of architecture in the United States. Conversely to the earlier central period, the penitentiary and its population were marginalised from society, both geographically and socially. It would no longer hold its 'central' position. The adjunct period, ranging from the late twentieth century to the present, has emerged out of this marginality. It sees the carceral space of the prison leech out into the urban. The prison and the urban have come to act as adjuncts to each other. They are not simply parallel sites, but of one another. Yet what is the importance of Sing Sing in examining these processes?

Sing Sing's popularity as a film location in particular has seen it seep into popular consciousness. Its name has become synonymous with the prison experience. We can use it, as Soja (1996: 18) (acknowledging Proust) would put it, as a 'geographical madeleine'. To put this differently, lacunae of meaning build up in space over time. As they do so, some elements are lost whilst others remain visible. An analysis of the space of a prison in the early twenty-first century will reveal glimpses of the spaces of the generations of penal regime, architecture and philosophy that preceded it. Likewise, an examination of those earlier prisons can illuminate our understanding of contemporary concerns. By peeling back the layers of this spatial palimpsest we can see the on-going development of key phenomena (Fiddler, 2006). Namely, the progression and changing demands of modernity can be mapped onto the space of the prison. Indeed, the periodisation I outline here maps onto Sing Sing as it does the history of imprisonment more broadly. We can use Sing Sing as a lens to view the production of a modern (carceral) space. In so doing we can position the penitentiary in its wider socio-economic and political context. This illuminates these broader processes to a greater degree than a simplistic chronological recounting of a given institution's history. More pertinently, it causes us to rethink the prison's relation to modernity itself.

Examining the history of Sing Sing

My analysis of the history of Sing Sing takes its lead from de Certeau (1988). Specifically, one cannot recount a narrative of the past 'as it really was'. In looking back we apply filters of present day thinking onto what we perceive to have occurred. Yet, de Certeau did not think of history as a simple 'construction' of the present. He described a tension between the 'real' and 'known'. In other words, that which the historic wishes to 'bring back to life' and the 'modes of comprehension', the models, to be applied to it (de Certeau, 1988: 35). Weymans cogently describes de Certeau's (1988) metaphor of the 'staging of the past through historiography' as being like 'the work of a museum guide':

> On the one hand, the guide organizes the paintings on the wall; he or she relates a story about them, following a set route that connects all the pictures together. On the other hand, the guide cannot speak

definitively... [T]he museum guide must also refer to what he or she cannot fully describe in words: the picture itself. The museum guide and the pictures are dependent on each other: the picture receives its meaning through the tale that the museum guide tells about it, while the museum guide cannot tell anything about the picture without showing it (Weymans, 2004: 176).

This then links models and events. So, the 'text is always held together by various concepts and organising structures that enable historical understandings' (Weymans, 2004: 175). I pick out what I consider to be 'key' events in Sing Sing's history before offering my analysis of them and overlaying an 'organising structure'. As such, my selections are like the paintings of de Certeau's metaphor, and my concepts and organising structures are the 'museum guide' to these 'paintings'.

I will frame this chapter by examining the role of three wardens (Elam Lynds, Thomas Mott-Osborne and Lewis Lawes) and their varied influences upon the creation of a 'modern' Sing Sing. Their periods of wardenship map onto key passages of centrality and marginality. This periodisation brings with it epistemological issues (*inter alia*, Kelly, 1977; Bentley, 1996). That said, I do not claim that these are discrete periods apprehended as such by actors at given points. Instead, they emerged, organically, from the processes of modernity. Themes relevant to one stage in this model can appear in another stage, albeit in a subtly different form. There are echoes, repetitions and circularities. It is Sing Sing itself that we turn to now and, as Beaumont and De Tocqueville put it, 'the way in which it was executed is of a kind that deserves to be reported' (1833/1979: 43).

Central: the wardenship of Elam Lynds (1825–1830)

Elam Lynds, the former warden of Auburn penitentiary, was given the responsibility of finding a site and building a 'new, more modern prison' in 1825 (Gado, 2004: 1). He 'explored sites at Manhattanville on the Spuyten Duyvil', Staten Island and the Bronx (Panetta, 1986: 39). However, it was a location at Mount Pleasant on the banks of the Hudson in Westchester County that was selected.

There was a small village near the site called 'Sing Sing'. Sing Sing was derived from 'Sint Sincks', the name of a local native American tribe. Sint Sincks itself was taken from an earlier phrase, 'Ossine Ossine' which meant 'stone upon stone' (Lawes, 1932). This is oddly prescient given that the penitentiary would be built by inmates from the stone from the quarry next to the prison site. Once the plan was approved, the state legislature provided $20,100 for the purchase of the land. The regime and building itself would be based on the Auburn model, the latter being 'the latest word in penal institutions' (Lawes, 1932: 78). The aptly named John Carpenter was appointed by Lynds as Sing Sing's architect. The cells were positioned back-to-back in a freestanding, central core. This distance from the exterior walls afforded a greater degree of security and represented the then 'unique contribution' of the Auburn-Sing Sing design (Johnston, 2000: 78). Sing Sing further drew upon the regime established by Lynds and others at Auburn's northern wing in the early 1820s. This saw the prisoner work silently in association during the day and then return to their cell at night. This was known variously as the congregate, silent or Auburn system (for use in England, see Chapter 4). As Lynds would state, '[t]he point is, to maintain uninterrupted silence and uninterrupted labour' (Beaumont and De Tocqueville, 1833/1979: 162).

Sing Sing was some thirty miles north of New York. Its location next to the Hudson ensured that there was a route for supplies and products could be sent either down river to New York or up river to Albany. The river formed one side of the compound and was useful as a security barrier. The other elemental force was seemingly Lynds himself. Beaumont and De Tocqueville describe Lynds as 'having no other means to keep [the prisoners] in obedience, than the firmness of his character and the energy of his will' (1833/1979: 43). The English Captain Basil Hall visited Sing Sing during its construction and described his 'astonishment' at seeing 'only two sentinels pacing along the height, from whence I looked down upon two hundred convicts at work' (1832, cited by Gura, 2001: lxiv). There was a 'perfect feeling of security, though we were walking around unarmed amongst cutthroats and villains of all sorts' (*ibid*.: xi).

There was also a more brutally practical aspect to his wardenship of Sing Sing. When asked if it were possible to manage without resort to corporal punishment, Lynds replied 'I am completely convinced of the opposite' (cited by Conover, 2001: 177). Levi Burr published the splendidly titled *A voice from Sing Sing, giving a general description of the state prison, a short and comprehensive geological history of the Quality of the Stone of the Quarries; and a synopsis of the Horrid Treatment of the Convicts in That Prison* in 1833 (Conover, 2001: 177). In the book he describes the 'cat-ocracy', whereby a cat-o'-nine-tails was used for a range of offences. On the ground floor of the completed cellblock was an area called the 'Flogging Post' (*ibid*.). Here '[t]wo irons had been fastened to the wall' and the cat-o'-nine-tails hung nearby (*ibid*.). An 1841 legislative report offered the following gruesome detail: '[t]he whipping post was never dry' (*ibid.*: 178).

These then were the means by which Lynds was able to control the early prison population and construction of Sing Sing. Once the prisoner-cum-builders had completed the first two tiers the convict population of New York's Newgate transferred into the prison. This influx of new inmates meant that each cell was swiftly inhabited. By 1830 the population was some 800. In those first few years the prison simply consisted of the enormous cellblock. In contrast to Auburn there was 'no administrative center; no main entrance' (Panetta, 1986: 39). All there was, in Lawes's (1932: 82) telling phrase, was a 'mausoleum with niches arranged in galleries'. Plates that remain also depict the warden's house, styled after a large colonial house, stood at one end of the block. Industrial shops were latterly built close to the river. Cheli (2003: 17) notes that, before the exterior wall was eventually erected, the prison '*looked like an industrial village* on the banks of the Hudson river' (emphasis added).

In many ways the Sing Sing of the first half of the nineteenth century could be deemed a success. The system originated in Auburn was further refined in Sing Sing. It then became the template upon which other state penitentiary systems were based. The ill-effects of association between criminals; which 'renders their moral reformation impossible, and becomes even for them the inevitable cause of an alarming corruption', had been countered through rational, yet cost-effective means (Beaumont and De Tocqueville, 1833/1979: 55). A report of the Prison Commissioners concerning Sing Sing stated that '[n]o better penitentiary prison was ever built at any time in this or any other country' (cited by Lawes, 1932: 82). This then was a state-of-the-art prison and a symbol for the utopic project of the New Republic.

Central: discipline and labour

It is the confluence of modernity, industrialisation and the prison that I turn to now. Simply put, industrialisation required workers. As Faucher (1838, cited by Melossi and Pavarini, 1981: 99) stated:

> ...labour is the fate of the modern peoples...Labour must become the religion of the prisons. A society-machine requires purely mechanical means of reform.

The prison became the central site where the discipline of repeated micro-actions on the body of the prisoner produced a modern labourer.

The repetitious gestures and actions of the prisoner inculcated the physical skills needed to work in the industrialised workplaces of the eighteenth and nineteenth centuries. Inculcating industrious patterns of behaviour and 'the habits of society' became the 'principal object[s] of punishment' (Beaumont and De Tocqueville, 1833/1979: 58). Foucault's description of the importance of these measured (in both senses) movements focuses attention on what I argue is the true essence of the centrality of this period. It is the importance of the small gesture (or rather, as Foucault (1977: 152) corrects, 'the best relation between a gesture and the overall position of the body, which is its condition of efficiency and speed') which arcs out and up, across the social body. As Wright suggests,

> [i]deology is not merely produced in written texts but inscribed in and on the flesh, in the ritual moving of the body in social settings... (1997: 60–1).

In this way, prisoners themselves took on an 'abstract exchange value'. As Melossi and Pavarini (1981: 185) elaborate, the prisoner is denied a *'quantum of liberty'* (original emphasis). This represents 'the most simple and absolute form of "exchange value"' in a capitalist society (*ibid.*). The denial of liberty is achieved in its most powerful and abstract form in the prison. The labourer/prisoner is not simply alienated 'from/by the means of production', but is also expropriated 'from his own body' (*ibid.*: 187). Melossi and Pavarini's (1981) reading follows on from Rusche and Kirchheimer's (1939) influential, if not now somewhat simplistic, work. Whilst it has been argued that to place heavy emphasis upon the training of workers to populate factories is misguided (*inter alia*, Garland, 1990; Rothman, 1990), this writer would suggest that re-evaluating their work with reference to that of Pashukanis (1980) is valuable.

Pashukanis's (1980) idea of crime and its punishment was premised on them being part of the capitalist system of contracts and exchange. Crime was a 'contract concluded against one's will' (Pashukanis, 1980: 112). The punishment, it then followed, is a contract which is an act of exchange in relation to the harm inflicted upon the victim. The systems of punishment then became a means, if not *the* means, by which the class system is maintained. For Pashukanis (1980: 116), '[e]very historical system of punitive policy bears the imprint of the class interest of that class which realized it.' The relation of the prisoner to the space of the prison, be it mediated by labour or architecture, is directly linked to the prison's location amidst changing systems of capital. During this initial period of the prison 'experiment', the disciplining aspect of the prison grew out of the requirement for a workforce. Pashukanis (1980: 115) points to the changing character of justice as society moved from a natural economy to the 'development of commerce and the organisation of a class state' and with it 'the concomitant increase in the exploitation of the peasantry.' Through these systems, the subordinated class was kept 'in obedience' (*ibid.*).

The exchange value that is manifest in the prisoner is their capacity to work. Applying a quantum of time to be 'taken' in exchange for a crime is related to the amount of labour to be achieved during that period of time. The prisoner is thought of in terms of 'the abstract man' and of 'abstract human labour time' (*ibid.*: 120). For Pashukanis (1980) it was not coincidental that such a system should develop and be normalised during the nineteenth century, a period which saw the consolidation of bourgeois society. Thinking of the prisoners in terms of abstract human labour time is a reductive device. Simplifying and abstracting reduced the individual to their most base level. One need not consider them as anything other than their abstract capacities.

There are dissenting voices to the ideas espoused here. Rothman (1990) dismisses the link between industrialisation and the role of the prison. Preferring to draw upon the apparent collapse in social ties rather than an explanation borne of the changing demands of modes of production, Rothman (1990: xxxviii), citing Sutton's (1988) stance, airily dismisses the work of Rusche and Kirchheimer (1939) and Melossi and Pavarini (1981):

> The reformatory is not efficiently explained either as a functional outcome of modernization or as a simple instrument of class control and industrial discipline.

Further, he uses Ignatieff's (1978) claim that the factory and prison came to resemble one another not out of a simplistic reading of class control, but

> ...because both public order authorities and employers shared the same universe of assumptions about the regulation of the body and the ordering of time (cited by Rothman, 1990: xxxvii).

The fear that prompted the birth of the penitentiary was itself not a reaction to 'the aggressive demands of a submerged labouring class', but a sense of 'moral dissoluteness' at the collapse of the imagined communities that had characterised America a century before (Rothman, 1990: xliii). Thus, it was the institutions of family and church that informed the Jacksonian-era prison, not the factory.

Cheli's (2003) comments as to the superficial likeness of Sing Sing to an industrial village aside, my intention here is not to provide evidence for a 'simple translation' of the prison to the factory (*ibid.*: xxxvii). Such a uni-dimensional response would not take us much further than Rusche and Kirchheimer's work. However, it is clear that Rothman and Sutton selectively ignore the impact of the broader processes of industrialisation and modernity itself. Rothman (1990) becomes entangled in the argument that questions whether the modern prison was profitable (*inter alia*, Durham, 1989). The material benefits to the prison system of inmate labour were of secondary importance. At one point Rothman (1990: 105) does stumble across the fundamental point that '[t]he idea of labour, even more than the calculations of profit and loss, made it central to the penitentiary'. I propose that, with reference to Pashukanis, the importance lay in the *practice* and not necessarily the *product* of labour. Indeed, it is *the idea of labour* that is the key. As Lynds stated, the importance lay in the message to be taken from 'uninterrupted labour' (Beaumont and De Tocqueville, 1833/1979: 162). Sutton's criticisms entirely ignore the pivotal role of the modern prison in the construction of industrialised America. The construction of the prison and the discipline of the prisoners held a position of ideological centrality. It is a rather simplistic rebuttal to Rothman, but the following quote from Beaumont and De Tocqueville neatly encapsulates my argument:

> Perhaps, leaving the prison [the inmate] is not an honest man, but he has contracted honest habits. He was an idler; now he knows how to work (1833/1979: 90).

There was indeed a syncretism between factory and prison (and the other 'total' institutions such as the workhouse, hospital or school) as Ignatieff (1978) rightly suggests. I am not suggesting that the prison and factory's relationship was unique. They did, indeed, exist within an atmosphere, a 'universe of assumptions'. The same new sciences of the body impacted on institutions throughout the social body. This was a function of the broader processes of modernity. To deny the importance of these as Sutton and Rothman do (and which, arguably, produced the very conditions that they highlight as producing the prison) is grossly remiss. The docile body was constructed in numerous ways, but most evidently within the prison walls.

Central: discipline and citizenship

...the emergence of the penitentiary in the United States was a project constitutive of liberal democracy. That is, the penitentiary system formed the epistemological project of liberal democracy, creating conditions of knowledge of self and other that were to shape the political subject required for liberal and democratic values to be realised in practice...we could in a sense say that the American penitentiary was erected by the Founding Fathers of the Nation as an imposing and monumental Gateway to the Republic (Dumm, 1987: 6).

The production of these docile, compliant bodies was achieved within the individualised space of the cell. This was a function of the broader development of a 'science of the individual' (Foucault, n.d., cited by Mills, 2003: 105). The individual became 'the object of possible knowledge' (Foucault, 1988, cited by Mills, 2003: 104). The emergence of 'Man' as an area of study marked an 'episteme shift, a dramatic change in the way that societies conceptualise' (Mills, 2003: 104). Broadly, it was the 'carceral texture of society' that allowed for the surveillance of the body (Foucault, 1977: 304). More narrowly, it was the prison that was the main instrument in this new constellation of power-knowledge that took the body as its focus in the late eighteenth and early nineteenth century. The core unit of liberalism is the individual. The penitentiary project was constitutive of individuals and the cell was the central component in these individualising processes. However, it is not entirely correct to talk about the docility of these incarcerated individuals. To paraphrase Dumm (1987: 90), these selves were to rule as much as be ruled. The penitentiary, working at the level of the individual (and democratically so given that 'the same operations applied to each individual' (*ibid.*) saw the inculcation of the practices and understandings of 'government', as Foucault (1993: 203–4) put it. Its end point sees 'the modern sovereign state and the modern autonomous individual co-determine each other's emergence' (Lemke, 2002: 2). In other words, the penitentiary was intended to produce the conditions and the capacity for citizenship.

As such, the American penitentiary was central in constituting the New Republic. This centrality is not a retrospective piece of artifice recognised by Dumm or argued by this writer. Its importance was recognised at the time. As Rothman (1990: 81) states, by 'the 1830s, the American penitentiary had become world famous.' Talking of 'asylums' as a whole, which he takes to have included institutions for the mad, bad and sad, Rothman goes on to state that '[r]ather than stand as place of last resort, hidden and ignored, these institutions become *the pride of the nation*' (emphasis added, *ibid.*: 79). Indeed, we might be reminded of the words of the Prison Commissioners who stated that Sing Sing was the pinnacle of prison design, not simply in America, but globally.

In no small part, *On the Penitentiary System in the United States*, as well as the broader scope of De Tocqueville's (1835) *Democracy in America*, served to highlight the place of the penitentiary in American society for European readers. Prisons were a vehicle by which they could explore the broader concerns of the political, social and economic. I would contend though that the prison was the most logical point of departure for such broad themes. As Dumm proposes, the penitentiary was a 'project constitutive of liberal democracy' (1987: 6).

Marginal: the wardenship of Mott-Osborne (1914–1916)

...the quickest way out of Sing Sing is to come in as a warden (popular joke of the 1910s, cited by Gado, 2004).

Just as Elam Lynds was the central figure around which the newly built Sing Sing revolved, so Thomas Mott Osborne and Lewis Lawes loom large in the history of Sing Sing. Both men brought a reforming agenda to their position, but with varying degrees of explicitness and success.

Osborne's tenure as warden was brief although not atypically short. Between 1900 and 1919, for example, there were ten wardens, some of whom 'stayed as little as a few weeks' (Gado, 2004: 7). He was a major political figure in Auburn, being its mayor and chairman of the State Commission on Prison Reform, as well as a newspaper publisher and manufacturer. His entry into Auburn's penitentiary in September 1913 is best described as unusual. He elected to go in as an 'inmate'. Going under the name Tom Brown, he spent a week inside Auburn:

...to learn what I can first-hand...I am coming here to live your life; to be housed, clothed, fed, treated in all respects like one of you. I want to see for myself what your life is like, not as viewed from the outside looking in, but from the inside looking out (Osborne, 1913, cited by Conover, 2001: 196).

Although his intention had been to remain anonymous, his identity was revealed to staff and inmates the day before his arrival. Conover (2001: 197) describes Osborne's account, published as *Within Prison Walls*, as being one of sentimental naivety. His fellow inmates were depicted as a 'swell bunch of guys', whereas those guards who were not actively brutal were likened to the 'honorable and kindly...slave owners before the Civil War' (*ibid.*: 197–8). His sense of the oppressiveness of prison rules and the possibility of finding 'something far better to take [the] place' of the penitentiary enamored him to inmates and distanced him from guards (*ibid.*). It also led to Osborne's later position within the penitentiary system becoming increasingly precarious.

Osborne was made warden of Sing Sing on 1 December, 1914. His major achievement was the establishing of the Mutual Welfare League (M.W.L.). This had taken on nascent form during his wardenship at Auburn. The M.W.L. was a means of allowing inmates a degree of self-governance. In a public address in 1905 he had criticised the penitentiary system for forcing men to work in a system that 'brutalizes the men and the keepers' (cited by Conover, 2001: 196). He declared, quite simply, 'this is not reformatory' (*ibid.*). Under the M.W.L. system inmate representatives were allowed input on the regime under which the penitentiary operated. His thinking was that responsibilising the inmates would inculcate those sentiments that the congregate system and its like had manifestly failed to do. Inmate representatives advised the prison authorities on matters of discipline in addition to organising sporting events and a commissary. Two stores were opened by the league in 1919 and used their own currency. The notes carried Osborne's motto: 'Do good, make good'.

As Lawes (1932: 115) puts it, a warden must be a 'benevolent despot as well as the understanding leader'. Whilst conceding that Osborne's wardenship 'ended too soon', Lawes (1932: 115) does condemn it as resulting in 'chaos.' Principally, Lawes criticises Osborne's weak leadership, seen as a function of devolving power to the inmates, and a fatal misunderstanding of the prison population. Indeed, Osborne's political grandstanding, 'coddling' of the inmate population and anti-capital punishment pronouncements had done little to endear him to his political rivals. Conover (2001) describes a series of conspiratorial plans designed to discredit him. In 1915 he was accused of committing 'various unlawful and unnatural acts with inmates' (*ibid.*: 199). An inmate ('Fat Alger'), who had been labelled as an informant for the Superintendent of Prisons and been transferred away from the prison, had made the allegations. Osborne was indicted on the charges, but they were subsequently dismissed. He returned to the prison, but resigned in 1916. As Lawes (1932: 114) argues, whilst Osborne's influence diminished in the following years, he had nonetheless 'introduced the prison to the public. He made it a subject of free and popular discussion in the Press and on the platform.'

Marginal: the wardenship of Lewis Lawes (1920–1941)

Lewis Lawes's (1932) book, which encompassed the history of the prison, his somewhat self-aggrandising reminiscences over his time as Warden and his own progressive thoughts on penal thinking, was entitled *Twenty Thousand Years in Sing Sing*. The title was derived from the aggregate sentence facing the 2500 men contained within the prison walls at his time of writing. As Lawes powerfully put it,

> [w]ithin such cycles worlds are born, die and are reborn. That span has witnessed the evolution of the intelligence of mortal men (1932: 244).

In 1920 Lawes became warden of Sing Sing. He would stay in the post for some 20 years and became 'America's most famous and admired warden' (Conover, 2001: 199). His initial course of action was the steady dismantling of the M.W.L.. Lawes withdrew the element of self-government from the prisoners, replacing it with the administration's 'despotism', albeit 'an enlightened one' (Conover, 2001: 200). Initially there was one cell block and a dormitory. Lawes then presided over an extensive building program in the 1920s that would radically change the shape and face of Sing Sing.

In 1926, the state approved a budget of $2,775,000 for the construction of two colossal new blocks (A and B). They had a combined capacity of 1,366 and were the largest cellblocks in Western prison systems. A visitor in the 1930s described them as 'beautifully finished and very light and airy' (Cox, 1986: 50). By 1930 a mess hall, chapel, new Death House, laundry, bathhouse and barbershop had been built whilst the industrial plant workshops were rebuilt. Between 1920 and 1932, some eight million dollars had been spent on construction at Sing Sing and cell capacity stood at 1,752. During Lawes's wardenship, the acreage of the site rose from 14 and a half to 47 and a half.

Sing Sing remains the only prison in the world where commuter train tracks run through prison grounds. The train tracks act as a marker, dividing the old cell block from those constructed under Lawes's wardenship, further up the hillside. It became evident in the early 1900s that the original, century-old cellblock was fast approaching the end of its usefulness. Overcrowding made living conditions untenable. The State Prison Improvement Commission had described it in 1905 as 'verily...far worse than living in a sewer' (Conover, 2001: 202). A bid in 1917 to demolish the cellblock led to the removal of a 'floor and a half' (*ibid.*). However, the demolition remained incomplete and prison numbers dictated that the partially demolished cellblock remain open. Conover (2001: 202) quotes the official departmental history as describing how, in a wonderful turn of phrase, the old cell block 'continued to swallow thousands of inmates into its malevolent, malodorous maw.' By 1943 the old cell block was finally closed. The bars and doors, 'of which there were many,' were melted down for the war effort (Gado, 2004: 8). The roof burned down in 1984 leaving an outer shell. It has since been 'listed on the National Register of Historic Places and can never be removed' (Cheli, 2003: 126).

During Lawes's wardenship there was an intriguing juxtaposition of the construction of the brute monumentality of the prison buildings and the work of a number of inmates to improve their environment (the celebrated 'Roseman of Sing Sing' being a notable example). In a way, this echoes the juxtaposition of prison and landscape. As Lawes poetically states,

> [o]ne can follow for miles the wide sweep of the Hudson, as it eddies its endless flow and disappears around a distant bend, majestically unconcerned with the problems of the variable human who clings to its shore in intermittent cycles of its countless years (1932: 209).

The old cellblock was built on 'a foundation of crushed rock, trodden cinders and old scrap iron' (Lawes, 1932: 232). It was built, in other words, on (and by) the exhaust of industrialisation. With no apparent irony, Lawes wrote, '[i]t is scarcely the sort of thing to support plant life' (1932: 232). Nor, we might imagine, to support the countless lives of the prisoners housed there.

Sing Sing took its place in popular culture by appearing as the backdrop to several Hollywood gangster films. *The Big House* (dir. G. W. Hill, 1930), *Angels with Dirty Faces* (dir. M. Curtiz, 1938) and *20,000 Years in Sing Sing* (dir. M. Curtiz, 1932) used the penitentiary as a character.

The trailer for the latter describes Lawes as '[t]he man who lives on the volcano of human passion'! The cinematic countenance of Sing Sing 'helped to form an image of the prison in the public mind that exists even today' (Gado, 2004: 13). During and after Lawes's wardenship film stars and entertainers were brought into Sing Sing and encouraged to speak to the inmates. These included James Cagney (the lead in *Angels with Dirty Faces*), Spencer Tracey (star of *20,000 Years in Sing Sing*) and Harry Houdini (we might wonder what *his* talk concerned). Lawes allowed filming within the prison and Warner Bros. reciprocated by paying for a gymnasium to be built in 1934. It was, apparently, 'on par with any collegiate gym of the time' (Cheli, 2003: 75). The building now stands idle. Curiously it resembles a sound stage and so expresses rather neatly the syncretic relationship of cinema and location.

Where the Lawes era had been one of a perverse prosperity with the popularity of the prison on film allied with the 1920s/30s building boom, the post-war period marked a down turn. Symbolically this is reflected in the use of the industrial shops and power plant. The power plant was built by inmates and represented a $1 million 'state-of-the-art' venture (Cheli, 2003: 64). For Lawes it had embodied the 'spirit of the new Sing Sing' (1932: 209). Down by the river's edge it rose up 'in a commanding gesture toward the heavens' (*ibid.*). Lawes used Beaumont and De Tocqueville's reference to 'honest habits' a century earlier to describe its utility:

[t]o me it is a symbol of what we hope to make of Sing Sing – an industrial plant where men will labour willingly and hopefully; where they will learn to perfect themselves in the ways of honest toil (1932: 209).

During the 1960s 'most of the industrial shops and buildings in the lower yard were torn down to make way for a proposed new state road' (Cheli, 2003: 68). The new road never materialised. The now vacant power plant has become yet another layer of industrial sediment on the shore of the Hudson.

Marginal: defining the 'monumental' prison

The first half of the twentieth century saw the beginnings of what I will refer to as the 'monumental' prison. I wish to focus here on the meanings that we can take from the cell blocks that were constructed under Lawes's wardenship. The 'look' of the monumental prison, as I shall refer to it, was typified by the telegraph pole and self-enclosed designs. The former consisted of a central spine or corridor off which cell blocks and other services were located at right angles. The latter saw the cellblocks themselves form part or all of the prison enclosure. The first telegraph pole design in the United States was at the Minnesota State Prison (completed 1913–14). Subsequently, the 1930s saw the 'enthusiastic' adoption of the design by the federal government (Johnston, 2000: 141). Sing Sing's A and B blocks offered a truncated version of this.

Rotman (1995: 165) bluntly refers to the 'superficiality of Progressive reforms in recreation, work, and assimilation with the open society' within the Big House. This was another failed penal experiment. Instead of reform, 'in the world of granite, steel, and cement, the dominant features were stultifying routines, monotonous schedules, and isolation' (*ibid.*). This description encapsulates the starkly functional, monolithic nature of the Big House with its huge, elongated cell blocks. The irony of the term itself is acute. There is little sense of domesticity in the vast blocks at Sing Sing. Yet, this world also describes that outside the prison walls. Aside from the Depression, this was a time of the construction of an entire world of granite, steel and cement. Incarceration, on the grand scale of the Big Houses, simultaneously distanced the prison population from this swiftly developing world whilst locking them within one of it vast symbols.

Jencks (1993: 75) uses the term 'mono-architecture' to describe those buildings that are 'reduced, exclusive...sealed off from life and change'. These are the properties I envisage the monumental building to possess and, by extension, so too the monumental prison. The blankness of the monumental prison contrasts starkly with that of the elaborate gatehouses of prisons built in the late eighteenth and early nineteenth centuries during the 'central' period. What I mean by the 'monumental' prison is that it combines the extreme functionalism of New York's tenement buildings of the late nineteenth century with the scale of the City Beautiful ethos and the modernist utopia of Le Corbusier's Ideal City. Let us start with Le Corbusier. I do not wish to add to the 'monotonous regularity with which Le Corbusier has been represented as a malevolent, all-powerful force for evil' (Sudjic, 1993: 18). Rather, I wish to simply illuminate the similarities between the Corbusian living block and the filing cabinets of stone of the Big House. Hall, P. (2002: 226), for example, describes the plans of Soviet architects, the urbanists, who had been influenced by Le Corbusier: '[t]hey wanted to build new cities in open countryside, in which everyone would live in gigantic collective apartment blocks...'

For Le Corbusier, the house-machine would consist of 'cells' and be one amongst many other mass-produced 'units'. Each would be like the last without 'any kind of individual idiosyncrasy' (*ibid.*: 224). The cell would be the base form with nothing 'more or less than the minimum necessary for efficient existence' (*ibid.*: 225). This echoes, of course, the rigorous equality of the prison. We also see in Le Corbusier's designs, the same metaphor of the machine and the regimented, disciplined life that had been applied to the prison. These were to be machines for living in, representing a 'normalizing morality that seeks to reduce all differences to an economic order of the Same' (Smith, 2001: 31).

The Big House looked back to Burnham's 1893 Chicago World's Fair designs and forward to those of Speer's Berlin and Lutyens and Baker's New Delhi. Yet it was not in any elaborate detail of design that the Big House spoke, rather it announced itself through its scale. It took on an 'iconic role' (Lefebvre, 1974/5, 2003: 152). It acted to produce consensus by offering 'each member of a society an image of that mem bership' (Lefebvre, 1991: 139). The monumental prison projected for those people outside of its walls the message of inclusion or rejection thereby imposing consensus upon those outside. Lefebvre (1991: 225) points to the 'two "primary processes"' of the monument: it displaces and condenses. In the instance of the monumental prison, it condenses the incarcerated into an undifferentiated mass. As such, they are deemed fit to be housed in these gigantic housing blocks.

Yet why should we not also consider those prisons of the earlier 'central' period to be 'monumental'? It is the stripping of the architectural artifice, what Benjamin (1936) would refer to as the 'aura', and the simultaneous leap in scale that lends it this monumental characteristic. The prison no longer needed those accruements to tell the massed throng how to react to it. Indeed, their own 'folk' readings of the prison carried with them elements of the 'Gothic' (see Fiddler, 2006, 2007). This was a blank canvas upon which condensing and displacement could occur. This is what made it so powerful on film. The scale was imposing, but the blank façade made it susceptible to displacement by the mass audience. The 'monumental' prisons were not just physically marginal in that they were increasingly constructed away from cities. They also distanced the incarcerated from those outside by the messages that they projected and that were, in turn, projected upon them.

Further, we can use Bauman (1995) and Young's (1999) reading of phagic and emic strategies to describe the difference between the periods of centrality and marginality. The initial period of centrality could be seen as an attempt to assimilate the unreasoned, unproductive Other into the productive labour force. As the nature of capitalism and modes of production altered, so the requirements of industry changed. A disciplined workforce of the type, in part, created by the prison was no longer required. The inclusive strategy of the prison had ended. So that waste would be minimised, the inclusive strategy (of the prison) swung around to an exclusive one. Alternative inclusive strategies were employed that ran in parallel with the prison (Simon, 1995). The workforce could now be placed in reserve. Those individuals representing disorder would remain in the monumental space of the prison.

The prison no longer occupied its central position in relation to factories and similar such institutions. A modern workforce was no longer going to be disciplined or created within its walls. The offender was to be removed from society and stored in the 'Big House'. Berman (1982: 19) powerfully states that the processes of modernity are 'capable of the most spectacular growth, capable of appalling waste and destruction.' So it is that the marginal prison was produced to contain those 'left behind'. The prison became an essential feature in channelling this human waste, this exhaust of modernity.

Adjunct: a prison *and* urban population of redundant 'republic machines'

Berman talks of the various 'symbolic expression(s) of modernity': the Brooklyn Bridge, Times Square and the Bowery (1982: 289). It is quite possible to add Sing Sing to such a list. Penitentiaries were, as one contemporary critic put it, 'grand theatre[s], for the trial of all new plans in hygiene and education, in physical and moral reform.' (unknown, cited by Rothman, 1990: 84). Certainly during the central period discussed earlier, the penitentiary (and Sing Sing more narrowly) was envisaged as just such a 'grand theatre' to demonstrate the 'project of Enlightenment' (Dumm, 1987: 5–6). The marginal period that saw the development of what I have called a 'monumental' aesthetic, also saw the purpose of this 'theatre' change. As a marginalised space, the prison acted as the end-zone repository for the 'Other(s)' of society.

The marginal space created a 'segregated and insulated institution [making] the actual business of deviancy control invisible, but it did make its boundaries obvious enough' (Cohen, 1996: 401). Now we might talk of a continuum where it is difficult to define 'where the prison ends and the community begins' (*ibid.*). It is no longer the case that these populations are subject to either-or phagic and emic strategies. Rather they encounter varied and alternating types of both from a range of institutions. Where Garland (1985) described the positioning of the prison at a terminus point, the far end of a continuum of institutions of punishment and welfare, the twenty-first century prison is an adjunct to the contemporary urban environment. To appropriate Lefebvre's (1991) metaphor of the permeability of the space of a house, so the prison is a node in a series of outward and inward energies, carceral and otherwise. The prison walls give the 'appearance of separation', but there is also an 'ambiguous continuity' (*ibid.*: 87). There is now an uncanny confusion of interiority and exteriority.

It is not simply that the urban and carceral mimic one another's aesthetic or that contemporary 'Metropolitan Detention Centers' bring the penitentiary back toward the city (Fiddler, 2006, 2007). Wacquant (2001) talks specifically of the socio-cultural syncretism of ghetto and prison (where once we would have spoken of the socio-economic syncretism of prison and factory, also see Concluding Remarks). As such, instead of the discipline of the 'central' period or the deskilling of the 'marginal', we presently see the *un*disciplining of this population in the 'adjunct'; a stripping away of expectations. The urban and incarcerated populations are no longer required to participate in the labour market (save for perfunctory 'workfare requirements now imposed upon the free poor as a requirement of citizenship' (Wacquant, 2002: 54)). As such, the disciplining of the workforce is a redundant concept. We see a gravitational pull between these adjunct or '"residual" spaces' of the urban and prison, between that of welfare/workfare and incarceration (Allen, 1999: 250). In essence, this is a type of training, but only to be stationary in a late-modern period that values mobility. The goal is no longer to produce 'republic machines', but merely to contain (Dumm, 1987: 95).

2
Reconceptualising Social Control: A Case-Study in Gender, Punishment and Murder

*Anette Ballinger**

It is not difficult to demonstrate that a casual usage of 'social control' metaphors leads to non-explanation and incoherence. There is no political or ideological institution which could not in some way be interpreted as an agency of social control. There is no indication in the phrase of who the agents or instigators of social control may be: no constant criterion whereby we may judge whether social control has broken down – certainly not conflict, for this may ultimately, or even inherently, be a means of reinforcing conformity. Nor finally is there any fixed yardstick whereby we may know when social control has been reimposed (Stedman Jones, 1983: 42).

Lacking any precise definition and consistent use, the concept was aptly described by Cohen (1985: 2) as 'Mickey Mouse' and by Lowman *et al.* (1987: 4) as 'a skeleton key opening so many doors that its analytic power has been drained ... a spectral category which becomes all things to all theorists' (Wilson, 2006: 392).

First popularised by Edward A. Ross in 1901 who intended it to refer to 'a constraining social element which held in check man's darker animal side' (Stedman Jones, 1983: 44), the term 'social control' has been described as 'a poorly defined concept which has been used to describe all means through which conformity might be achieved – from infant social-ization to incarceration' (Wilson, 2006: 391). It is therefore the aim of this chapter to offer a critical reappraisal of the concept in order to explore whether it alone has the ability or potential to offer an adequate explana-tion of the complexities of the interactions between individual women and powerful arms of the state such as the criminal justice system. More specifically, the chapter explores how useful the concept is as an analytical tool through the case-study of Ada Allen who stood trial for the murder of her husband Donald in 1945.

Until the arrival of second-wave feminism in the UK during the 1970s, the concept 'social control' had been mainly associated with the relationships between different social classes, with specific focus on the impact that middle class reform movements had on the lower classes. Thus, the activities of various nineteenth century welfare, relief and reform movements have often been interpreted as having a hidden agenda of transposing middle class moral values onto working class populations through charity. This interpretation maintains that industrialisation and urbanisation led to a breakdown of the pre-industrial social order which traditionally had been community-based. The perceived crisis generated by this breakdown led to the middle and upper classes designing new social control measures to be imposed on the working class in general and its 'disreputable' elements in particular, in order to teach them 'self-discipline, industry, punctuality, thrift' and temperance (Mayer, 1983: 17–18). Much of the work in this area has therefore been developed by conceptualising social control in a 'top-down' manner, emphasising the functionalist aspect of the concept and over-emphasising the homogenised motives of the 'controllers' at the expense of the agency and perspective of the 'controlled' (Morrison, 2005: 69).

Social control and feminism

With the arrival of second-wave feminism during the 1970s the concept underwent a theoretical modernisation as feminist theorists embarked on the process of genderising it. While feminists recognised from the beginning that within a society deeply divided by social class, *both* men and women 'are subject to material, repressive and ideological forms of social control', writers such as Smart and Smart noted in their classic text *Women, Sexuality and Social Control*, that women's experience of social control is related specifically to discourses embedded within the social construction of femininity – namely those of sexuality, respectability, domesticity, and motherhood. Furthermore:

> The social control of women assumes many forms, it may be internal or external, implicit or explicit, private or public, ideological or repressive (1978: 2).

Smart and Smart further identified four specific areas within which women alone are socially controlled – those of the reproductive cycle;

the double standards of morality; a subordinate social and legal status within the family and the ideology of woman's place which lies at the heart of 'the separation of "home" and "work"' (1978: 3).

Together with other early influential works such as Hutter and Williams's (1981) edited collection, *Controlling Women*, Smart and Smart's *Women, Sexuality and Social Control* had thus established analytical concepts which were to become the cornerstones of feminist challenges to the dominant heteropatriarchal nature of criminology 'for decades to come, and which helped to expand the criminological agenda by emphasising the gender-specific social control experienced by women in both the public and private spheres' (Ballinger, 2008: forthcoming).

Building on such early work, Heidensohn explored the role that women themselves had played in dispersing social control through nineteenth century charities and reform movements. Through charitable work, and later through 'the semi-professions of nursing, midwifery, social work, etc.', middle and upper-class women gained a public role within 'the system of social control' (1985: 172–3).

However, women's public connections with various agencies of social control can be understood as interpositions 'between the state and the people, strategically softening the sternness of [state] power,' and making 'life for the poor a little more acceptable.' In that sense, such agencies remained within overall 'patriarchal control' (Heidensohn, 1985: 173, 172).

The 1980s also saw the publication of influential studies on the subject of women and punishment by authors such as Rafter and Carlen who identified the gender-specific nature of social control within reformatories and prisons.

Rafter employed a gendered version of the concept in order to explore its impact on institutionalised women in her historical study 'Chastising the Unchaste' which focused on the social control mechanisms being utilised in a New York reformatory for women in the period 1894–1931. She identified a range of non-criminal behaviours which could result in incarceration in the Albion reformatory. Such behaviour included 'promiscuity, vagrancy and saloon-visiting', which, when engaged in by men, did not result in similar penal interventions (1983: 288, 291). Through a policy of 'rescue and reform' Rafter identified how mechanisms of social control legitimised the double standards of morality as 'a new segment of the female population' – those who cared little for conventional notions of female propriety' – was deemed in need of being taught 'the values associated with the lady

– refinement, propriety, decorum' (1983: 291, 293). Rafter concluded that this net-widening of penal institutions for those who failed to display acceptable standards of femininity arose as a consequence of 'the solidification of gender roles in nineteenth century America as well as the hardening of divisions between social classes'. Within this context reformatories taught working-class women 'to accept a new concept of gender which entailed restriction of their sexual and vocational choices' (1983: 306, 307).

In her contemporary study, Carlen noted that female defendants are not only judged according to the crimes they have committed, but also according to 'the court's assessment of them as wives, mothers and daughters (1988: 10). This assessment would inevitably focus upon issues related to the discourses of femininity identified above – sexuality, respectability, domesticity and motherhood.

In 1987 Green, Hebron and Woodward articulated a definition of social control which captured its gender-specific nature:

> Social control is defined as an ongoing process, one element in the struggle to maintain male hegemony which sets the limits of appropriate feminine behaviour (1987: 79).

Hence, by the end of the 1980s a host of pioneering feminist and other critical work had provided detailed analyses which demonstrated not only the gender-specific nature of social control, but also the role that such control plays in constructing 'normal' versus 'deviant' womanhood. In particular, the discourses of respectability sexuality motherhood and domesticity were identified, as both the means by which women can be socially controlled, and 'as key variables when women come into contact with the criminal justice system – whether as victims or perpetrators' (Ballinger, 2008: forthcoming).

The demise of social control

The increasing influence of postmodern feminism and identity politics during the 1980s and 1990s played an important role in the demise of the concept of social control. As feminism became pre-occupied with issues of 'difference' between women – in turn resulting in the destabilisation of women as a category – the idea of women being 'socially controlled' became increasingly unfashionable. Instead the concept became associated with the accusation that it had contributed to the 'over-generalisation' and 'over-simplification' of the complexity of women's oppression. McNay, for example, argued 'that gender is not the only determining influence on women's lives'. Rather:

> any individual's life is determined by multiple factors which conflict and interlink with each other, producing differential effects ... against this background of multiple determinants, individuals act upon themselves and order their own lives in numerous and variable ways (1992: 64, 65).

Thus, attempts to conceptualise female oppression within a general 'patriarchal' framework was now itself the target of feminist critique due to its 'North-American/Euro-centric' nature:

> An insistence on women as passive victims of male oppression oversimplifies the complexities of women's subordination by placing too great a stress both on the universal nature of oppression and the common undifferentiated enemy of patriarchy (McNay, 1992: 64).

Yet, it is important to note that the portrayal of early feminist social control theory as over-generalised and universal – branding 'all men as the upholders of patriarchy' (Tosh, 2004: 45) and locking all women into the role of eternal and passive victims – was itself an over-simplification of the core arguments of second-wave feminism. For example, Hartmann recognised in 1979 that not all men are equal or necessarily located in positions of power. Instead 'patriarchy is a set of social relations which has a material base and in which there are hierarchical relations between men and solidarities amongst them, which enable them to control women' (cited in Tosh, 2004: 46). Thus, there are examples in feminist literature during the 1970s and 1980s which demonstrate that the concept of social control never referred 'to a crude or conspiratorial model of oppression' in which all women are perpetual victims – kept in a subordinate position by the iron fist of patriarchy (Ballinger, 2000: 41). Instead postmodern feminism and identity politics can – with hindsight – be conceptualised as having *over-played* issues of 'difference' and ethnocentricity: at the expense of the structural inequalities that early feminism identified and campaigned against. Tosh has observed:

> Multivalence and contingency can ... be overplayed. The virtual absence of 'patriarchy' from the scholarly lexicon at the present time points to a disconcerting shift away from those deep-set and

enduring inequalities between men and women which informed scholarly work in the 1970s and 1980s (2004: 56).

Perhaps a fairer evaluation of the gender-specific analysis of social control in early feminist literature is the rather cursory attention paid to issues relating to its impact on the construction of respectable and disreputable masculinities, as well as the state's role and interest in the maintenance of such control and gender conformity as far as *both* women and men are concerned. Furthermore, this early work has also been accused of being reluctant to deal with the agency of women who commit violent crime, preferring instead to rely on stereotypes of women's passivity, or that they had little or no idea of what they were doing – their actions understood as unintentional – 'the result of pathology rather than reason and rationality' (Ballinger, 2005: 70). According to Wilczynski:

... criminality in women is rarely, if ever, seen as a rational reaction to life stresses, or as a response to social, political or physical inequalities, as is often the case with men (cited in Morrissey, 2003: 33; Ballinger, 1996; Allen, 1987).

While the portrayal of female violence as unintentional and irrational may help to ensure a favourable sentence for individual female defendants, it harms the wider cause of feminism because it 'undermine[s] a concept of women in general as fully fledged moral subject and responsible agents', and therefore as citizens equal to men (Morrissey, 2003: 35). As I have documented elsewhere, it is relatively unproblematic to demonstrate the influence of androcentric law as a social control mechanism in cases where women have refused to present themselves and their violent act through the dominant discourses of acceptable femininity. For example, the execution of Ruth Ellis is widely regarded as being the result of not only her crime, but also her failure to conform to the discourses of respectability, domesticity, sexuality and motherhood discussed above (Ballinger, 1996, 2000). Yet, if feminism is to engage with notions of social control at all, it is vital that it has available an analysis so robust, rigorous and complex that it can also encompass cases like that of Marie Fahmy who – despite being a woman with a 'past' very similar to that of Ellis and having committed a crime in almost identical circumstances – nonetheless left the court a free woman after being found 'not guilty' on all counts (Ballinger, 1996).

To meet this demand, the analysis in the remainder of this chapter will avoid the use of a universal and generalised 'top-down' conception of social control and will instead incorporate an additional two key themes – those of masculinity and agency. First, I shall demonstrate that it is not only women who can be socially controlled through discourses around appropriate femininity, men who fail to conform to the social construction of 'respectable masculinity' may also be perceived to be problematic to the dominant social order, and may subsequently suffer the loss of both 'manly' honour and status as a victim, despite having been killed by their female partners. In doing so, I shall argue that a message is sent out to men as a category about their personal conduct and responsibilities within a heteropatriarchal social order which may also be regarded as a form of 'social control'. This is not to say that men and women are *equally* socially controlled. As will become apparent, it is the gender-specific production and re-production of the male and female subject, and their place within the overall heteropatriarchal social order which is at issue. More specifically, with respect to the Ada Allen case analysed below:

> We need ... to consider the ways in which law constructs and reconstructs masculinity and femininity, and maleness and femaleness, and contributes routinely to a common-sense perception of difference which sustains the social and sexual practices which feminism is attempting to challenge (Smart, 1995: 79).

Second, I shall explore the limitations of the concept 'social control' by placing it within the context of women's culpability, responsibility and agency when they commit crimes of violence. The central arguments presented in this chapter therefore seek to emphasise and elaborate upon the complexities and limits involved when applying the concept of social control to particular social groups, thereby avoiding the over-generalisation and over-simplification implied by the term as outlined in the opening quotes of this chapter.

The case of Ada Allen

Ada Allen killed her husband Donald in June 1945 after 12 years of marriage. Donald was frequently away from home for long periods of time due to his employment as an RAF pilot. Whilst home on leave Donald and Ada spent the evening of the 9th June drinking in a bar when Donald commented that another women in the bar had 'nice legs'. According to Inspector Hills, Ada described the sequence of event leading up to the murder in the following terms:

> We were so happy this afternoon. We went to the Wellington this evening. My husband kept on remarking what nice legs a girl there had got until I couldn't stick it any longer and I left in disgust and came back home. He came later and said he had decided to walk out on me at last and that he really meant it this time. I said 'Donald Darling do you realise what you are doing'. He repeated that this was final and that he was going. *I reached for the revolver and did not realise it was cocked. I held it towards him. It went off.*[1] (emphasis added).

While giving her statement to Inspector Hills:

> the accused who had been sobbing bitterly broke down completely and leaned against me for support ... Still crying she said, 'I loved him. He knows I wouldn't hurt a hair on his head. How is he? Let me go to him. I can't live without him; he is my life. He knows I love him and he plays me up.'[2]

She offered a rather different version of events to Inspector Price:

> Don kept looking at other women's legs. I did not like it. He gave me two or three brandies. I left him at the Wellington and came home. He followed me home and when we got home we quarrelled. *I took the gun out of the top drawer of the cabinet. I knew it was half cocked and I pulled it. I meant to shoot him in the legs.*[3] (emphasis added). [Donald was shot in the groin].

Both Inspectors Hills and Price agreed that when they arrived at the murder scene Ada was in a 'very distressed' condition, and Chief Superintendent Wakefield agreed that she was 'suffering with emotional strain' when she arrived at the police station.[4] Similarly, nurse Sheppard stated that when Ada sought medical help for Donald after the shooting, 'her condition was very distressed and distraught', explaining that:

> ... she and her husband had been quarrelling and that they were always quarrelling. He told her he was going to leave her and she

did not know what she was doing and shot him in the stomach with his Service revolver.[5]

Night sister Mary Downs agreed that 'she was extremely distressed and agitated beyond words' and said:

> I have shot my husband in the stomach. We are always having fights and I have just shot him in the stomach.[6]

Finally PC Trinder who interviewed Ada, confirmed that 'she was very agitated' and deeply concerned about the condition of Donald.[7]

Witnesses also gave evidence relating to the immediate aftermath of the shooting before either police, or hospital staff, were called. Clive Jones who lived in the flat above the Allens' basement flat testified that when he arrived at the scene of the shooting after being called by Ada, 'she was very distressed and very hysterical'. After arriving with her at the hospital to seek help she 'became more hysterical than ever'.[8] Clive's friend, Kenneth Hyett, agreed that Ada 'was very hysterical, crying and holding her head in her hands':

> She kept saying, 'Oh Ken oh, Ken' ... She bent over the deceased and said, 'Oh darling I love you, I love you'.[9]

When Ada stood trial for the murder of Donald at Birmingham Assizes one month later, she testified that:

> Her husband was pummelling her; she tried to get away, and reached out for something with which to protect herself. Her husband ... struck her again and 'the gun went off'. She had no intention of firing the shot.[10]

After an hour and a half of deliberations the jury returned 'a verdict of "Not guilty" of murder, but "Guilty" of manslaughter'. The verdict was followed by 'half-an-hour packed with drama' when Mr Cartwright for the *prosecution* revealed further details of Ada's 'wretched life' as a result of having discovered letters amongst Donald's belongings which indicated he had been 'grossly unfaithful'.[11] These letters had been passed to the defending counsel who told the court that Donald had been using 'pen clubs' as a means to befriend women with whom he would subsequently have affairs:

> She has had to go through all that and has had to leave him on two or three occasions owing to his ill-treatment of her ... the man was reduced from the rank of squadron-leader to that of flight-lieut. Because of similar things happening with women on the aerodrome ... In view of the fact that she has been a decent clean-living woman and done her duty; and also in view of the jury's recommendation of mercy, I appeal to you to take a very lenient course.[12]

This glowing character reference was echoed by the *prosecutor*, Mr Cartwright Sharp:

> On behalf of the prosecution I can say the prisoner is a woman of excellent character ... [who has] had a wretched life owing to her husband's association with other women.[13]

After listening to these additional statements by both the defence and prosecutor, the judge too became extremely sympathetic to the plight of Ada, remarking:

> If the jury had known all we now know about your married life and you had been wise enough and honest enough to have told them ... they might have acquitted you altogether ... I am going to take a course I have never taken before.[14]

This unprecedented course of action took the form of the judge sentencing Ada 'to imprisonment for the term of the Assizes – nine days', consequently, she left the court a free woman.[15]

A picture had thus emerged of a 'clean-living', 'decent' and 'dutiful' wife who had obeyed all the rules associated with respectable, domesticated and obedient womanhood, and hence complied with the discourses around appropriate feminine conduct outlined above, yet was wronged by a brutal philanderer who repeatedly 'mistreated' and betrayed her. However, on closer examination a different picture emerged. Relatives and neighbours who saw and heard the couple on a regular basis such as Olive Jones, Ken Hyett and Lena Carpenter all testified that the couple 'gave the impression that they were quite happy together'.[16] Robert Page, the licensee of the couples' local pub agreed that he 'neither saw nor heard anything to give me cause or reason to believe that the deceased and his wife were not on the best of domestic relations'.[17] This was further confirmed by a friend of the couple who was with them immediately prior to the shooting:

> They were on the very best of terms and during the quarter of an hour or so we were in their company I did not hear either of them make a complaint. There was certainly no suggestion of any friction between them. They were in what I would describe as a cheerful and happy mood and jokingly referred to the fact that they had been drinking brandy at their home since six o'clock that evening.[18]

More specifically, Clive Jones who lived in the flat above, testified that immediately before the murder the radio was on 'and I could hear the accused singing'. When Donald returned 'I could hear them laughing.'[19] Kenneth Hyett confirmed that he too heard laughing immediately prior to the shooting.[20]

Thus, while Ada's sister, Lena Carpenter, made reference to the couples' differences in the past due to Donald's womanising, no evidence was presented in court to support the view that the couple were having relationship problems either immediately prior to the shooting or in the recent past. On the contrary, Lena testified, that 'when he came home [on leave] they used to go out together and were happy' and on the afternoon of the murder 'they were quite happy'.[21]

At a different level, the medical condition of Ada upon arriving in prison did not support her claim that Donald had repeatedly 'pummelled her in the face'[22] prior to the shooting – the doctor finding only 'a small bruise upon' her thigh.[23]

In terms of the period leading up to the shooting, while indisputable evidence of Donald's unfaithfulness was available to the prosecution in the form of letters written by two women he had associations with, a number of other letters written by Ada to Donald were also available. These letters do not support either Ada's own, or the court's presentation of herself as the innocent, respectable and dutiful wife, who 'had had a wretched life owing to her husband's association with other women'.[24] Instead they reveal a woman in possession of considerable agency who did not shy away from an active social life and the company of other men when Donald was away. For example, she wrote in one letter:

> I had quite a good evening dancing Saturday night ... everyone including myself got very boozed and ended the evening singing for

the boys which they enjoyed very much ... I am being very good – well as good as you could be if you were here.[25]

One week later she wrote:

I was wolfed by Bill Nash ... he had a beautiful line and looked amazed when I told him so. I didn't get tight darling and was only kissed very hard, don't you think I'm a good girl.[?]

In the same letter she referred to two American army captains who had asked her for a date, whilst also reminding Donald of the temptations facing him while away in France:

Hope you haven't been getting too fond of any french [sic] dames – I shall get awfully mad if you don't take care dear, even if they do look nice – I shan't fancy myself very much with no eyes and a nose eaten away with disease.[26]

Several other letters described Ada and her friends' busy social lives which included getting drunk frequently in various pubs and bars and coming 'home with a strange yank'.[27] In one letter she reassured Donald that '[I] haven't bothered about finding anyone to take your place ... in any case the men are lousy so I'm not worried', whilst again warning Donald about catching a sexually transmitted disease: '... be careful of the wolverines and dont [sic] get any extras to bring home to me'.[28]

Finally, she wrote to one of the women Donald had an affair with, identifying herself as his wife – presumably to deter this woman from seeing Donald again – but also admitting 'that she [Ada] was having an affair with another man'.[29]

Taken together, Ada's correspondence therefore challenged her portrayal in court as a passive, meek, much put upon victim being brutalised by a faithless husband, and instead suggested a more complex relationship within which Ada's personal conduct was not dissimilar to that of her husband. Furthermore, her relaxed and humorous accounts of her busy social life – including references to other men she was seeing – does not suggest a woman terrorised by a brutal husband. How then, can we explain her nine-day sentence? Women, however obedient and compliant, do not as a rule receive nine-day sentences for shooting dead their husbands, even in circumstances where there are other mitigating factors, as for example, the aforementioned Ruth Ellis case demonstrates, who was executed in 1955 for shooting her faithless lover (Ballinger, 2000, 1996). While headlines such as the *Daily Herald's* '"Excellent Wife" Shot Brutal Husband: Freed'[30] demonstrate the importance of Ada being able to present herself through the discourses of appropriate femininity discussed above, any suggestion that the 'social control' aspects of these discourses are always and necessarily repressive in nature and work in favour of the 'controllers', and thus to the detriment of the 'controlled', is clearly challenged by the outcome of her trial. As can be seen from the evidence above, her construction as a helpless, victimised wife in need of protection became particularly effective as a result of being juxtaposed against Donald's construction as a philandering, violent brute, a discourse in direct conflict with 'respectable masculinity'. In the following section I therefore explore issues around the social construction of masculinity and its impact on the final verdict in Ada's case. This analysis will allow for the exposure of both contradiction and conflict within the criminal justice system, which in turn challenges the top-down application of the concept 'social control' outlined earlier.

Theoretical implications: masculinity and social control

Just as concerns have been raised about 'over-generalising' the complexities involved in the process of socially controlling women, so the concept of masculinity cannot be reduced to a unitary, self-explanatory term (Hearn, 1996: 203). Instead it is the existence of 'multiple masculinities' (Strange, 2003: 311), embodying 'multiple dimensions' which should be recognised (Haywood and Mac an Ghaill, 1996: 51). Nonetheless, it has been widely acknowledged that 'within the broader changes in family structure' which the Industrial Revolution initiated, the masculine ideal was transformed into the 'man of law' still recognisable today (Collier, 1995b: 207; Naffine cited in Collier, 1995a: 208; Wilcott and Griffin, 1996: 86). Thus, while women experienced new forms of social control through the 'modernisation of patriarchy' (Bartky, 1990), a process which involved the elevation of 'the cult of domesticity' (O'Donovan, 1985), men also had to be disciplined in order to achieve the goal of '"respectable" familial masculinity' now required to ensure the prosperity of the new social, economic and political order – industrial capitalism (Collier, 1995a: 218; Clark, 2000: 27). Youth organisations such as the Boys Brigade and Baden-Powell's scouting movement, helped to communicate a new standard of middle-class masculinity which emphasised the qualities 'of directness, honesty, decency, duty and honour' (Warren, 1987: 200; Springhall, 1987). Thus, while bravery and courage remained important qualities within this new construction of 'manliness', respectable masculinity could not be achieved through brute force; on the contrary, the nineteenth century brand of masculinity now emphasised that 'a man is not the less strong for being gentle' (Springhall, 1987: 66). Through self-discipline and self-control, as well as marriage and work, this new man of 'reason' and 'rationality' could achieve respectable masculinity, a process which gave him a new status as the sole provider of the 'family wage' (Hammerton, 1992; Collier, 1995a; Clark, 2000).

Connell's concept of hegemonic masculinity highlights the complexities involved in the social construction of masculinity:

> The public face of hegemonic masculinity is not necessarily what powerful men are but what sustains their power and what large numbers of men are motivated to support (1987: 185).

In other words, as long as hegemonic masculinity is accepted as the dominant cultural form of masculinity to which all men should aspire, deviations in actual behaviour is relatively unthreatening to the social order. This is a key qualification because it demonstrates the emphasis on maintaining the interests of hegemonic masculinity rather than the interests of men, which in turn challenges simplistic explanations with regard to both the social order and the criminal justice system within that order, as being based on 'a rigid system of male domination' (Smart, 1995: 130). It therefore also challenges the traditional top-down application of legal control mechanisms by demonstrating that the law does not operate solely in the interests of men, just as men do not operate solely in the interests of each other.

A similar argument can be made about Connell's concept of 'emphasised femininity' which he defines as the subordination of women to men, 'oriented to accommodating the interests and desires of men' (1987: 183). In particular, compliance as one aspect of emphasised femininity, 'is given most cultural and ideological support ...' (Connell, 1987: 187). As with hegemonic masculinity, women's actual behaviour may not necessarily match this key characteristic of emphasised femininity as long as the *performance* of it is sustained: 'This kind of femininity is performed, and performed especially to men' (Connell, 1987: 188).

Ada's performance of emphasised femininity was brimming with compliance as she constructed herself as the long-suffering, put-upon, self-sacrificing wife, who had lied in court – despite this being to the detriment of her defence – for the sole purpose of protecting the good name of her faithless husband:

> Had I only made a full statement of my husband's associations with other women in the first days of the case, I have been told I would have been discharged altogether ... But I did not want to. My only thought at that time was to shield Don's name from being besmirched by gossiping. Only a few weeks ago I painted all the inside of the caravan and put in new fittings, so that Don and I could spend our summer holidays in it. No one can say I did not try to make our lives happy. Everything I had or earned I gave up to help him in his career. No sacrifice was too great.[31]

Meanwhile, Donald was constructed as having failed to comply with the two key components of hegemonic masculinity – those of marriage and work. While no evidence was presented in court that he had ever been physically abusive towards Ada, Mr Griffiths, for the defence, claimed that:

> As far back as 1936 he would not work, so she had to get a job as a cook-general and while working to keep both of them she found that he was associated with professional dance partners at Hammersmith. When she left him he thrashed her.[32]

Throughout the following years Ada 'had stuck to him and had had to leave him on two occasions because of his ill-treatment'.[33] Despite this level of loyalty, Ada claimed that immediately prior to the shooting Donald announced: 'I have decided to walk out on you at last. This is final. This time I am going.'[34]

Hammerton has argued that since the nineteenth century, the manliness of husbands has increasingly been tested by their marital conduct and breadwinning capacities (1992: 3). If their 'failure to maintain their wives adequately' was combined with 'physical assault', they risked being regarded as 'monstrous ... unmanly and cruel' (1992: 48). Ada's, and indeed the court's ability, to construct Donald through the discourses of philanderer, wife-beater and poor provider ensured that it was not only Ada's femininity, but also Donald's masculinity which was on trial in the courtroom. Ada's testimony presented above, indicated that he had broken every one of the qualities of 'respectable manliness – directness, honesty, decency, duty and honour'. His failure to live up to respectable masculinity therefore played a significant part in constructing him as a 'cruel', 'brutal' and dishonourable man[35] who preyed on 'lonely women', despite his marital status, thereby humiliating Ada still further.[36]

Meanwhile, Ada's ability to construct herself as not only the long-suffering, compliant wife who had to write to these lonely women telling them: 'This man is my husband',[37] but also as a stereotypical hysterical female who was lacking in both agency and intent as far as her crime 'against a man who had been a brute to her for years'[38] was concerned, helped to ensure that the prosecutor, defence and judge all displayed a deep measure of sympathy towards her. In the following section I elaborate upon the second theme to be considered in the 'reconceptualising' of social control – that of agency and its relationship to the social construction of femininity and masculinity, the state and the social order.

Women's violence, agency and rationality

Since the arrival of second-wave feminism several authors have analysed the labelling of female murderers as 'mad', 'bad' or 'tragic victim' – more 'sinned against than sinning' – 'to be pitied rather than punished' (Ballinger, 2005: 70; see also Allen, 1987; Ballinger, 1996, 2000; Morrissey, 2003; Lloyd, 1995; Wilczynski, 1991; Worrall, 1990). Feminists have also investigated the impact that surrounding discourses of femininity have in determining which of these labels are applied to individual female criminals. For example, those who adhere to traditional constructions of emphasised femininity are likely to be perceived through the 'victim' label. The utilisation of such labels can be understood as a strategy for reducing the threat that female agency presents when women kill. As Kennedy has explained:

> Women are still the glue that cements the family unit, providing cohesion and continuity, and we do not like to admit to the possibility that there is a potential for crime in Everywoman (1993: 23).

The victim stereotype has been particularly noteworthy in analysing the predicament of battered women who eventually retaliate by killing their abuser and has undoubtedly benefited *individual* women as they make their way through the criminal justice system (Allen, 1987; Ballinger, 1996, 2005, 2007). Yet such benefits have been to the detriment of women as a *category* since the over-emphasis on women as helpless, passive victims, whose actions are unintentional, serves to reinforce existing stereotypical beliefs about female conduct and behaviour – that women are irrational and over-emotional, rather than responsible agents. In short, emphasising women's helplessness and victimisation reinforces their inequality and lack of full citizenship (Ballinger, 2007: 475; Morrissey, 2003: 25), and hence stands in direct conflict with the feminist struggle for gender equality. This construction of women as passive non-agentic beings also reinforces the 'top-down' model of social control which, as noted above, over-emphasises the motivations of the controllers whilst simultaneously marginalising the voices of the controlled (Morrison, 2005: 69). It thus fails to recognise the complexities involved in women's oppression. For example, as far as the criminal justice system is concerned, it fails 'to recognise that the main sources of women's oppression do not originate within the criminal system *per se* but "arise from prevailing material conditions, cultural values, customs and social practices"' (Smart and Smart cited in Morrison, 2005: 69). Thus, feminist theorists have rejected a simplistic equation of social control with repression:

> Rather it [social control] came to signify those ongoing processes by which femininity was constructed, in language, sexual and social relationships and law ... Feminism's role in the imputation process [of social control] and its consequences, namely the construction of new social problems, was usually acknowledged, and responsibility was taken for the ambivalent results this might lead to. Thus feminists tended to view themselves, and women in general, as actors, rather than merely acted upon, and very early on rid themselves of the oppression paradigm ... (Pitch, 1995: 89).

The Ada Allen case demonstrates both the limitations of traditional 'top-down' models of social control as well as how those limitations can be remedied through a more complex gender-specific 'reconceptualising' of the concept. Morrissey has argued that 'many portrayals of women who kill depict them as so profoundly victimised that it is difficult to regard them as ever having engaged in an intentional act in their lives' (2003: 25). Ada can be understood as falling into that category because, despite the conflicting evidence presented above as to whether the shooting had been intentional or accidental, she was able to construct herself as an 'excellent' but 'wronged' wife through the discourses of 'emphasised femininity'. Moreover, despite there being no independent evidence to support Ada's claim that she was a battered wife, she was treated as such. Thus, Ada's ability to gain the sympathy of the court through discourses of emphasised femininity, rather than actual evidence, can be seen as an example of how social control should be understood as 'an ongoing process by which femininity is constructed' rather than as 'repression' (Pitch, 1995: 89). That is to say, this feminist analysis can account for the fact that, within a framework which regards women as actors and agents, social control mechanisms may achieve a positive outcome for individual women like Ada – thus illustrating Pitch's point that outcomes may be 'ambivalent'. In short, such an analysis has avoided over-generalising women's oppression, and has instead proved capable of taking into account the 'multiple determinants' that individuals utilise to 'act upon themselves and order their own lives in numerous and variable ways' as discussed above (McNay, 1992: 65).

In turn, the process of creating such ambivalent outcomes can be linked to Morrison's point above, that it is not the criminal justice system *per se* but the prevailing cultural values, customs and social practices which create women's oppression. For example, Kennedy notes:

> Judges are not aware that they allow preconceived ideas about 'good' women to affect their decision-making. ... However, hidden expectations creep in unawares ... The compulsion to make women fulfil accepted criteria of decent womanhood is a great temptation to lawyers, who in colluding with it succumb to a paternalism which effectively marginalises women (1993: 70, 75).

In Ada's case, this compulsion was noteworthy for uniting judge, jury, defence and *prosecution* in constructing her as a 'tragic victim', 'more sinned against than sinning'. Yet, as noted above, the 'leniency' following on from this construction of individual women like Ada, comes at a heavy price – the maintenance of the heteropatriarchal social order within which women remain subordinate to men, for it is only through playing the role of the subordinate female, ruled by emotions and lacking in agency and rationality that sympathy can be sustained.

Referring to the case of Sarah Tisdall,[39] Kennedy notes how she 'was described as 'misguided' and a 'silly girl' during her trial (1993: 75), strongly mirroring Judge Humphrys' statement in Ada's case when he chastised her for telling 'silly stories':

> ... [if] 'you had been wise enough and honest enough to have told [the jury] ...all we know now about your married life ... they might have acquitted you altogether.' She had, he said, done herself no

good by telling the 'silly story' of having no intention to shoot and should have told the jury the truth.[40]

In short, an extremely light sentence may be secured through the infantilisation of the female defendant, even when she has admitted her intention to shoot her husband, as implied by the judge's comments above. While at first glance, this suggests a large measure of sympathy and leniency towards a defendant whom the judge considered to 'have been punished enough already',[41] ultimately, this can be understood as a highly conservative strategy because it reinforces both the unequal power relationship within marriage and the gendered social order more generally (Morrissey, 2003: 20). This is therefore a strategy which does nothing to further women's equality as citizens (Morrissey, 2003: 95), nor secure their emancipation, but, on the contrary, it secures the production and re-production of the gendered subject which in turn facilitates the maintenance of the social order, whilst simultaneously preventing new discourses being created through which the agency of female murderers can be articulated without falling into either the mad/bad or victim categories.

Conclusion

In this chapter I have highlighted the important contribution that early feminist work made to our understanding of how women are socially controlled through discourses around appropriate femininity, and how that socially constructed femininity may impact on the final outcome of trials of female defendants. In doing so, I have argued for a 'reconceptualising' of 'social control' by incorporating two added dimensions which were lacking in traditional top-down uses of the concept – those of masculinity and female agency. Adding these two dimensions has allowed for an analysis which does not regard the concept solely in negative terms, but instead can account for 'ambivalent outcomes' as illustrated by the Ada Allen case.

In the case-study I have also responded to the critique that traditional social control over-emphasises the perspectives of the controllers at the expense of the controlled by stressing that heteropatriarchy is not a monolithic immutable force. On the contrary, it allows for the existence of 'sacrificial men' such as Donald, who, by failing to measure up to the qualities of 'respectable masculinity', paid the price in terms of loss of reputation, and who could thus be 'sacrificed' for the greater good of preserving the gendered social order (Ballinger, 2007: 477).

Conversely, the purpose of this expanded analysis has also been to demonstrate the validity of preserving women as a *category* whilst simultaneously avoiding over-simplified explanations of marital relations which centres on 'all men's potential to abuse power' and all women's potential to become victimised (Segal, 1990: 260). In short, the analysis of women as a category may be enhanced when examined within the context of masculinity and agency. The Ada Allen case-study has demonstrated how 'representations of the murderess as victim ... function to deny her responsibility, culpability, agency, and often her rationality as well' (Morrissey, 2003: 25). Yet that representation would not have had such a powerful impact had Ada not been able to construct herself through additional discourses of emphasised femininity. In turn, that emphasised femininity would not have such a powerful impact, had it not been constructed against a disreputable masculinity – a discourse which united court personnel in the discrediting of Donald.

Connell has argued that 'the state is indeed the main organiser of the power relations of gender', but not in a simplistic or conspiratorial way which leads to 'futile searches for Patriarch Headquarters' (1996: 148, 146). Instead, 'patriarchy is embedded in *procedure*, in the state's way of functioning ... It locates sexual politics in the realm of social action, where it belongs, avoiding the speculative reductionism that would explain state action as an emanation of the inner nature of males' (1996: 146). To this we can add that the 'reconceptualised' concept of social control proposed here also does not operate in a simplistic or conspiratorial way. On the contrary, a feminist analysis of the concept which incorporates the added dimensions of masculinity and agency has enhanced the development of an analysis which is robust and rigorous enough to encompass those cases of female violence which do not fit easily into pre-existing stereotypical categories of femininity, but which feminism cannot afford to ignore if it is to continue to engage with notions of social control. This analysis therefore avoids oversimplifying women's subordination by taking into account the multiple factors which contextualise their lives as well as the numerous ways in which individual women order their lives, *without* losing sight of women as a category and their position within the wider male-dominated social order. Moreover, it is an analysis which is able to recognise women's subordinate place within that social order *without* arguing on the same terrain as heteropatriarchal traditionalists who have perpetuated sexist myths regarding women's 'nature' – that they are incapable of experiencing the full range of human emotions, and *without* relying on more contemporary victim stereotypes which undermine women's ability to respond to their emotions as rational agents:

> Such an approach acknowledges the reality of power without presenting women as eternal victim and insists on the agency of the oppressed without denying the reality of oppression (Connell, 1987: 149).

Although written over two decades ago, Connell's words remain as relevant to a twenty-first century feminist 'reconceptualising' of social control as they were to twentieth century authors interested in developing new legal narratives which focus on female agency within the wider context of gendered oppression in a heteropatriarchal social order.

Notes

* The research for this chapter was funded by the *Nuffield Foundation*. I am grateful to the Foundation for its support, both financially and emotionally. I am further indebted to the staff in the National Archives, Kew, for their professional assistance. A big thank you also to Helen Johnston for her patience and to Joe Sim for his support and encouragement.

1 NA, DPP 2/1377: 23–4.
2 DPP 2/1377: 24.
3 *ibid.*, 26.
4 *ibid.*, 25, 26, 29.
5 *ibid.*, 16, 17.
6 *ibid.*, 18.
7 *ibid.*, 21.
8 *ibid.*, 9, 10.
9 *ibid.*, 12, 13.
10 *Birmingham Gazette*, 20 July 1945.
11 *Birmingham Gazette*, 20 July 1945; *Telegraph*, 20 July 1945.
12 cited in *Birmingham Gazette*, 20 July 1945.
13 cited in *Birmingham Gazette*, 20 July 1945; *Daily Herald*, 20 July 1945.
14 cited in *Birmingham Gazette*, 20 July 1945.
15 *Birmingham Gazette*, 20 July 1945.
16 DPP 2/1377: 11, 14, 6.
17 *ibid.*, 2.
18 *ibid.*, 3.
19 *ibid.*, 8.
20 *ibid.*, 12.
21 *ibid.*, 5, 6.
22 *Daily Herald*, 20 July 1945.
23 DPP 2/1377.
24 *Daily Herald*, 20 July 1945.
25 DPP 2/1377.

26 *ibid.*
27 *ibid.*
28 *ibid.*
29 NA, HO 144/22230; DPP 2/1377.
30 *Daily Herald*, 20 July 1945.
31 *Daily Mirror*, 21 July 1945.
32 HO144/22230.
33 *Daily Herald*, 20 July 1945.
34 *Daily Express*, 20 June 1945.
35 *Manchester Guardian*, 20 July 1945; *Daily Express*, 20 July 1945.
36 *Daily Express*, 20 July 1945.
37 *Daily Express*, 20 July 1945.
38 *Birmingham Post*, 20 July 1945.
39 Sarah Tisdall was charged in 1984 under the Official Secrets Act for leaking 'information about the deployment of American missiles in the UK' (Kennedy, 1993: 75).
40 *Birmingham Gazette*, 20 July 1945.
41 *Daily Herald*, 20 July 1945.

3

An Honourable Regime of Truth? Foucault, Psychiatry and English Criminal Justice

*Tony Ward**

Psychiatry has played an important part in the history of punishment and social control over the last two centuries. It has contributed to shaping particular practices of punishment (Sim, 1990), to the development of ostensibly non-punitive forms of social control (Scull, 1993), and to the discourses and practices by which the boundary between punitive and non-punitive institutions, and penally responsible and non-responsible subjects, is defined. This chapter focuses on the last of those three roles.

Unquestionably the most influential historian of the interface between medicine and punishment is Michel Foucault. The work of Foucault most directly relevant to the concerns of this chapter is *Abnormal,* published in English in 2003, and comprising transcripts of a series of lectures delivered at the Collège de France in 1975, around the time that *Discipline and Punish* (Foucault, 1977) was published. Some of the lectures prefigure themes of the *History of Sexuality* (Foucault, 1990) but the main subject of the first six lectures is the development of psychiatric expert evidence in French criminal trials in the nineteenth and twentieth centuries.

On reading the opening pages of *Abnormal* one is immediately struck by their uncharacteristically clear normative purpose. Foucault launches a polemical attack on medico-legal expertise as it operated in the France of his day, while carefully explaining that this is not a general assault on psychiatry or law:

> ...it would be absolutely unjust to judge modern law (or, at any rate, law as it functioned at the beginning of the nineteenth century) by such a practice, and it would be unjust to assess medical knowledge

and even psychiatric knowledge in the light of this practice (Foucault, 2003: 41).

The words in parenthesis are significant. Foucault is highly critical of French criminal law *for departing from the principles of the enlightenment reformers*. In particular, he castigates it for distorting the principle of *intime conviction,* under which evidence was to be assessed not according to legal rules which stipulate quantitative measures of proof, but rather according to its persuasive effect on the conscience of the individual judge or juror (Taruffo, 2003: 667). For Foucault, this principle replaced 'the arithmetico-scholastic and ridiculous regime of classical proof' (discussed in Foucault, 1977: 35–42) with a 'common, honourable and anonymous regime of truth for a supposedly universal human subject' (Foucault, 2003: 8). This 'rule of common truth' (Foucault, 1977: 96) was essential to demonstrate to the public the consistent and predictable link between crime and punishment that the enlightenment reformers sought to achieve. The French courts, according to Foucault (2003), progressively subverted the rule by the use of 'extenuating circumstances' to convict people whose guilt was less than certain and, more importantly for our purposes, by according some expert evidence 'an effect of power, a demonstrative value, greater than other evidence and independently of its own rational structure' (Foucault, 2003: 10).

Again, it is important to notice how narrowly focused is Foucault's criticism. He is not complaining about the use of scientific evidence in general; indeed he sees empirical scientific enquiry as instantiating the 'rule of common truth' (1977: 97) and implicitly accepts that some such evidence has a 'rational structure' capable of producing 'profound conviction' (though he would deny that the rationality it appeals to is in any way natural or innate: Foucault, 2002a). Foucault's target is what American lawyers often refer to as 'junk science' (cf. Slobogin, 1998): 'statements...having the status of true discourses with considerable judicial effects...[despite] being foreign to all, even the most elementary, rules for the formation of scientific discourse' (Foucault, 2003: 11).

In the unlikely event that an English judge had been in Foucault's audience, he would probably have nodded in agreement at the speaker's mockery of French forensic psychiatry. The lectures, after all, are roughly contemporaneous with the Court of Appeal's decision in *R* v *Turner*,[1] which set strict limits to the use of psychiatric evidence in English criminal trials. Foucault, however, does not explain the problem of 'grotesque' medico-legal evidence in terms of any peculiarities of French legal culture or procedure, but rather explains it as the result of an interplay between certain very general features of modern law and psychiatry. Given the nature of Foucault's explanation, it is fair to ask how far it applies to England. In fact, English law and psychiatry in the nineteenth century did have the general features that Foucault described, and yet, as this chapter will seek to show, the interplay between them worked out quite differently.

The rule of common truth

There is little doubt that Foucault exaggerated the abruptness of the change in methods of proof in France and other civil-law jurisdictions. Langbein (1977) has shown that sixteenth and seventeenth century courts were often able to evade the formal requirements of the Roman-Canon law of proof and impose non-capital punishments on the basis of a free judicial evaluation of the evidence. Decision-making based on what French judges call *intime conviction* seems to have arrived earlier and more gradually than he supposed.

When transposed to England the idea of a 'rule of common truth', together with Foucault's (2002a) suggestion that the development of 'juridical forms' contributes to the formation of new subjects (in both senses) of knowledge, nevertheless captures an important feature of the development of criminal justice between the seventeenth and the nineteenth centuries. As Barbara Shapiro (1991, 2000) has argued, trial by jury helped institutionalise the idea that men of the middling sort could arrive at 'moral certainty' about questions of fact ('fact' itself being originally a legal concept) on the basis of evidence and argument, and thus helped develop a common epistemological foundation for legal, scientific and other forms of inquiry. The idea of 'moral certainty', or the 'satisfied conscience' of the juror, seems to correspond quite closely to the historic meaning of *intime conviction* (Taruffo, 2003). In his study of the nineteenth-century adversarial system, David Cairns argues that Foucault's 'rule' 'describes a specific instance of the need for harmony of the law and public feeling recognised by early nineteenth century reformers.... The spectator must leave court in no possible doubt of the correctness of the verdict', and adversarial procedure was the means the English courts developed to achieve this (Cairns, 1998: 94). The way English criminal procedure developed on the basis of private prosecutions, with adversarial procedure as a check against abuses, and continued to develop this adversarial procedure as prosecutions were progressively taken over to the state, was in marked contrast to the development of the highly centralised inquisitorial system in France (Langbein, 2003; Hodgson, 2005; Vogler, 2005).

One important consequence of the way English procedure developed was the marginalisation of the accused, to the point where an early nineteenth-century French observer remarked that 'his hat stuck on a pole might without inconvenience be his substitute at the trial' (quoted by Langbein, 2003: 6). In contrast, French defendants were, and still are, expected to play an active part in the trial (Hodgson, 2005) and inquiries into their character are far more central to the trial than in England (Field, 2006). As Harris (1994) argues, the Napoleonic codes created a tension between the rigid tariff of sentences, fitted to the offence rather than the individual, and the thorough investigation of individual life-histories and motives encouraged by inquisitorial procedure. The nature of French inquisitorialism helps explain Foucault's observation that, in the criminal courts of his own day, when the accused refused to explain his conduct, 'the machinery jams, the gears seize up. Why? ...The accused evades a question that is essential in the eyes of a modern tribunal, but which would have had a strange ring to it 150 years ago: "Who are you?"' (Foucault, 2002b: 177). It would hardly have such a dramatic effect in a common-law trial.[2]

Perhaps the clearest statement of the 'rule of common truth' in English jurisprudence is that of the pre-eminent Victorian theorist of criminal law and evidence, J. F. Stephen. He defended trial by jury as upholding the principle 'that no one shall be punished unless his guilt be proved on grounds which the bulk of the nation at large can understand' (Stephen, 1863: 213).

There is a curious parallel between Stephen's view of expert evidence and Foucault's. Stephen thought that juries, and laypeople in general, necessarily accepted many propositions on the basis of 'mere authority', because such acceptance was a practical necessity 'in the transaction of the common affairs of life, however momentous may be the conclusions which rest upon them' (1863: 210). Similarly, Foucault maintained that courts and other institutions routinely accepted statements as true merely on the basis of the status of their maker, even in matters of life and death, because this was practical necessity for the working of the machinery of power. The authoritarian Stephen approved what the libertarian Foucault deplored; but his argument was put forward mainly with toxicology in mind and did not extend to psychiatry. Psychiatry, however scientific it might become, could never provide authoritative answers to the law's questions about the state of an individual's mind at the moment of a particular act (Stephen, 1863: 87–8).

Insanity, deterrence and delinquency

Psychiatric evidence, according to Foucault, functions within modern penal discourse through the 'doubling' of offenders and offences. The theme of the double 'always haunted Foucault' (Deleuze, 1986: 97), and can be understood in at least two senses in the context of crime. One is the formulation of two types of statement which are similar on the surface but function within different discourses. The legal statements by which a series of offences is attributed to a particular legal subject are 'doubled' by medical statements identifying the same acts as manifestations of a pathological trait. These overlapping sets of statements provide a 'switch point' between legal and medical discourses (Foucault, 2003: 16–18, 33). In another sense, the human subject is 'doubled' by the human being as an object of positive knowledge (Foucault, 1970: Ch. 9): the offender as author of his crimes is doubled by the delinquent, the bearer of the pathological trait of criminality.

Such doubling is necessitated, according to Foucault, by a fundamental paradox in the classical theory of deterrence. Deterrent punishment is supposed to provide a sufficient incentive to induce a rational person to refrain from offending. If punishment is correctly calibrated but some people nevertheless break the law, then either those people have unusually strong motives or they are irrational. Thus, although the legal codes of the enlightenment reformers (and the rationalised English common law of the nineteenth century: Norrie, 2001) addressed themselves to a rational, calculating, legal subject, those who were punished could not be adequately conceived as such subjects. 'Delinquents', as Bentham put it, must be 'a peculiar race of beings, who require unremitted inspection. Their weakness consists in yielding to the temptations of the passing moment. Their minds are weak and disordered' (quoted by Wiener, 1995: 254).

At first, this paradox only presented an embarrassment to the courts in the rare cases of homicidal 'monsters' whose acts appeared motiveless or patently irrational. (As an English example, Foucault's *History of Madness* (2006: 643n.) mentions the trial of Bowler for attempted murder in 1812, apparently the first time the concept of 'delusion' was used by a medical witness: Eigen 1995: 136–40.) In time, according to Foucault, the medico-legal knowledge that emerged in these cases was extended to a much wider range of 'abnormal' delinquents.

Wiener (1990) argues that English legal culture in the early Victorian period resolved the problem of the irrationality of everyday delin-

quency to its own satisfaction by assuming that although most criminals were not rational, calculating subjects, the best way to teach them
and others to become such subjects was to treat them *as if* they were.
Even when faced with seemingly irrational homicides, some judges
held fast to the logic of deterrence:

> The homicidal maniac has a morbid craving for taking life. The not
> doing so is painful to him, the doing so pleasurable. We may
> wonder that it is so, but so it is.... Why should persons who commit
> offences under the influence of their vicious desires or appetites – or
> 'manias', if that is the right word – not be punished, i.e. not be
> threatened with punishment? ... Should the law not direct its threat
> against one who stands so much in need of it, who, unless fortified
> by it, is so likely to do wrong? (Baron Bramwell, 1872, quoted by
> Fairfield, 1898: 43–4)

The insanity defence, as formulated by the judges in 1843,[3] removed
the threat of punishment only from those who were so insane that
they could not understand that they were doing what the law declared
punishable – those who did not know what they were doing or did not
know it was (legally) wrong. The medical argument that insane criminals were not simply acting on vicious desires but rather were physically incapable of controlling their conduct (Smith, 1981) made no
headway at all at the level of legal doctrine; the so-called McNaughton
(or M'Naghten) rules are still law today (see Mackay, 1995).

The restrictive wording of the legal definition of insanity, as compared with the undefined concept of *démence* in the *Code Napoleon*
(Art. 64: 'there is neither crime nor offence [*délit*] where the accused is
in a state of insanity [*démence*] at the time of his act'), had significant
effects in limiting expert authority. According to Robert Nye, 'It was
the very generality of the [Napoleonic] code that called forth the
expert medical witness and made him a partner in the judicial process,'
(Nye, 1984: 30, 128). By contrast, it was a perception on the part of the
public, and more particularly the Law Lords, that the judges at the trial
of Daniel McNaughton (a political assassin acting from seemingly irrational motives) had been too willing to allow the medical witnesses to
step 'from the witness-box to the jury-box' that led the judges to for-
mulate their restrictive definition of insanity.[4]

The McNaughton rules made the crucial issue the state of the
accused's mind at the precise moment of the act, which in the nature
of things was something about which the medical witnesses could not

give direct testimony.[5] This produced one of two results, depending on how strictly the judge interpreted the law of evidence. Either the medical witnesses were confined to speaking about events before and after the act – insane relatives, previous fits or eccentric conduct, etc. – drawing a conclusion that the accused was or was not of sound mind before and after the crime, and leaving the jury to draw its own conclusions as to how someone with that history might have come to act as he did;[6] or, as was the usual practice in the late nineteenth and early twentieth centuries, the witnesses gave the same kind of evidence but were allowed to explain to the jury how they inferred from it that the accused did or did not fit the legal definition of insanity (see Ward, 1997, 2001, for examples).

Such evidence located the criminal act in a series of acts which resembled in it in some way; but rather than 'a para-pathological series that is close to being an illness, but an illness that is not an illness since it is a moral fault' (Foucault, 2003: 20), it constructed a pathological series that absolved the actor from moral fault. 'The vicious act or crime is not itself proof of insanity; it must, in order to establish moral insanity,[7] be traced from disease through a proper chain of symptoms, just as the acts of a sane man are deduced from his motives; and the evidence of disease must be found in the entire history of the case' (Maudsley, 1874: 173). Medical evidence intended to show the defendant as sane and responsible usually relied not on any series of deviant acts but simply on an absence of signs of insanity while remanded in prison, under observation by the prison medical officer or a visiting psychiatrist. As we shall see, the 'delinquent' whose offences showed a pattern of character defects or 'weak-mindedness' falling short of insanity was certainly not unknown to medical discourse. But though occasionally evidence of weak-mindedness was given in relation to an insanity defence, it was usually more as an appeal for mercy, or a limited concession to the defence, than as a medical ground for responsibility or irresponsibility.[8]

The trial of Lucy Samways for drowning her three-year old illegitimate child (reported by Mercier, 1904: 591–3) provides a striking exception to this generalisation, but one which could be said to prove the rule. A medical officer of health (not a mental specialist) called Samways 'a moral degenerate....She would think no more of putting her child in the water than of eating her dinner'. Another doctor could find no 'mark of mental disease' but the 'history of her life' and 'moral character' (the fact of having an illegitimate child) pointed to her being the kind of person who would act 'automatically', without knowing what she was doing. The judge, however, made it very clear that the jury should take no notice of this evidence, and the only medical witness 'worthy of attention' was the asylum superintendent who said that the prisoner showed defects of memory and 'did not morally appreciate in its true sense the nature and quality of the act' (thus, typically, bringing her almost, but not quite, within the letter of the McNaughton rules). The jury was quick to bring in a verdict of guilty but insane, which reflected the generally merciful attitude of juries to poor women who killed their illegitimate children (Ward, 1998).

There were also cases where evidence that was intended to demonstrate insanity was probably taken by the jury to demonstrate only depravity (see Smith, 1981). Two well known examples were the murder trials of William Dove in 1856 and Ronald True in 1922. In his recent study of the Dove case, Owen Davies (2005: 127) argues that the whole defence case was constructed to fit James Cowles Prichard's profile of moral insanity, using evidence of his unconventional farming methods, belief in the supernatural, volatile behaviour and emotional cruelty to the wife he eventually poisoned. The judge, Baron Bramwell, told the jury that 'none of the instances of strange conduct, adduced when he was a boy, [were] evidence of insanity, more than might be found in a perverse, ill-conducted boy', and that the jury were as capable as the medical men of judging the facts on which the medical evidence was founded.[9] Similarly, the editor of the published transcript of Ronald True's trial was almost certainly right when he remarked that 'the facts which to the medical men were so eloquent of profound medical disorder would convey to the jury only the picture of a depraved, callous monster who, being in need of ready money, thought to raise a few pounds by robbing a defenceless woman' (Carswell, 1925: 38).

Between these two cases there was, to be sure, a marked increase in the receptivity of judges and juries to psychiatric evidence. By the 1890s, the change in mood was apparent to both legal and medical commentators. The lunacy law expert A. Wood Renton (1890: 317–18) called it a 'silent revolution…every barrister who has gone on circuit knows that the "rules in MacNaghten's [sic] case" are, avowedly, manipulated by judges and, if need be, defied by juries.' The Medico-Psychological Association (1896), the alienists' professional body, abandoned a campaign for reform of the insanity defence on the grounds that the relaxed interpretation of the rules made it unnecessary, and any proposal for change would alarm public opinion.[10] The percentage of those charged with murder who were found either unfit to plead or legally insane climbed steadily from 14.6% in the decade 1861–70 to 34.3% from 1901–10 (Chadwick, 1992: 399).

The nature of medical evidence and its reception in turn-of-the-century English murder trials was, however, very different from Nye's description of France in the same period, with judges and juries so baffled by 'esoteric expert testimony' that 'magistrates out of desperation importuned the justice minister to ask psychiatrists to pronounce directly on the question of responsibility' (Nye, 1984: 251). The minister's response was a circular requiring prosecutors to ask experts to what extent any 'mental anomalies' *not* amounting to *démence* under Article 64 of the penal code affected the defendant's responsibility (*ibid.*: 248). It was to such questions that the experts (after initially protesting that responsibility was not a medical question: *ibid.*: 251–2) responded with the 'grotesque' evidence castigated by Foucault. British justice,[11] by contrast, liked to congratulate itself on its robust common sense (see Ward, 1997, 1998). A *Times* leader, commenting on a long discussion of the insanity defence in its letters pages, summed up the attitude well:

> It is [the] adaptation of doctrine to the totality of the impression made not only by the evidence, but by a thousand details of appearance and demeanour, which is the sphere of that common-sense, the application of which to responsibility fills some medical minds with scorn. But that common-sense, instructed and enlightened by judicial processes, is the main element of our whole system of jurisprudence, and is every day called upon to decide the state of mind in which sane people did particular acts. If medical men wish to convert lawyers and the laity to their views, they would do well to give up the idea of over-riding this great moderating factor by expert authority.[12]

As Foucault (2003: 161) notes in the French context, these claims to authority (best articulated in England by Maudsley, 1874) rested on a view of madness as a biological condition akin to epilepsy and characterised by various forms of involuntary conduct (see Young, 1970; Clark, 1982; Oppenheim, 1991). Psychiatry allied itself to biological science and in particular to degeneration theory (see Pick, 1996) while finding itself isolated from the medical mainstream (Oppenheim, 1991; Scull, 1993). As in France (Nye, 1984; Harris, 1989) psychiatry was able in this way to cultivate a reassuringly scientific and socially conservative image. As Wiener (1990) argues, it also reflected a broader cultural mood which was more inclined to see weakness rather than wilfulness in the misconduct of the lower classes. In the trials of this period, however, one gets no sense whatever of judges and juries being over-whelmed by scientific theory and jargon. In some cases, quite flimsy and tentative evidence that the accused might have been suffering from some form of epilepsy was sufficient in the light of the pro-secution's failure to show a plausible motive (for a good example, see Smith, 1901). In others, even unanimous evidence from eminent witnesses would not secure an acquittal where the accused did seem to have intelligible motives.[13] Such individuals would be promptly certified insane after the trial and sent to a criminal lunatic asylum instead of the gallows (Chadwick, 1992). But while in the adminis-trative processes of punishment expert opinion was often decisive, in the public ritual of the trial the 'rule of common truth' was staunchly upheld.[14]

Mental deficiency

By the 1870s, in what can reasonably be considered some of the earliest criminological texts (Davie, 2005), we find the observation of prisoners beginning to produce a form of medical knowledge of the lesser forms of delinquency. Nicolson (1874) proposed a categorisation of prisoners based on their crimes and response to discipline. He summed up the 'habitual or thorough criminal' as '[m]ostly unintelligent, wilful and impulsive. Moral depravity and grossness, with low selfish cunning. (Criminal minded.)'. The 'weak-minded criminal', on the other hand, showed '[e]vidences of a mind morbidly defective or disturbed, requir-ing the relaxation of prison discipline, but not warranting or rendering expedient a certificate of lunacy' (Nicolson, 1874: 168). These 'evid-ences' were nothing but his repeated failures to be deterred by prison discipline: 'No prisoner whose mind is fairly regulated will lay himself open to such punishment by resisting as will be likely to affect him seriously' (*ibid.*: 172). Thus prison discipline could double as 'a test of mind' (*ibid.*: 167).

The problem with this kind of reasoning was that the prisoner who repeatedly defied discipline might be just the sort of prisoner who most needed it:

the good-for-nothing scoundrel... whose insubordinate and violent tendencies... are equalled only by his utter callousness in the matter of punishment. To hold that all such are irresponsible and not pun-ishable would be a dangerous doctrine, and would simply provoke more numerous assaults on the part of criminals, with the view of

obtaining the specially mild treatment accorded to the weak-
minded class... (*ibid.*: 172–3)

Such considerations, as Davie (2005) argues, led prison-based criminologists to be cautious in confining any suggestion of a lack of
responsibility to a relatively small group of weak-minded prisoners.
They also made prison administrators unwilling to allow medical officers
to determine prisoners' responsibility for breaches of discipline.[15]

Nicolson's 'weak-minded' prisoner was weak in self-control. In the
evidence of prison medical officers to the Royal Commission on the
Care and Control of the Feeble-Minded, which sat from 1904–8, weak-
mindedness began to be equated with low intelligence (Watson, 1994),
but was still identified by prisoners' failure to appreciate the seriousness of their crimes and by their conduct in prison:

> The committal of semi-impulsive acts; assaults; destruction of furni-
> ture, clothing, etc., breaking of windows, self-mutilation and the use
> of threatening, abusive and obscene language for trivial and quite
> inadequate causes; extreme obstinacy, idleness and laziness; sullen
> or defiant moods alternating with periods of cheerfulness and sub-
> mission; untidy, dirty or filthy habits; tendencies to threaten suicide
> or make feigned attempts at suicide.[16]

Criminal records collated in prisons formed 'para-pathological series'
by which not only weak-minded individuals but whole families could
be identified:[17] 'These weak-minded prisoners... are mischievous and
predatory and propagate their species thus doing incomparable evil'.[18]

The administrative and legal dilemmas posed by these offenders were
explained to the Royal Commission (1908) by Sir Charles Troup, assistant under-secretary at the Home Office. The proper verdict in such
cases would be one of 'guilty but not fully responsible and in need of
care and restraint', but it was impossible to ask a jury to return such a
verdict because it would require consideration of the prisoner's previous convictions, which were excluded from evidence on the ground
that they were prejudicial.[19] (The Commission was informed that the
judges were unanimously opposed to juries deciding this question.)[20]
The Home Office's powers over criminal lunatics depended on juries
'finding them insane on evidence which, strictly speaking, does not
quite amount to that', but Troup nevertheless felt that the question of
insanity should be left to a jury, not to 'a body of experts'; and the
Home Office was very reluctant to transfer accused persons to asylums

without trial.[21] (At one time some 40 prisoners a year had been dealt with in this way, but the practice was changed in the light of judicial criticism.)[22] The Home Office had also urged on magistrates the necessity to send alleged minor offenders who were certifiably insane to lunatic asylums rather than convicting them, but many weak-minded offenders were not certifiable and 'in the very nature of the case the punishment of imprisonment has no deterrent effect'.[23]

We can see here quite clearly the underlying logic which according to Foucault led courts towards an increasing reliance on medico-legal expertise. Punishment is supposed to deter, but those who are punished repeatedly (as demonstrated by prison record-keeping) show that they have not been deterred, and it is only by acting on the basis of a knowledge of the criminal's career, character and heredity, that the courts can identify offenders in need of segregation or cure. But this knowledge constructs a subject who eludes legal categories:

> With his irregularities, his lack of intelligence, his failures, and his unflagging infinite desires, a series of elements are constituted concerning which the question of responsibility cannot be posed, or simply cannot arise, since ultimately, according to these descriptions, the subject is responsible for everything and nothing. (Foucault, 2003: 21)

Foucault saw the response to this dilemma as the emergence, from the end of the nineteenth century, of the 'doctor-judge' – the doctor as judge and the judge as doctor – who practiced 'the fine profession of curing' the individual delinquent (2003: 23). But there was little appetite for such a role among the judiciary, or in the legalistic culture of the Home Office. A retired senior judge told the Royal Commission: 'Imprisonment for punishment is one thing; segregation for imbecility is another, and I do not think the two things should be mixed'.[24]

As Simmons (1978) and Johnstone (1996a) have argued, while 'idiots' and 'imbeciles' were seen as needing care by reason of their intellectual disabilities, the 'feeble-minded' were objects of concern primarily because of their criminal or feckless behaviour. The Royal Commission constructed a theory of the feeble-minded offender as *partially* responsible, which meant in effect that he or she would be treated *both* as a responsible legal subject to be punished *and* as an irresponsible object of preventive detention once the sentence had been served.

> Of course, if it could be suggested that no such mentally defective person could be in any degree responsible, the course suggested here

could not be defended; but all the evidence goes to show that in these cases there is no fixed line in regard to the sense of responsibility any more than there is a fixed line in the nature and extent of mental defect.... Recognising these variations, therefore, we suggest that the element of punishment should be retained, so far as it is valid, but that ...care and control should follow.[25]

The Commission did not define what it meant by the 'sense of responsibility', but saw it as being correlated with the degree of 'defect of the brain'.[26] Whatever it was, it was too subtle for juries to determine: 'a jury who may well deal with the question whether or not an act was committed by the defendant, can hardly be expected to decide also the very much more complicated question, whether the act was a voluntary act done by a responsible agent'.[27] But despite this frontal assault on the rule of common truth, the Commission accepted that *legal* responsibility would continue to be determined by juries applying the McNaughton rules.[28] A modified version of the Commission's proposals was enacted as the Mental Deficiency Act, 1913. In place of the Royal Commission's combination of punishment, care and control, the Act adopted a compromise between medical and penal approaches which is still broadly reflected in English law today. The decision whether an offender was a mental defective was separated from the decision as to legal responsibility and treated as part of the sentencing process. Alternatively, the judge could adjourn the case and let the local authority apply for a civil commitment order (from a specially appointed magistrate). The magistrates' courts had the power (giving statutory effect to a long-established practice) to detain a mentally defective offender without conviction. The Act also introduced a power (s. 9) to transfer mentally defective prisoners to hospital.

In practice, the impact of the Act on criminal justice was relatively limited, reflecting the views of prison medical officers that only a small minority of prisoners were so weak-minded as to need detention elsewhere (Walker and McCabe, 1973). The annual number of detention orders made in criminal courts (predominantly in magistrates' courts) was initially in double figures, and although this rose to 332 in 1938, it was offset by a decline in transfers from prisons (East, 1949: 41). The provision of the Act which seemed to mark the most radical step towards the medicalisation of crime had even less practical impact. This was the inclusion of the 'moral imbecile' in the list of categories of mental deficiency.

The 'moral imbecile' was largely, though not exclusively, the product of medical theorising about repeat offenders and those who resisted prison discipline (Watson, 1988). Johnstone (1996a) has distinguished between two strands in this discourse – one which attributed moral imbecility or something like it to a large section of the criminal class (e.g. Maudsley, 1874) and one which applied the term more restrictively to offenders whose conduct showed a quite startling absence of prudence or 'common sense'. The leading theorist of moral imbecility, Mercier (1905: 201), defined it as 'an original defect of character displayed from an early age' and manifested 'in an inability to be deterred by punishment, however severe, certain and prompt, from wrongful acts', or at least in a failure to be deterred 'by the punishment which would ordinarily be awarded'. In the evidence to the Royal Commission, however, moral insanity or imbecility – some witnesses did not clearly distinguish between the two – were associated with sexual deviance and financial irresponsibility among the classes of people whose families could afford to consult private specialists.[29] As Watson (1994) argues, the diagnosis of moral imbecility suited the methods of observation employed by prison doctors, but did not find favour with outside experts who preferred to diagnose mental deficiency using intelligence tests. Moral assessment, however, remained important in the certification of all forms of mental deficiency (Thomson, 1998: 245).

The magistrate as 'doctor-judge'

Though the senior judiciary in England never bore the slightest resemblance to Foucault's 'doctor-judge', 'the fine profession of curing' did appeal to some magistrates in the inter-war years. Magistrates were more deferential to psychiatric expertise than judges and juries, and would 'usually exempt from punishment those certified as insane' (East, 1927: 27). A few magistrates made extensive use of psychiatric reports. After the Great War the Birmingham justices established a scheme by which defendants were examined in a specially adapted wing of the local prison or, more rarely, by a psychologist outside the prison (Birmingham Justices, 1921; Lancet, 1919; Smith, 1922). But despite official encouragement for magistrates to obtain more medical reports, especially for juveniles, the use of reports remained uneven (Bailey, 1987).

The magistrates most likely to sympathise with a psychiatric or psychological approach were those who joined the Magistrates' Association established in 1921, in its early days a small, reform-minded body which 'adopted and championed an entirely new image of the magistracy which was based upon scientific skill' (Vogler, 1990: 80). The new breed of magistrates did not claim scientific expertise in their own right, but rather a sufficient working knowledge of psychology to be able to steer a common-sense, practical course between science and law (Clarke Hall, 1926: 13–14). What they wanted, according to the stipendiary magistrate for Bradford, was 'a medical examination interpreted from a common-sense point of view'; specialised psychiatric knowledge 'was not required in the case of the great majority of these petty delinquents' (quoted in Magistrates' Association and BMA, 1939).

The leading exponent of this approach where juveniles were concerned was Sir William Clarke Hall, a metropolitan stipendiary magistrate who 'incurred the ridicule of old-fashioned legal critics for the psychiatric "circus" said to attend his court' (Lancet, 1936). Clarke Hall gained the support of at least two of his fellow metropolitan stipendiaries, Claud Mullins and John Watson, but not of the Chief Metropolitan Magistrate who denounced him to Mullins as 'a dangerous man' (Watson, 1942; Mullins, 1948: 163).

Rose (1985: 174) sees these developments as the beginning of 'a new psychological jurisdiction'. Cox (1996), however, has stressed how limited was the impact of psychology on juvenile justice between the wars, as has Donzelot in his study of France (1979: 133–4). Donzelot's argument that philanthropy was much more significant than psychiatry in observing and controlling delinquents in this period can be applied to the position in England of the charitable (though state-supervised) probation officers and certified schools (Bailey, 1987). Only Birmingham, Bradford and London had schemes for assessing defendants psychologically in a non-custodial setting; juveniles could not be remanded to prisons, the main centres for the medical observation of adults; and plans for a network of State Observation Centres were dropped from the 1933 Children's Bill owing to financial pressures (ibid: 189–91; Bailey, 1987: 31). The 'doctor-judge' was still a marginal figure, albeit sometimes one with a certain flair for self-promotion.

Conclusion

My discussion of some aspects of nineteenth and early twentieth century legal practice in England has suggested that the 'rule of common truth' was not subverted by medico-legal expertise to anything like the extent that Foucault's account of the French system suggests (for a critical examination of contemporary practice in these respects see Johnstone and Ward, forthcoming, Ch. 5). In confining my attention to the legal system I do not mean to deny the importance of all the '[s]mall-scale legal systems and parallel judges' involved in the punishment and treatment of crime (Foucault, 1977: 21), such as prison discipline, the 'transcarceration' of delinquents between, for example, industrial schools and colonies for defectives (Thomson, 1998: 257) or, perhaps most importantly, the granting of reprieves from capital punishment. The psychiatrist William Sargant tells an instructive anecdote in this respect. After a case where he and a colleague managed to get an epileptic found guilty but insane in blatant defiance of the McNaughton rules,[30] he met Dr Norwood East, head of the prison medical service and a key adviser to the Home Office on reprieves:

> He remarked that we had been very 'naughty' at the trial – he actually used that word – to behave as we did, since it was his special work to decide, though only after conviction, whether prisoners were medically as well as legally sane. Norwood East went on to say that he deplored any attempts like ours to secure a murderer's medical acquittal in Court, these being matters that should best be decided by him and others later on (Sargant, 1967: 187).

As East's remark illustrates, English criminal justice was and is based on a separation between the trial, as an inquiry into the act, and subsequent judicial and administrative inquiries into the offender as an individual. This is reflected in the often passive role of the defendant, the restriction of evidence to that deemed directly probative in relation to the specific act charged, and the separation of roles between the judge and jury. Being less interested in defendants' characters than their French counterparts, English judges were less inclined to call upon medico-legal expertise. These peculiarities of national legal cultures are an important dimension of the 'scientifico-legal complex' (Foucault 1977: 23) which is neglected in Foucault's analysis.

Foucault's main interest was not in court procedures but in disciplinary institutions and the ways in which they created new forms of knowledge of the individual, and his insights have undoubtedly been immensely helpful in understanding phenomena such as the emergence of mental deficiency in England (Rose, 1985; Sim, 1990; Watson, 1994). The idea of the 'doubling' of knowledge of the offence by knowledge of the offender is also helpful in understanding how this knowledge circulates in the courts; but again there is a dimension to this phenomenon that seems to receive insufficient attention. As Foucault and his collaborators (particularly Riot, 1978) showed in their study of the Pierre Rivière case, it is not only in medical and legal discourse that incidents from a person's life are selected and arranged to construct a portrait of his character; the same is done in various forms of 'popular knowledge' (Foucault, 1978: 206), including broadsheets, journalistic accounts, and sometimes (as in Rivière's case) the offender's own words.[31] All these accounts produce alternative narratives of the crime (Smith, 1985), and it would not be difficult to show that in some respects they all follow similar 'rules' of narrative construction (Jackson, 1988). But this casts doubt on Foucault's claim that the effect of psychiatric evidence is independent of its 'rational structure'. In the historical or contemporary English context, as in the French cases discussed by Harris (1989), it is surely more likely that judges and juries assess(ed) such reports in terms of their narrative coherence and plausibility, against a background of cultural assumptions or stereotypes about gender, class, etc. (Ward, 1998, 1999). I suspect that this also goes for the kind of French reports that Foucault (2003: 2–6) quotes at length, which beneath their pretentious jargon simply attempt to construct a plausible, speculative story of the accused's character and motives. In discussing the relation between legal and medical knowledge, we should not overlook the lay knowledge that makes the 'rule of common truth' workable.

Notes

*I am indebted to Daniel McCarthy and Gerry Johnstone for their comments on a draft of this paper, and to Joe Sim for his advice on the aspects of my PhD thesis on which the paper is based.
  1 [1975] QB 834. The ruling was substantially reaffirmed in *R v Henry* [2006] 1 Cr. App, R. 6.
  2 For a striking example, see Morrissey's (2003, Ch. 4) account of the Australian case of the supposed 'lesbian vampire' Tracey Wigginton, whose 1991 trial for the apparently motiveless murder of a stranger lasted approximately nine minutes, based on a guilty plea and a confession that gave nothing more than the bare facts. Wigginton's detailed confession, which Morrissey discusses in Foucauldian terms, was made to a journalist five years later.
  3 *M'Naghten's* case (1843) 10 C. & F. 200.
  4 See Moran (1981), which includes the House of Lords' debate on the McNaughton case. The only speakers were the four Law Lords (Lords Lyndhurst, Brougham, Campbell and Cottingham) who conducted most of the House's appellate work (Stevens, 1979: 30, 37–8). Moran argues, not entirely convincingly, that McNaughton's motives were rational. The quotation is from Lord Brougham (Moran, 1981: 160).
  5 What follows is based on my study (Ward, 1996) of trials where insanity was pleaded which were reported in the medical press (*British Medical*

Journal, Lancet and *Journal of Mental Science* between 1883 and 1939, and on Smith's (1981) and Eigen's (1995, 2003) studies of earlier Victorian trials.

6 A good example of this type of trial is *R v Watson* (1871–2) *Old Bailey Sessions Papers* (3rd Sess.) 147. Beryl Bainbridge ingeniously incorporates much of the trial transcript in her novel *Watson's Apology* (1984). See also Chadwick (1992).

7 'Moral insanity' was characterised by immoral conduct at variance with the patient's previous character.

8 *R v Cross,* (1898) 44 *Journal of Mental Science* 439; *R v Viney, The Times,* 16 Sep. 1898: 10 (prison medical officer, cross-examined by the defence, conceded 'that the prisoner was of weak mind, but he could not certify him as a lunatic at the present time').

9 *The Times,* 21 July 1856: 10.

10 The report was drafted by two very well-informed, but conservative, alienists, Drs Orange and Mercier, and may not represent the views of the profession as a whole. See Medico-Psychological Association (1895).

11 Including Scottish justice (Ward, 2001).

12 *The Times,* 1 September 1894: 9.

13 In addition to *True,* discussed above, a particularly striking example is the case of William Cromwell (1896), NA, HO144/266/A57742.

14 In the inter-war years, both the administrative power of medical experts and the judges' determination to resist their claims to authority in court were even more strongly marked. See Ward (2002).

15 See NA, HO144/170/A43422 (1897). A Home Office proposal that the Medical Officers be required to state not only that a prisoner was fit for punishment but that there was no reason to doubt his/her responsibility for the relevant act was watered down after opposition from the Prison Commission.

16 Dr. O. F. N. Treadwell, Medical Officer, HMP Parkhurst, evidence to the Royal Commission on the Care and Control of the Feeble-Minded [hereafter RCCCFM] Minutes of Evidence (vol. 1), PP, 35: 83, q. 4301.

17 *Ibid.,* written evidence of Dr J. H. Parker Wilson, Medical Officer of Pentonville, q. 4440, p. 258 (with a family tree to illustrate the point).

18 Sir J. Crichton-Browne, psychiatrist and Lord Chancellor's Visitor in Lunacy, *ibid.,* q. 6,000.

19 RCCCFM Report, PP, 39: 159; Minutes, q. 1323.

20 *Ibid.,* 458 and Minutes of Evidence, vol. V, Appendix.

21 RCCCFM Minutes, vol. 1 q. 1,359, q. 1,346; q. 1,483.

22 *R v Marshall, The Times,* 10 February 1885; NA, HO144/148/A38399.

23 RCCCFM Minutes q. 1,327.

24 Sir Edward Fry, RCCCFM Minutes q. 5,789.

25 RCCCFM Report, para. 463.

26 *Ibid.*

27 *Ibid.,* para. 459.

28 *Ibid.,* para. 458.

29 See the evidence of Drs Savage, Mercier and Ferrier, RCCCFM.

30 The unnamed case is clearly *R* v *Lees-Smith, Daily Telegraph*, 17–18 March 1943.

31 Harris (1989: 126) points out that nineteenth-century French criminal procedure encouraged the production of such autobiographical narratives, which magistrates perused with interest. She also argues that 'an unusual degree of cultural interchange' occurred in *fin de siècle* France between popular narratives and medical theory, for example in discussions of crime under hypnosis (*ibid.*: 158).

Part II

Penal Policy, Prison Practice and Discourses on Offenders

4
Moral Guardians? Prison Officers, Prison Practice and Ambiguity in the Nineteenth Century

*Helen Johnston**

The theoretical work on the birth of the prison in the late eighteenth and early nineteenth centuries focuses on the transformation of punishment, the movement away from torturous, public punishments, to the increasing use of imprisonment to deal with the majority of offences by the mid to late nineteenth century. Frequently, this work is concerned with the regimes, policies and practices of the prison environment, and the experiences of those confined. Whig or orthodox accounts see this change as the progressive movement away from past barbarous practices. Whereas, revisionist accounts argue that the institutions that emerged were part of a wider strategy of social control, through which discipline was dispersed throughout society, and have questioned the motives of reformers and the resulting practices (Foucault, 1977; Ignatieff, 1978; Melossi and Pavarini, 1981; Rothman, 1971; see Introduction).

Research on local imprisonment in England and Wales during the nineteenth century has challenged revisionist accounts by arguing that the implementation of prison policies, at the local level, often fell short of the 'national' showpiece penitentiaries (Saunders, 1986) on which these theoretical accounts were based. They have also questioned the extent to which these prisons ever met up to the vision of the 'machine for grinding men good' (DeLacy, 1981: 211).

This chapter is concerned with understanding the role and working lives of turnkeys, warders, prison officers[1] between 1835 and 1877 period, and to examine this role within a broader understanding of the nature of local imprisonment at this time. Over this period, England and Wales experienced a significant change in penal philosophy moving from the use of the 'reformatory' practices of separate system, enacted in the Prison Act 1839[2] to a more deterrent regime, based on low diet, harsh living conditions and hard labour from the 1860s, which only begins to ameliorate by the end of the nineteenth century. This, to some extent is generalising; it is a gesture to the philosophies of punishment that dominated prison legislation during this period. As noted above, not all prisons around the country adhered to such practices, until forced to by centralisation. However, what was significant over this period was the changing role of the government. From the beginning of the nineteenth century, the government began a slow but increasing vigorous intrusion into the administration of local prisons. This began with the establishment of the first government run penitentiary, Millbank, the implementation of prison inspectors in 1835, and culminated in the centralisation of the local prisons in 1877. The changing relationship between local prisons and the government ensured increasing bureaucratic control and an emphasis on uniformity in prison regimes that manifested itself most significantly after the 1860s (see Chapter 9).

This chapter seeks to extend an argument, begun elsewhere, that prison policy and practice was ambiguous, contradictory and paradoxical, and this can be exemplified by understanding the role and working life of the prison officer within these penal transformations (Johnston, 2008). Despite the considerable amount of research on prison history, it is often concerned with prisoners experiences of confinement, and rightly so, but the prison officer was central to this experience. It was not the magistrates, prison inspectors, policymakers or, to some extent, the governors, that had the most contact with the confined, but the officers who walked the wings, delivered the food, and monitored labour and exercise. Prison officers remain relatively unresearched in historical accounts and 'left few accounts of their views and experiences' (Forsythe, 1987: 113). Despite the focus of attention on Bentham's blueprint for the Panopticon and the scandals of insanity in the newly created penitentiaries, there has been little consideration of prison staff who implemented these regimes on a day-to-day basis. Moreover, in the growing official discourse, aspects of prison life are hidden by stock phrases; 'officers have performed their duties with intelligence, zeal and fidelity' (Pratt, 2004: 79), which reveal little about the working lives of officers. Thus, 'it is necessary to attempt, from very little evidence, to piece together an impression of the reformatory work of by far the biggest body of prison staff' (Forsythe, 1987: 113).

This chapter seeks to understand the role of the prison officer within the changing prison policies and practices of the nineteenth century and to locate this discussion within a broader argument concerned with the ambiguous nature of policy and practice in local prisons. It seeks to understand this ambiguity, alongside the increasingly bureaucratic and controlling arm of the state, which concludes in the secrecy and dominance of state power, evident in the 1860s, but exemplified in the features of prison life from 1877.

Prison regimes in the 1830s and 1840s

The dominant penal philosophies over the early to mid nineteenth century focused on the degree to which prisoners could be reformed or altered during imprisonment, or at the very least, not further contaminated by their incarceration. Predominantly, the regimes used sought to prevent contamination using either the separate or the silent systems of punishment. Both systems were imported philosophies from the United States (see Chapter 1) and were based on the idea that through either isolation or silence prisoners could be transformed. Under the separate system, prisoners were isolated in a cell, where they would work, sleep and eat, and they were only able to leave the cell to attend the chapel or exercise. In such circumstances, they were to be masked, to prevent recognition, and the regime also contained a strong emphasis on religious conversion. Under the silent system, prisoners associated during hours of work but were to be silence at all times.

Documentation suggests that in the early 1830s, most local prisons were operating a system based on classification. Prisoners were classified by offence and gender (as set out in the Gaols Act 1823[3]), or were subject to the 'silent system', or at least some variation of the silent system. Under the silent system, prisoners had to be closely observed by a number of officers or guards during the long hours of labour, thus the system required high levels of staffing. For example, at Coldbath Fields House of Correction, Governor G. L. Chesterton, a leading advocate of the silent system, had trouble overcoming the subculture of the overcrowded prison when he first took charge. Before implementing the system, he spent a number of years gathering evidence to dismiss corrupt guards and attempted to ban all 'fraternization between guards, prisoners and their families' (Ignatieff, 1978: 191):

> Turnkeys ... are strictly forbidden to hold familiar conversation with the prisoners or to communicate with them on any subject whatsoever unconnected to their duties ... Moreover, it is expected that they will carefully abstain from forming intimacy or acquaintanceship with discharged prisoners of any class or description but

maintain their respectability by avoiding the company of all such people (cited in Ignatieff, 1978: 192).

The silent system required a higher level of staffing, and often prisoners were used as guardsmen or wardsmen to help oversee the large number of prisoners in workrooms. At Millbank Penitentiary, it was argued that these wardsmen undermined the prison officers; warning prisoners of their approach, and preventing officers 'from restraining or detecting misconduct or irregularity' (cited in Ignatieff, 1978: 193). Yet the poor staffing levels persisted at some prisons in the following decades. Chesterton reported to the local magistrates of Warwickshire on their prisons in 1847. At Warwick, he observed the poor condition of the buildings, large number of prisoners, and few officers, which he argued was a 'serious obstacle to the enforcement of wholesome discipline'.[4] He thought that to continue to use these prisons in their faulty condition would be 'to consign to contamination and in all likelihood to total ruin, those who are so unfortunate as to be committed to them'.[5]

The returns, under the *Select Committee on Gaols and Houses of Corrections*, in 1835, show information for 40 counties in England and 12 in Wales. They cover 125 county gaols and houses of correction.[6] What is apparent from these sources is the considerable diversity in the number of staff, and therefore the operation, of many of these prisons. The overwhelming majority of these prisons were small, 68 of these prisons in England were staffed with three turnkeys or less; in Wales, 16 of the 25 prisons listed had no turnkeys. In a number of these prisons, the staff consisted of the gaoler or governor and a matron, often the gaoler's wife.[7]

After the Gaols Act 1823, which forced certain policies on local prisons, notably classification, appointing a chaplain and surgeon, and requiring female staff to supervise female prisoners, an influential step taken by the government in 1835 was the appointment of prison inspectors. The reports made by these inspectors demonstrate the diversity in local prisons across the country. Two of these inspectors, William Crawford and Reverend Whitworth Russell were strong supporters of the separate system and although, the other inspectors did not share this view, they were very influential in the implementation of the separate system in the Prison Act of 1839, and used their reports in early years of inspection to champion this position.

However, in the early to mid 1830s, evidence suggests a range of practices in local prisons. The Inspector of the Northern and Eastern district noted in 1836, that the construction of prisons was based on classification rather than separation, that sleeping cells were not sufficiently divided to prevent communication, and that solitary confinement was often nominal, without the constant presence of a day and night watch in the passages. He had not found the slightest difficulty in maintaining communication with a person in an adjoining cell. The construction of prisons were 'favourable to the propagation of sound ...and the sense of hearing in prisoners becomes so acute, that the approach of the officers is constantly anticipated, by the noise created by their footsteps, while yet distant'.[8] Bisset Hawkins, Inspector of the Southern and Western district presents a rather different picture of the silent system, he had 'not been able to trace a single mischievous consequence ... all those conversant with the interior of prisons ... pronounced decidedly in the favour, and entertain an expectation of its probably efficacy in increasing repugnance to incarceration'.[9]

Although these prisons claimed to operate a silent regime it is difficult to see how the prisoners would have been prevented from communicating at all times, especially where there might only be a handful of prisoners and few staff, or even in larger prisons, where the prisoners were numerous, but the staffing levels low. What this suggests is that despite the growing ideas of the use of different regimes, to ensure the conformity and possible reform of prisoners, practice varied considerably. Whilst the prisons of Coldbath Fields and Pentonville, marched forward with the silent and separate regimes of punishment, many rural prisons although structurally and physically better, than the prisons observed by John Howard, still suffered problems of poor management, dilapidated buildings, and were ill-constructed for the new philosophies of punishment. The opposing system of separation could be enforced with fewer staff, but did require architectural alterations to buildings. Local magistrates were often reluctant to spend the money required to construct cells that were properly ventilated and heated, and to the standard required by the prison inspectors. Yet under the separate system, the degree to which prisoners could be controlled by staff was obviously much higher. Therefore, there was considerable difference in experience of imprisonment for prisoners and staff across the country. As Ireland notes when discussing the separate and silent systems, 'despite what the Governor may have told inspectors [Carmarthen Gaol] had for many years neither the architecture to employ the former nor the staff to enforce the latter' (2007: 43).

Changing role of prison staff

Even after the Prison Act 1839, which, in theory, required the adoption of the separate system in all prisons across the country, practice still varied. But these changing ideas about imprisonment, and the ways in which they could be used to alter the minds of offenders, also signified, changing ideas about the role of officers. In the early years of government inspection, prison discipline was found wanting and there is scant reference to prison officers in these years. It is evident from the early reports, that there was criticism directed at those responsible for appointing and discharging officers. It was recommended by Inspector Williams in 1837 that magistrates should appoint and dismiss officers, and that the keeper or governor of the prison should only have powers of suspension.[10] He thought it a great inconvenience that officers were retained when incapable of undertaking their duties, due to age or infirmity. He thought officers needed to be rewarded and magistrates were unwilling to discharge them, and that 'the absence of any provision for old age or infirmity must prevent a more respectable class of persons from seeking such offices'.[11] Williams was also concerned that officers were 'not unfrequently preferred for possessing qualifications as gardeners, or grooms' demonstrated a relationship similar to master and servant rather than officers performing public duties, and that 'prisoners had no respect for the turnkeys, beyond that which physical force inspires'.[12] What begins to emerge is the notion that a superior class of men need to be secured in the position of turnkey.[13] This is reiterated by the Inspectors for the Home District who stated that:

> of late years increased attention has been given to the selection of Prison officers of every description, and a very favourable change has occurred in their general character. It is a great object to make the situation of Prison officers respectable in the public estimation. They have highly responsible duties to perform, and much must depend on their zeal and fidelity for the success of the discipline which is enforced. Every effort should, therefore, be made for bringing into and retaining in this department of the public services persons of sound principles, respectability and intelligence, who are capable of being trained to the higher duties of Prison management.[14]

It was thought that, since 'penal discipline is sustained by moral rather than physical agency',[15] a more respectable and superior person was required to fulfil the role of prison officer. At Millbank Penitentiary, the governor-chaplain Reverend Daniel Nihill, 'required his staff of tough turnkeys to turn overnight into religious missionaries' (Henriques, 1972: 75). He dismissed officers for swearing and unbelief and those who remained walked around carrying Bibles, and were nicknamed 'the Pantilers' (cited in Henriques, 1972: 75–6).

Increasingly evident in this period is a change in the language of discipline. The eighteenth century 'keeper' had been replaced with the 'governor', turnkey with 'warder' and 'apartment' with 'cell'. As Ignatieff notes, 'discipline replaced economy' and commands became 'increasingly military in derivation' (1978: 190; Thomas, 1972). Under the Prison Act 1839, local prisons were to turn their attention to enabling the use of the separate system and within this regime; the role of prison staff was to redirect prisoners from a tendency towards 'evil'. It was believed that prisoners lacked 'firm and virtuous familial care' and 'had not experienced the redirection of their natures in religious and moral families towards God and virtue' (Forsythe, 1987: 60–1). During imprisonment, as Forsythe notes, this deficiency was to be rectified through moral example and benevolent human relationships, with 'prison staff providing what ought to have occurred at a much earlier stage of life' (1987: 61). As Joshua Jebb (Director of Convict Prisons) remarked, warders 'must strive to acquire moral influence over the prisoners by performing their duties conscientiously but without harshness. They should especially try to raise the prisoner's mind to a proper feeling of moral obligation by example of their own uniform regard to truth and integrity even in the smallest matters' (cited in Forsythe, 1987: 61). Warders were not to be familiar with prisoners, but were to treat them with human dignity, and lead them through example of 'strict integrity and truthfulness in word and act' to a 'higher standard of moral conduct' (cited in Forsythe, 1987: 61).

As Ignatieff notes, the ideological origins of the prison were rooted in the ideas of the new industrialists; 'the fathers of the factory system and scientific management' (1978: 62). These principles were also directed at the prison staff, particularly the lower ranks, and not only the prisoners. It was not just the morals and manners of the prisoners that needed reform, 'the surveillant was himself an individual subject to the same rules of the new disciplinary regime as those in his charge' (O'Brien, 1982: 224). Prison officers would be distinguished from their charges by their strict adherence to qualities of hard work, sobriety and respectability, traits which would set them apart from moral weakness, idle habits and drunkenness; the precursors of a life in the 'criminal classes' (Emsley, 2005b; see Chapter 6). As Forsythe notes, it was clearly necessary for 'warders to understand and exemplify the reformatory aspiration' (1987: 114). This was particularly the case for female warders on whom high expectations of feminine, maternal, and compassionate behaviour were placed as a means of effecting reform in their charges (Zedner, 1991).

Prison officers worked long hours and often residing in the prison under constant surveillance and regulation. They were encouraged or required to attend chapel; Sunday schools were promoted, as were saving banks for officers' families. These were all endeavours 'plainly similar to that of the approach to offenders themselves: education, religion and proper moral pursuits were essential to the creation of an attitude of attachment to the prison and fidelity to the state' (Forsythe, 1987: 114).

The main problem for the prison authorities was that the 'rank and file' officers were working in an environment that was seeking to discipline and control the very communities from which they were drawn. Those in charge of the prison, and the newly established police forces sought 'the creation of a reliable cadre of working class disciplinarians, demarcated from their class by the regimens of their corps [but] it proved difficult in practice to find sufficient men capable of adopting the controlled institutional persona envisaged by prison and police reformers' (Ignatieff, 1978: 192–3).

To speak of the separate system as the prevailing philosophy of prison regimes in this period is misleading. Whilst the government pressed for such regimes, local magistrates were slow to implement and practice varied widely across the country. However, the new philosophies of imprisonment did require a different officer to that of the eighteenth century 'turnkey'. But it is important to note that practice varied, and the role and duties of officers were determined by the degree to which these regimes predominated in the prison where they were employed, the number of prisoners, and the structure of staffing. Thus a large number of staff under the separate system at Pentonville overseeing the confinement of hundreds of prisoners would clearly be different to a small rural house of correction which only held a dozen prisoners under the silent system.

Disciplining prison officers

The records of local prisons in this period are peppered with cases of prison officers who were dismissed, fined or suspended for various deficiencies in their duties; these were punishments meted out by either the governor, the visiting magistrates, or in some cases, the Quarter Sessions court. The slow, but growing implementation of the separate system and the strict routine made infractions of the rules more observable and surveillance of staff was more regulated, especially in the prisons which had converted the architectural structure to such regimes. One of the most prevalent problems was drunkenness, records show officers being dismissed for being drunk on duty, arriving at the prison drunk, or being found drinking and smoking with prisoners or debtors (Johnston, 2006a). They were also dismissed for neglecting their duties, not returning to the prison at night, improper conduct to senior officers or the chaplain, and the most serious offence against discipline 'allowing a prisoner to escape' (Johnston, 2006a). At Lincoln prison, questions were asked in relation to the negligence of officers when prisoners escaped, particularly how the prisoners had known where to look for the key.[16]

Some local prisons had minutely detailed lists of the fines against officers who neglected their duties. For example, at Shrewsbury prison in 1840 fines listed that neglecting to communicate any order of the Governor to another turnkey, or neglecting to execute any order given to them, inattention to the cleanliness of prisoners under their charge, and carelessly leaving provisions unguarded within the reach of prisoners, or neglecting to search each prisoner once a week, resulted in a sixpence fine. Heavier fines were set down for allowing a criminal prisoners to converse with a visitor out of hearing, or leaving the prisoners without being properly relieved, or being asleep in chapel, or on duty, and these resulted in between a one and one shilling and sixpence fine. All serious cases and second offences were reported to the visiting justices.[17] Regulators or 'tell-tales' clocks were used to ensure officers or nightwatchmen completed the correct patrols and to maintain close supervision of staff (McConville, 1981). At Liverpool prison in the 1860s, fines of up to five shillings could be levied on officers for neglect or violation of duty by the Governor and heavy fines or reduction of rank or pay could be dealt with by the visiting magistrates.[18] Fines of these amounts could make a substantial impact on the household budget of a turnkey, and in some cases, officers had their rank reduced to junior, for a set period of time (Johnston, 2006a).

It appears that these practices were fairly widespread, 38 prisons in England and Wales, levied fines for negligence or misconduct before centralisation.[19] The Commissioners wanted to implement the system across all local prisons and laid out a new scale of fines in 1879. These fines ranged from sixpence to one shilling, for being late on duty, inattention or carelessness in duty, slovenliness on duty or in uniform, allowing prisoners to communicate to between one and two shillings for disobeying orders, gross neglect of duty or carelessness or neglect affecting the security of the prison. Repeated offences, or grave offences, such as trafficking with prisoners, sleeping on duty, being absent without leave, insubordination or permitting the escape of prisoners, could be dealt with by a heavier fine of up to two weeks pay, besides loss of pay for suspension from duty, or other punishments which may be awarded.[20]

As noted above, prison officers were not to leave the prison day or night without permission, on doing so they were required to leave their keys and journal with the Governor. Overnight guests were only allowed with express permission from the Governor and many prisons insisted that officers lived within or near the prison. It was thought necessary to keep the officers away from working-class neighbourhoods from which many of the prisoners came (McConville, 1981). After the centralisation of local prisons, living accommodation had to be built in areas in where rents were beyond the means of most prison officers (Thomas, 1972).

Prison staff and local imprisonment, 1850–1877

By the mid-century the increasing pressure from the government was beginning to pervade life in local prisons. Prison officers' working lives became highly regulated within the changing discipline of the regime, away from the reformatory ideals of the separate and silent systems, towards the deterrent system which was to permeate the prison experience at least until the end of the nineteenth century. Between late 1840s and the 1860s, the reformative powers of the separate system had collapsed and attention had turned to a more deterrent regime of 'hard labour, hard board, hard fare' where discipline was enforced through low diet, long hours of hard labour and sparse living conditions. Some local prisons were still in the process of adapting the construction of the prison to the separate system (Johnston, 2004) and never caught up with the shifting dynamics of the prison philosophy from above. The use of separate cells remained; it was the 'reformative' powers of the separate system that were lost as public and official discord with the system grew (Henriques, 1972; Johnston, 2006b).

It is at this point that prison life for officers becomes increasingly regimented and constrained. Rules and regulations which governed their working lives, and the stricter prison regime and timetable became more regulated. Primarily, their role continued as before; the day to day operation of the prison, to obey directions of the governor, to examine the state of the cells, bedding, locks and bolts, and to seize prohibited articles from prisoners.[21] They were not permitted to leave the prison without permission or to have any visitors. The hierarchical organisation of the prison and its architectural structure of surveillance allowed those in authority to 'spy on all employees that were under his orders: nurses, doctors, foremen, teachers, warders; he will be able to judge them continuously, impose upon them the methods he thinks best' (Foucault, 1977: 204). The increasing hold of the government over local prisons was beginning to manifest itself more significantly, and this affected the lives of prison officers as well as prisoners.

In turn, the day to day working life of the prison officer was also influenced by another contradiction. Despite pressing for uniform practices; it was thought that some groups should not or could not be subjected to the rigours of such regimes; namely, debtors, prisoners suffering from mental illness, juveniles and mothers with babies. In some cases, for example, debtors, they were not 'criminal' prisoners, but being detained until a debt was settled, and in others, like juvenile prisoners, it was thought the rigid application of such regimes might be damaging to the minds of young people. Thus prison officers were pressed on the one hand to implement reformatory, and then later deterrent regimes, but were confronted by various groups of prisoners to whom such regimes could not be applied, and their role was perceived differently.

A further ambiguity in the application of prison regimes was the use of short sentences, often for minor offences, such as petty larceny or drunkenness (see Chapter 7), which resulted in days or weeks' imprisonment, rather than months. During this short time, it was thought the reformatory aims of the system were simply impracticable, and in the latter period, often ensured severe conditions for short term prisoners. These two issues continued to haunt the application of prison policy for much of the remainder of the nineteenth and into the twentieth century.

Whilst there is not room here to discussion the complexities of scandals which occurred in some local prisons during the mid century, minutes of evidence and reports concerned with the treatment of prisoners at Leicester and Birmingham in 1854 do provide us with a deeper glimpse into the working lives and daily activities of the officers and the ways in which discretion and relationships with prisoners manifested themselves.

The minutes of evidence contained in the investigation at Leicester reveal that the warders duties consisted of delivering food to prisoners, taking prisoners to and from chapel, and exercise, and supervising them in the chapel, and under hard labour. Hard labour at Leicester was the central issue in the investigation, the warder in charge of the crank ward came under scrutiny and was severely criticised, at least by the prisoners who gave evidence, as was the regime, under which prisoners had their meals withdrawn as punishment. The reports by the Commissioners noted that the 'intensity of the labour ...[was] in the hands of the prison officer'[22] as the officer controlled the weight at which the cranks were set, this may, they thought engender feelings of irritation in prisoners who conceive the intensity of the labour to be arbitrarily set. This method of setting of cranks appears to indicate the origin of the term 'screw', used to refer to prison officers. The Commissioners noted that almost every one of the prisoners subject to this regime stated his belief that the warder 'had been in the habit, wantonly and cruelly, of increasing the hardness of the cranks, and gave utterance to expressions of bitter resentment against him for his supposed cruelty in doing so'.[23] However, they noted that the prisoner being under the direct control of the warder may excite in the prisoner feelings of resentment, the expression of which may lead the warder to 'further severity until this ends in systematic cruelty'.[24] The discretion of this crank warder was called into question, but the prisoners' evidence was often, at least implied to be unreliable, and the Commissioners praised the warder for his 'discretion, humanity and veracity'.[25]

The day-to-day activities of the officers also show that officers were responsible for reading the rules of the prison, or hard labour to the prisoners, and that prisoners had to be told when they had completed the labour (as the counters were outside the cell) and prisoners' also claimed that officers prevented them access to the surgeon or Governor. Although the surgeon went round the prison daily, a number of prisoners claimed that he went so quickly through the ward, without stopping, that it did not allow them time to call his attention.[26]

During this investigation, the Commissioners held a thorough examination of the daily report book by the officer in the crank ward, indeed this provides meticulous details of the prisoners' hard labour as the below example, of the failure to meet the required daily target of 14,400 revolutions per day, highlights:

No 2228, Joseph Allsop, received the 24th of May. May 25th, 'reported idle, first report; 7200 bad.' The 27th, 'reported idle, second report;

3300 bad'. The 28th, 'breakfast at 8am by mistake; dinner at 2pm; supper kept back; reported idle; 1300 bad'. The 29th, 'had last night's supper at 6pm today; reported idle; 7700 bad'. The 30th 'had yester-days' breakfast at 8am; dinner and supper at usual time; has done better today' On June 2d, he is reported 'for being idle yesterday, fifth report, 2800 bad', June 3d, 'breakfast at 9am; dinner 1pm; supper kept back'.[27]

Similarly, at Birmingham Gaol, the governor, surgeon and visiting justices were severely admonished for the cruel regime which had resulted in the death of a fifteen year old prisoner, Edward Andrews. Chief Warder, Freer, and father and son warders', Thomas and Edward Cotterill, came under scrutiny and evidence given at the inquiry alleged their maltreatment and physical violence towards prisoners. This resulted in the dismissal of some of the subordinate officers and only one warder, William Brown was praised by the Commissioners, 'who felt that he had exhibited great sympathy towards the prisoners under punishment and had attempted to relieve their suffering' (Roberts, 1986: 329).

By the 1860s the parameters for the prison officers working lives were being more tightly drawn. Inspector Perry, giving evidence to the Carnarvon Committee in 1863, thought that amongst the subordinate officers there were 'a great many very competent men'.[28] Although there were still dismissals, the Committee noted one case of a chief warder passing communications between two prisoners, this was his 'general' impression'. The Committee also discussed a case of a woman confined in a gaol where her husband was the warder. Perry thought that although these cases did not occur frequently, he did not see how they were to be avoided. This is another indication of the close relationship between the local prison and the community in which it was located.

In Goffman's assessment of the 'total' institution he maintains that the social distance between the inmates and the staff is 'typically great and often formally prescribed' (1961: 19). However, this does not appear to be the case between officers and prisoners in the decades before centralisation. Although, the relationship is formally prescribed there was little social distance between the two groups. As Sykes observed, in an early sociological account of the prison, officers closely associated with prisoners throughout the working day, they could not physically withdraw, there was no one else to bear the brunt of resentment when orders were disliked, and they were seen as 'a *hack* or a *screw* in the eyes of those he controls' (1958: 54, original emphasis). Therefore they possessed few of the 'devices which normally serve to maintain social distance between the rulers and the ruled' (Sykes, 1958: 54). However, social distance was more apparent between prisoners and superior officers and certainly the governor, in the nineteenth century.

Yet, there was concern about the moral character of the staff and isolating them from the working-class community. As Brown notes when discussing Hull prison, the inmate culture of the local prison was 'linked to the local community, bringing in both its negative and positive elements and contributing to the diversity of the local prisons' (2003: 79). McConville argues that the 'lingering localism of English life' meant that often there were 'ties of familiarity and sentiment between local officials and prisoners. Family names, backgrounds and places allowed officials and offenders to meet on a human plane (1998: 131). Even after nationalisation this was not eradicated, but 'prisoners and subordinate staff would be treated more by the book and less in terms of their individual characteristics or the customs of the locality' (McConville, 1998: 131) as senior prison officials were rotated through several prisons during their careers.

Documentation of prison officers working conditions reveal the long hours which they continued to work. A committee of magistrates at Wakefield reported a higher rate of mortality amongst prison officers during the preceding ten years, as compared to other large county prisons. The average hours of attendance in other prisons, deducting Sundays and leave of absence, was 74.5 hours per week and at Wakefield, 73.75 hours per week. However, the committee adopted a policy to reduce working hours to 70 per week in light of the higher mortality rate amongst their officers.[29] From the evidence collected on the larger county prisons, full hours of weekly attendance ranged between 67.5 hours at Warwick to 83.5 hours at Winchester and Birmingham. Most local prisons allowed 13 Sundays absence per year and 7 days leave of absence but practice varied. At Coldbath Fields only 4 Sundays absence were allowed, but 10 days leave, whilst at Wandsworth, 13 Sundays absence were permitted but only 3 days leave per year.[30] It is not difficult to see why commentators have referred to the officers as 'the other prisoners' (Hawkins, 1976: 81; see Chapter 5).

Long hours of work persisted into the early twentieth century. Petitions from officers at Bedford prison in 1899 called the Home Secretary's attention to the excessive hours of duty, no extra pay for working Sundays and Bank Holidays, when on evening duty they may have worked 36 hours at a time, without extra pay or time off.[31] The working hours in all local prisons were from 6am to 6pm weekdays, Sundays 7am to 5pm, allowing time for meals (40 minutes for breakfast and 1 hour, 10 minutes for dinner). Officers were off duty every other Saturday afternoon, and every other Sunday, but were liable to be called in if wanted. Officers were on duty all Bank Holidays, without extra pay, and without evening duty worked 82 hours per week (seven days). Furthermore, each officer took evening duty either once, twice or three times per week depending on the prison in which he worked. One evening duty resulted in 94 hours work, two evening duties, 106 hours work, and three evening duties 118 hours work per week. When on evening duty, officers left the prison at 4pm returning at 5.45pm they were then actively on duty until 8pm or 10pm and afterwards slept in the prison where liable to be called upon during the night.[32] It appears these petitions from Bedford prison were part of a wider submission of petitions emanating from eleven prisons, signed by 272 subordinate officers. In considering these petitions, then Commissioner, Evelyn Ruggles-Brise, thought that the expansion of prison staff would ease these problems, and issued a standing order instructing governors to try to ensure no officers was on duty for more than 24 hours. But the requests for an eight hour working day and extra pay for Sundays and Bank Holidays, he thought was not a demand widely shared by any considerable number of officers and 'cannot in any case... be entertained'.[33]

Despite the unremitting grind of the prison machine, it appears that many officers stayed in such positions for a number of years. Evidence from Wakefield in 1865 shows service of over fifteen or twenty years, in the male and female sides of the prison.[34] This was not uncommon, other research on local prisons shows that although some employees only stayed for two or three years, there was a substantial minority who served long periods. Prison work was secure, and it provided a pension, making it a stable position, especially in the rural or agri-cultural areas where employment was seasonal affected. Registers of Officers from Hull, Lincoln, Wakefield and Nottingham[35] from the late nineteenth and early twentieth century show that many officers remained in the service for long periods of their lives.

Conclusion

The control of the local prisons was transferred to the government in April 1878 when the Prison Act 1877[36] came into force. The system came under the control of the Prison Commission, the then Chairman

Lieutenant-Colonel (later Sir) Edmund Du Cane. The establishment of the Prison Service bought together the staff from local prisons, with those working in the Convict Service, which had been established in 1850. From then on, applicants who wished to join the service would apply centrally rather than being appointed by the local prison governor or magistrate. Pay was set at the national level and the staff supplied with uniforms. Those officers who wished to reside in the prison could do so and quarters were free.[37] The officers in local prisons were placed on a new pyramidal structure of staff, from the Governor at the top, followed by the Chief Warder, Principal Warders, Warders, and then Assistant Warders (Thomas, 1972). Centralisation also resulted in the closure of 37 prisons, bringing the total number of prisons in England and Wales to 69 by 1878.[38] Du Cane distributed the staff around the system; other staff saw this as the time to leave the service (Harrison, 2000).

After the Gladstone Committee in 1895, the rigid and uniform discipline of the Du Cane era was ameliorated, at least, for some prisoners. Juveniles, those with mental health problems and inebriates (see Chapter 7) were removed from the prison and the new policy ethos focused on 'rehabilitation' and welfare. The training of prison officers began in the 1890s, when schools opened at Chelmsford, Hull, Wormwood Scrubs and Manchester prisons (Johnston, 2008). In the opening years of the new century prison officers remaining active in voicing concerns over their working conditions and collective representation (Thomas, 1972; see Chapter 5).

During the nineteenth century, the role and duties of prison officers were affected by the size, structure and regime of the prisons, in which they worked. As government control over local prisons grew, the duties and working conditions of officers were more closely observed and administered. In the period of reform, advocates of the reformatory systems sought morally upstanding officers to provide an example to prisoners and lead them away from a life of crime. Yet this was often undermined by the close relationship between the local prisons and the community, the turnover of staff and the types of prisoners held. Many officers would have 'regarded reformatory endeavours as the preoccupation of their gentlemanly superiors, which had little effect on the nature of the criminal' (Forsythe, 1987: 115). As the century progressed, the movement towards more deterrent prison regimes, resulted in stricter controls on officers, with regard to respectability and the completion of their duties. Whilst there was less focus on moral example as a reformatory measure, adherence to the timetable, standing orders and regulations, and uniform prison practices was paramount in the professionalisation of the service. Thomas (1978) argues that through the prison hierarchy, staff discretion was clearly prescribed, this helped staff to understand what was expected of them and eliminated vagueness. Although some of the ambiguity in prison policy had been removed with centralisation, short sentences and groups of prisoners which required different provision were still evident in the system.

In the years following centralisation, the lives of prison staff and prisoners vanished behind the closed door of bureaucratic government administration, links with the local community, although not entirely severed manifested themselves in a different way. Local prisons operated more as walled islands within the community – only reached by some but unknown to many – where the prisoners and staff were located in, but isolated from the community.

Notes

*This research was supported by British Academy Small Research Grant Award No: SG 40723. The author would also like to thank the archivists at their respective record offices and museums for their assistance with this research.

1 In the early years of the century prison officers were frequently referred to as turnkeys, as the decades progressed this was replaced with warder and later 'prison officer', which was officially adopted in 1922 (NA, HO 45/11082/ 427916) although in common usage before this time.
2 2 & 3 Vict. c. 56.
3 4 Geo. IV. c. 64.
4 QS24/585 Warwickshire County Records Office, Warwick.
5 *Ibid.*
6 *Select Committee of the House of Lords on Gaols and House of Correction in England and Wales: First Report; Second Report; Third Report; Fourth and Fifth Reports, Minutes of Evidence, Appendices, Index*, 1835, PP, (438) (439) (440) (441), XI.1, 495, XII.1, 57, Appendix 22: 593–622 (This may not include other town, city or borough gaols and houses of correction).
7 *Ibid.*
8 *First Report of the Inspectors of the Prisons*, (hereafter RIP), Northern & Eastern (NE), 1836, PP, (117–II), XXXV.161, 4.
9 First RIP, Southern & Western (SW), 1836, PP, (117–III), XXXV.269, 2.
10 Second RIP, NE, 1837, PP, (89), XXXII.499, 3.
11 Third RIP, NE, 1837–8, PP, (134), XXXI.1, 2.
12 *Ibid.*
13 Third RIP, SW, 1837–8, PP, (135), XXXI.177, 1.
14 Fourth RIP, Home, 1839, PP, (210), XXI.1, iv.
15 Fourth RIP, NE, 1839, PP, (199), XXII.1, ii.
16 CoC 4/1/27 Letter 306, Lincolnshire Archives, Lincoln.
17 For a complete list of fines see QA 2/1/2, Visiting Justices Reports, Shrewsbury Prison, Shropshire Archives, 57.

18   347 JUS/4/2/2, By-Laws of Liverpool Borough Prison 1865 to 1874, Liverpool Record Office, Liverpool.

19   NA, HO 45/9517/21125A.

20   *Ibid.*

21   Regulations for the Government of Prisons under Prison Act 1865, 1867, West Yorkshire Archive Service [WYAS], QT1/3/43.

22   *Royal Commission to inquire into the Condition and Treatment of the Prisoners confined in Leicester County Gaol and House of Correction; together with the Minutes of Evidence*, 1854, PP, (1808), XXXIV.197, xiii.

23   *Ibid.*

24   *Ibid.*

25   *Ibid.*, xv.

26   *Ibid.*, Minutes of Evidence.

27   *Ibid.*, Minutes of Evidence, 86.

28   *Select Committee of the House of Lords on the Present State of Prison Discipline in Gaols and Houses of Correction* [Carnarvon Committee], 1863, PP, (499), XI.1, 32.

29   QD 1/354 Wakefield House of Correction, Documents relating to Prison officers, 1860–1865, WYAS.

30   *Ibid.*

31   NA, HO 45/9718/A51528E/57.

32   *Ibid.* When off duty on Saturday afternoon and Sunday and without evening duty the working week consisted of 66 hours on duty and this was the minimum hours that could be served.

33   HO 45/9718/A51528E/57.

34   QD 1/359 Wakefield House of Correction, List of Officers, 1865, WYAS.

35   DPHG/4/1 Register of Officers: HMP Hull, Hull City Archives; Lincoln Prison 5 Register of Officers: HMP Lincoln, Lincolnshire Archives; Register of Officers: HMP Wakefield, WYAS, Register of Officers: HMP Nottingham, Prison Service Museum, Galleries of Justice, Nottingham.

36   40 & 41 Vict. c. 21.

37   First pay scales in July 1878, Chief Warders received a minimum of £125 per annum, with an annual increment of £2. Principal Warders were paid a minimum of £85 per annum, Warders, £70 per annum, Assistant Warders (and Messengers and Watchmen) £60 per annum, all with an annual increment of £1. Female Warders were paid £55 per annum with an annual increment of £1 and ten shillings and Assistant Female Warders received £45 per annum with an annual increment of £1 (*Report of the Commissioners of Prisons*, 1878, PP, (C.2174), XLII.1, 31).

38   *Ibid.*, 36.

5

The Man, the Machine and the Myths: Reconsidering Winston Churchill's Prison Reforms

Jamie Bennett

It has been argued that the modern penal system emerged during the last years of the nineteenth century and the early years of the twentieth century, a system that recognised prisoners as frequently being the victims of social circumstances and sought to ameliorate harsh conditions in prisons and provide reformative services including education and training (Garland, 1985). This more liberal and humane prison system was controversial and contested as it was in marked contrast to previous ideas and practices, based on a moralistic view of offenders and the predominance of harsh punishment and segregation acting as both a deterrent, and an opportunity for personal reflection. Despite the momentous nature of the battle of ideas that was taking place during that period it has been subjected to relatively little research. In contrast, one individual from this period has attracted significant popular attention as a person who not only symbolised the changes taking place, but has been credited by many as single-handedly transforming the prison system in less than two years. That man was Winston Churchill.

Churchill first achieved fame not as a politician, but as a prisoner. Whilst working as a correspondent during the Boer War in 1899, the train he was travelling on was attacked and after a short gun battle, he was captured and taken to Pretoria as a prisoner of war. Twenty-eight days later, he escaped and successfully made his way to safety. This event was mythologised both in the press, keen for good news to cheer a nation depressed by the reverses against the Boer, as well as in one of the first of Churchill's self-penned books that sought to seal his own historical legacy (Churchill, W., 1900). When elevated to the position of Home Secretary in 1910, Churchill's responsibilities included prisons, and his personal experience of imprisonment was seen by many as providing him with an intense appreciation for the pains of imprisonment and a humanitarian concern for prisoners. His official biographers claimed that; 'the loss of freedom had irked him greatly, and he felt he had some affinity with the life of the prisoners...He sought to help prisoners in every way, short of escaping' (Churchill, R., 1967: 386) and; 'Underlying Churchill's prison reforms was a real understanding of the nature of imprisonment from the perspective of the prisoner' (Gilbert, 1991: 214). Churchill himself was happy to play up to this myth. In his original book about his experiences in South Africa, his description of the pains of imprisonment was limited, describing his frustrations at being placed on the sidelines, the monotony of life and his inability to concentrate on reading and writing (Churchill, W., 1900). However, following his time as Home Secretary, he came to revise and elaborate this tale, intensifying its vividness and depth, and promoting his reputation as a sensitive reformer inspired by personal experience (see Churchill, W., 1930).

The romantic myth, elaborated and maintained by Churchill and his official biographers, has become part of popular iconography. This is symptomatic of the problem of trying to understand and reconsider both Churchill and the period in which the modern prison system emerged. Churchill has achieved a status that has been compared, if a little flippantly, to a 'canonisation' (Benn, 1987: 24), he is depicted as being above and beyond his time, a figure that dominates and shapes his era. He has come to be depicted without context other than his own agency, where every act is seen to break the mould and challenge convention. However no man exists in a vacuum, all are shaped to some degree by the values, ideas and institutions of their age; the material and intellectual structures. This reconsideration of Churchill's Home Secretaryship will attempt to reconnect his work with the developments in criminal justice at that time. It will also attempt to appreciate how this era marked a stage in Churchill's own personal political development. Bringing these two ideas together, this chapter will attempt to cast light on the interaction between social structure and the individual, the mutually influential relationship between a man and the prison machine. This is an attempt to draw upon ideas of structuration (Giddens, 1984), which describes how structures and individuals interact to recreate and transform society. By examining these issues, it is hoped that the reader will be taken beyond the simple romantic myths, no matter how attractive they are, and can glimpse the events of 1910–11 with an appreciation of the tensions, the conflict and complexity that they hold.

Crime and prisons in 1910

Whilst the Edwardian era is sometimes seen as a tranquil golden sunset to the Victorian age before the harsh night time of the Great War, the reality is that it was a more turbulent time than this broad-brush portrait reveals. It was an era when many of the ideas of the modern state started to emerge into public policy, albeit challenged and contested (Hattersley, 2004). The most dramatic examples of this, were the constitutional battles that ultimately led to the supremacy of the Commons over the Lords being enshrined in the Parliament Act 1911, the development of a direction in social policy that has been described as a prototype welfare state, following the election of the Liberal government in 1906 (Hennessy, 1992), and a series of violent industrial and social conflicts that marked the emergence of a more assertive population such as the violent strikes at Tonypandy and the Suffragette and Irish Home Rule campaigns. These developments can be seen as moving towards a more democratic state where the whole population had a voice rather than being dominated by economic and social elites. However, these developments were intensely contested, sometimes violently, and the strength of the interests involved meant that the results were controversial, partial and incomplete. Changes in values and practices reflecting this broader social context can be seen in prisons and crime policy during the years leading up to Churchill's time as Home Secretary.

The early and mid-Victorian approach to crime and criminals was concerned with the problems arising from unregulated human conduct, particularly as the material and social developments of the age, such as improved transportation, greater urbanisation and growing material wealth, increased the opportunities for individualism and the ability to meet human desires (Wiener, 1990). This was perceived as the dark, anarchic side of the opportunities afforded by industrialisation, the destructive temptations of the new age. As part of this, crime was seen as an issue of individual weaknesses, taking on a moral character. People were expected to exercise restraint and self-control so as to resist the corrupting urges that they felt and which could more readily be satisfied than in the past. In order to enforce this, the apparatus of criminal justice emerged, including the growth of organised police forces and the expansion of imprisonment. General deterrence was seen to be best served by uniformity and certainty through detection, trial and punishment, and moral improvement was sought through religious teaching and harsh treatment including physically punishing work.

The later-Victorian era saw this orthodoxy start to be eroded as new ideas competed for dominance. This was partly due to the success of the strategies implemented to control the population, which led to a reduction in crime and therefore a greater sense of safety. The desire for control started to be superseded by a growing concern that people felt constricted. In crime policy this was increasingly felt by the middle classes as they started to find themselves directly affected, becoming embroiled in popular discontent such as Irish Home Rule, the Suffragette movement, anti-vaccination campaigns and the forceful evangelism of the Salvation Army (Wiener, 1990). Increasingly, influential individuals including intellectuals, professionals and the famous philanthropists started to highlight that crime and social conditions were closely linked. These factors combined to support the emergence of a more sympathetic image of offenders, where; 'the criminal was no longer a wicked individual but rather a product of his environment and heredity' (Wiener, 1990: 226).

These conflicting images and ideas were the background to the penal crisis of the 1890s. Ostensibly, this crisis was brought about by concerns about maltreatment and the ineffectiveness of imprisoning large numbers of poor people, and was fed by powerful advocates of reform such as William Morrison, Chaplain of Wandsworth prison (Harding *et al.*, 1985), but was essentially a battle of ideas between Victorian orthodoxy and the newer idea of a socially conscious criminal justice system. A Commission was established to examine the management of prisons, led by Herbert Gladstone (also see Chapter 9). This famous report, published in 1895, was widely seen as ushering in a new approach based upon greater concern for reform and rehabilitation. The man brought in to implement these reforms described this report as; 'mark[ing] the passage from the old to the new methods of punishment, and from those which rested upon severity and repression to those which looked more hopefully towards the possible reformation of persons committed to prison' (Ruggles-Brise, 1921: 76). However, the report did not focus exclusively on rehabilitation and concern for prisoners, but it established a twin aim of prisons, henceforth they were to both deter and punish crime on the one hand, and to reform the prisoner on the other. Thus whilst the report gave support to the new ideas, it did not reject the past instead it was an approach that institutionalised a duality that would inevitably cause tension.

The period from 1895 through to 1914 and beyond into the immediate post-war era, was one in which the role of imprisonment was sharply contested. On one hand, it has been described that this was an era in which, 'The penal-welfare complex' emerged (Garland, 1985:

159), marking a radical reinvention of the role and nature of punishment. This was manifested in policies including ameliorating and reducing harsh conditions such as separation and punishing physical labour, improving education, training and aftercare, and developing specialist facilities to divert the young, the mentally ill and those worst affected by social problems, such as drunkards and vagrants. However, it has alternatively been argued that the reality of the day-to-day experience of imprisonment changed little and the changes that did occur were not dramatic (Bailey, 1997) and that new ideas were less clear cut and more pragmatically adapted into older practices in prison management (Forsythe, 1995). This argument suggests that the changes were largely based on a desire to ameliorate the worst excesses and to graft new ideas into the existing system rather than marking a radical reinvention of prisons, and so it has been described as 'a development, on less repressive lines, of the older system of prison discipline' (Bailey, 1997: 296). That is not to say that such an approach could not have dramatic consequences, in particular that amelioration in this context encompasses the abatement in the use of imprisonment that was so spectacularly evident during this period.

This era can be described as one in which the purpose of imprisonment and the social ideas that framed it were being contested. As a result there was not a smooth, orderly, Whiggish procession, but instead it was 'fragile and contingent' (Pratt, 2002: 6) in as much as the extent and nature of any changes were dependent upon the degree of visibility at any particular time, and the outcomes 'fragmentary' (Garland, 1985: 162) in as much as they were often a pragmatic compromise. There were a number of reasons for this. First, criminal policy and many of the personnel involved clung to the ideas of the mid-Victorian era and sought to limit or prevent change (Forsythe, 1990). Second, there was no clearly defined strategy or leading strategist to take forward the new ideas (Garland, 1985). Third, there were competing ideas that influenced developments, including those of eugenics (Radzinowicz and Hood, 1990). Fourth, the newer developments may not have been as transformational as proponents suggested but could alternatively be understood as a reinvention of control strategies outside of prison in the wider community (Garland, 1985) or have regressive consequences such as disproportionate sentences justified on the grounds of rehabilitation (Pratt, 2002). This encapsulates the context of the criminal justice debate at the point Churchill became Home Secretary, an era defined by a penological competition raging between the positivist ideas of the mid-Victorian era and the emerging welfarist ideology.

For Churchill himself, this was also an era in which he was experiencing an internal battle of ideas. In 1904, he had crossed the floor of the House of Commons, leaving the Conservatives and joining the Liberals. Although he played a central role and along with David Lloyd George was one of the most belligerent new Liberals, he was not a natural radical. He was a member of the aristocracy, a patrician and part of the traditional order. The reforms which he played a role in were aimed at ameliorating the worst excesses of laissez-faire economics and social inequality, but by empowering excluded groups these policies also moved increasingly towards challenging the established order. This period therefore marked a point of some moment in his personal political development, where he explored the limits of his own radicalism.

When Churchill was appointed Home Secretary on 15 February 1910, it was in the midst of a professionally and personally turbulent period. The battle of ideas that was raging was one that took place as much within himself as it did within his department.

Churchill's prison reforms

On leaving the Home Office, Viscount Gladstone counselled caution to Churchill; 'As regards Prisons it won't be a bad thing to give a harassed department some rest' (Churchill, R., 1969: 1141). This reflected the fact that the system had already undergone significant changes since Gladstone's own influential report of 1895. However, Churchill had other ideas, and he set his stall out quickly, hoping that this would be an opportunity for him to make an impression. He showed that he would be unconventional, seeking advice from reformers such as Wilfred Scawen Blunt (Churchill, R., 1969) who had served a short sentence for offences connected to Irish Home Rule. Within six days of taking up his post, he also took Sir Evelyn Ruggles-Brise, Chairman of the Prison Commissioners between 1895 and 1921, to a performance of John Galsworthy's play *Justice* (Gilbert, 1991). This play was calculated to promote prison reform including exposing the pain of solitary confinement, and it was successful in subsequently generating public concern about the inhumanity of that practice (Nellis, 1996).

Churchill followed this on 10 July 1910 with one of the most famous and humane statements of the importance of imprisonment to the community as a whole:

[T]he mood and temper of the public in regard to the treatment of crime and criminals is one of the most unfailing tests of the civilisation of any country. A calm and dispassionate recognition of the rights of the accused against the State, and even of convicted criminals against the State, a constant heart-searching by all charged with the duty of punishment, a desire and eagerness to rehabilitate in the world of industry all those who have paid their dues in the hard coinage of punishment, tireless effort towards the discovery of curative and regenerative processes, and an unfaltering faith that there is treasure, if you can only find it, in the heart of every man – these are the symbols which in the treatment of crime and criminals mark and measure the stored-up strength of a nation, and are sign and proof of the living virtue in it (cited in Gilbert, 1991: 214–15).

With that powerful opening, it was anticipated that this was to be a truly dramatic and radical period of change, but what was the reality? What did Churchill achieve during his time, and was he able to shape the more positive and humane prison system he described?

Prison conditions

Following the new direction heralded in 1895, some of the harshness of imprisonment had been reduced, for example, separate confinement at the start of each sentence was reduced from nine to six months in 1899, and to three months in 1909, the treadwheel and crank were abolished 1902, and there was a dramatic reduction in the use of corporal punishment, falling from 301 floggings between 1894–98, to 92 between 1899 and 1903, and by 1909, there were only ten floggings throughout the year (Wiener, 1990). Churchill wished to go further in ameliorating the conditions, believing that, 'The whole process of punishment is an ugly business at best' (Churchill, R., 1969: 1152–3).

As described above, it has been suggested that Churchill was sensitised by personal experience to the harshness of prison life. He particularly resented the boredom and the difficulty in reading and writing he had experienced:

Meanwhile the war is going on, great events are in progress, fine opportunities for action and adventure are slipping away. Also the days are very long. Hours crawl like paralytic centipedes. Nothing amuses you. Reading is difficult; writing impossible. Life is one long boredom from dawn till slumber...Looking back on those days, I have always felt the keenest pity for prisoners and captives. What it must mean for any man, especially an educated man, to be confined for years in a modern convict prison strains my imagination. Each day exactly like the one before, with the barren ashes of wasted life behind, and all the long years of bondage stretching out ahead (Churchill, W., 1930: 256).

These words do, albeit romantically, encapsulate a sense of the experience of time in imprisonment, the sense of 'lives...suddenly emptied of time markers' (Cohen and Taylor, 1972: 104). He also describes the acts of resistance he performed including petitioning officials and, of course, his escape. However, his experience of a relatively short period of detention in a prisoner of war camp differed from that of prisoners in England and Wales in 1910 in significant respects. The most obvious was that a prisoner of war camp, with its less formalised structures lacked the characteristics of the 'Total Institution' (Goffman, 1961) that attempted to intensely regulate and supervise the activities of prisoners, a feature of prisons at that time. In addition, Churchill's experience does not encompass all of the pains of imprisonment (Sykes, 1958), although he lost his liberty and complained about the loss of goods and services, particularly books and entertainment, he made no comment about the loss of heterosexual relations, his autonomy was limited to a lesser degree than in total institution, and he did not suffer from the loss of security experienced by prisoners tossed into a sea of offenders in a civilian prison. Churchill's experiences should not be dismissed out of hand, nor should their significance be exaggerated. For example, inspired by his experiences he increased the availability of visiting lecturers and the performance of concerts, so that each prisoner could attend these every quarter, and he sought to improve libraries so that they were of a similar standard to those in the community. However, this library reform in particular had a limited benefit as at that time, prisoners were only allowed to borrow books after serving 28 days and 81% of prisoners were serving less than a month imprisonment (Forsythe, 1990). Whilst these can be considered positive, they are of secondary importance, and illustration of the limitations of romanticising Churchill's personal experiences.

The second issue that was arguably informed by his personal experiences of imprisonment was his desire to draw a distinction between prisoners whose offences carried an element of moral condemnation, and those whose offences did not. This was pressing due to the increasing number of people imprisoned for 'political' offences related to the Irish Home Rule and Suffragette movements. There was an attempt to create a distinguishing classification of offenders in 1898 and Gladstone had developed ideas for a policy on this issue. However, it was Churchill who realised this, creating prison rule 243A which recognised political prisoners and allowed them to wear their own clothes, be searched by special officer, exempted them from bathing and haircutting, allowed them to receive the best prison food and have food brought in, they were allowed to exercise in association twice a day, have a supply of books, receive letters and visits once a fortnight, and were allowed to pay for their cells to be cleaned. If this was, indeed, informed by his personal experiences, then it betrays a desire to distance himself from prisoners rather than create a greater intimacy.

Following the lobbying of Galsworthy and the dramatic attendance at the performance of *Justice*, it could have been anticipated that Churchill would abolish separate confinement at the beginning of sentences, particularly as he wrote to Galsworthy after attending the performance stating his; 'entire sympathy with your general mood' (Churchill, R., 1969: 1150). However, following discussions with the Prison Commissioners, he limited his ambitious, and even started to rethink whether his radicalism was really the right approach. He decided to reduce separate confinement from three months to one month, but stated to the Permanent Secretary at the Home Office that he was impressed; 'with the importance of making the first period of prison life a severe disciplinary course, of interposing a hiatus between the world which the convict has left and the public works gang which he is to join' (cited in Gilbert, 1991: 212). This illustrates official resistance to reform and also the limits of Churchill's radicalism, casting light on the personal and professional tensions between reform and conservatism.

In other areas, Churchill's conservatism was more apparent. When a private members bill was presented to abolish corporal punishment, he actively blocked it (Radzinowicz and Hood, 1990). He also was robust in his management of Suffragettes, taking a hard line towards the force feeding of hunger strikers. This had been a problem since 1908 and at the end of Gladstone's period as Home Secretary, there had been a scandal as a result of the conduct of force feeding without medical examination and arising from visceral reports of the brutality involved. Not only did Churchill reject these complaints when he came to office, but he set clear boundaries, first that force feeding would commence after 48 hours, then that it would commence after 24 hours (Addison, 1992). As with his justification for maintaining solitary confinement, he was impressed by the need for discipline and order.

Churchill's reforms of prison conditions expose the conflicts and contradictions both of the time and the man. There was an ongoing tension between discipline and welfare, liberalism and conservatism. He was, however, conscious of the limitations of changing prisons internally, in the Prison Vote debate in July 1910, he cautioned:

> We must not forget that when every material improvement has been effected in prisons, when the temperature has been adjusted, when the proper food to maintain health and strength has been given, when the doctors, chaplains, and prison visitors have come and gone, the convict stands deprived over everything that a free man calls life. We must not forget that all these improvements, which are sometimes slaves to our consciences, do not change that position (cited in Gilbert, 1991: 214).

The main battle for Churchill would not be in changing prison conditions, but in reducing the number of people sent there.

Reforming prisoners

One way in which Churchill hoped to reduce the number of people in prison was to reduce recidivism. In response to a request for budget cuts from Treasury minister Charles Hobhouse, he wrote that he wanted additional funds as; 'I have discovered that of the convicts discharged during the years 1903–4–5 three out of every four are already back in penal servitude. It is this terrible proportion of recidivism that I am anxious to break in upon' (Churchill, R., 1969: 1186).

One way in which he hoped to do this was to improve after care services for prisoners so that they were better aided to settle back into the community and establish a law-abiding life. In his letter to Hobhouse, he elaborated his thoughts:

> It is clear that the existing attempt at reform, aid on discharge, and police supervision, fail altogether to enable or encourage a convict to resume his place in honest industry. A supervision more individualised, more intimate, more carefully considered, more philanthropically inspired, is necessary; and for this purpose I propose to weave all the existing Prisoners' Aid Societies into one strong confederacy, to sustain them with funds on a larger scale than they have hitherto had at their disposal, to place them in contact with individual convicts long before these are again thrown upon the world, and only to use the ordinary methods of police

supervision in cases which are utterly refractory (Churchill, R., 1969: 1186).

This was not a new idea; it was a reform that the Chairman of the Prison Commissioners, Evelyn Ruggles-Brise had advocated (Forsythe, 1990) and also built upon ideas that had led to the establishment of probation services in 1907 to supervise offenders in the community. Nevertheless, this was an important achievement that over time improved after care services and set a welfare-orientated approach to post-sentence supervision that was to endure for almost a century.

Following on from this success, Churchill developed some ambitious plans for extensive reform of the prison system. He shared his thoughts with the Prime Minister, Herbert Asquith, saying that in his view, 'classification is the essence of penology' (Churchill, R., 1969: 1202). He went on to elaborate his plans for re-organising prisons:

> I should propose to survey them as a whole, and organise them (gradually, of course) into one complete series of carefully graded specialised institutions conveniently distributed throughout the country, and adapted to the suitable treatment of every conceivable variety of human weakness and misdemeanour...I should set up administratively a Board, (or system of co-ordinated Boards) of Classification, which would consider the cases of all offenders after being sentenced , and distribute them to receive their appropriate treatment throughout different penal corrective and curative institutions of the prison system: due regard of course being paid to the decision of the Court and provided always that no such modification or variation of treatment shall be in excess or in aggravation of the original sentence of the court (Churchill, R., 1969: 1203).

This idea of a more individualised and therapeutic prison system was in line with the ideas of the age as prisons moved away from simply being places of punishment. Gladstone had stated that 'our object' was 'a more scientific treatment of all classes of prisoners by [the] study of antecedents and by making treatment penal, corrective, educational according to classes *and* cases' (cited in Wiener, 1990: 376). The idea of adopting a more scientific approach to the reform of prisoners was also the foundation for the creation of the Borstal system for young offenders, given legal effect in 1908, which aimed to use systematic techniques with an educative and corrective aim.

What distinguished Churchill's idea was that he had created a vision for realising a more individualised and scientific approach for the prison system as a whole. When confronted with these plans, the Permanent Secretary at the Home Office reported that Ruggles-Brise's, 'breath was rather taken away...and he burst into Homeric laughter' (Churchill, R., 1969: 1196). The idea was not directly enacted and although it has been claimed that this vision became the basis of reforms carried out after the Great War (Wiener, 1990), there is no direct evidence that it provided an explicit blue print of this nature, rather than being the articulation of the notion that prison should provide an individualised, corrective facility, an idea that was emerging before 1910–11 and continued to grow afterwards forming what is now described as the model of penal welfarism.

As with prison conditions, there was also a darker side to Churchill's ideas, in particular, his engagement with criminological science led him to a flirtation with eugenics. He circulated a paper from *The Eugenics Review* to the Cabinet, was willing to see indeterminate sentences on medical grounds for the 'feeble-minded' (Radzinowicz and Hood, 1990) and was even attracted to idea of sterilising people in this group (Addison, 1992).

In relation to the reform of prisoners, Churchill can be seen as less of an innovator in the sense that the ideas he developed were not new but rather reflected the Liberal welfarist agenda. What is distinct about Churchill is his ability to energetically bring important changes to fruition and to vividly articulate those ideals. However, his conservative instincts can also be seen in his flirtation with eugenics.

Sentencing

Given his expressed distaste of imprisonment and the movement towards seeing crime as related to social conditions, the attraction of imprisonment to both Churchill and the public was on the wane and moves to reduce the prison population attracted broad support. There had been a period of significant decarceration after the establishment of the national prison system in 1878. In that year, there were 31,000 prisoners on any day, ten years later this fell to 21,200 and by 1898 it reached 17,600 (Rutherford, 1984). However, the next decade, saw an increase to 22,000 in 1908 (Home Office, 2003). Thereafter, a sustained period of prison reduction took place, with the prison population dropping below 10,000 by 1917. Although the most dramatic reductions took place from 1912, after Churchill had left the Home Office, his period did see the start of a downward movement to below the 20,000 mark.

In handing over the Home Office, Gladstone had offered Churchill his advice:

I venture to make one suggestion in conclusion. The most responsible work which falls to the Home Secretary is the supervision of sentences. The final judgement subject to the law, is in his hands. Many cases are interesting enough, but the mass mean a great deal of irksome and minute examination. The office presents, as a rule, the traditional view of treatment, which in most cases is quite right. But they cannot bring to bear the outside, impartial view of human nature and human society which necessarily belongs to the Home Secretary. It very often happens that examination of the sordid affairs of rather discreditable and useless people involves a great deal of time. But you will find that if you give this generously you will be repaid by being able to lift up not a few miserable creatures out of trouble and disgrace (Churchill, R., 1969: 1141–2).

Churchill was fully in accordance with this and much has been made of his willingness to interfere with judicial decisions. The scale of 'The Churchillian onslaught' (Radzinowicz and Hood, 1990: 770) can be seen from the fact that in 1909 Gladstone mitigated 203 cases, whereas Churchill mitigated 395 from February 1910 to July 1911. He actively scoured the reports of criminal cases seeking out cases of perceived injustice. As important as the scale of his intervention was the very public way in which he did this. For example, the pardons he issued during his visits to young offenders at Pentonville prison, and to David Davies, the so-called Dartmoor Shepherd, attracted wide press coverage. He was also thorough in his review of capital cases, and exercised mercy in 21 of the 43 cases presented during his period in office, a greater proportion than his predecessor (Addison, 1992). He also persuaded the King to offer a partial remission to all prisoners serving a month or more as part of his accession celebrations. This resulted in 11,000 prisoners receiving a reduction in their sentence (Addison, 1992).

As well as this interference, Churchill tried to develop more systematic limits on sentencing. A particular example of this was his distaste for the use of extended preventative detention sentences under the Prevention of Crime Act 1908. This allowed judges to impose an additional period of detention for offenders considered to be habitual or professional offenders. Churchill was concerned that this measure was being used too easily and was therefore creating disproportionate sentencing for those who were 'merely a nuisance to society' (Ruggles-Brise, 1921: 51). He said;

> I have serious misgivings lest the institution of preventative detention should lead to a reversion to the ferocious sentences of the last generation. After all preventative detention is penal servitude in all essentials, but it is a very grave danger that the administration of the law should under softer names assume in fact a more severe character (cited in Radzinowicz and Hood, 1990: 283).

He interfered in individual cases, issued a new circular regarding the use of the sentence and warned judges that if they did not change their practice he would legislate (Radzinowicz and Hood, 1990). As a result, the use of preventative detention reduced from 177 cases in 1910 to 53 cases in 1911 and it continued to decline thereafter. His actions ensured that this form of sentencing was curbed and constrained.

Churchill also issued guidance regarding sentencing in the most serious cases (Radzinowicz and Hood, 1990) and gave consideration to establishing binding sentencing guidelines (Churchill, R., 1969), although this never made it to any firm proposals.

Although he tackled these long sentences, the vast majority of sentences were for short periods of time. He wrote to the Prime Minister, Asquith citing that of the 205,000 committals to prison annually, 61% or 125,000 were for a fortnight or less, and half were being imprisoned for first time. He described this as, 'a terrible and purposeless waste of public money and human character' (Churchill, R., 1969: 1199). He proposed four measures that he anticipated would reduce committals by a third and lead to a net reduction of 10–15%. The first strand of his strategy was to divert juvenile offenders from custody. This was a long standing policy direction, and the Children Act 1908 had led to a reduction from over 1,000 children under the age of 16 in prison in 1906, to only 143 by 1910. Churchill sought to extend this to those aged 16 to 21, and between 1910 and 1919, the number of young people aged under 21 in prison fell from 13,565 to 4,236 (Churchill, R., 1967). He also wanted to create a specific alternative to imprisonment known as the defaulters' drill, which is described below. The second strand was to abolish imprisonment for debt, which Churchill argued was usually the result of genuine need. This was immediately dismissed by Asquith due to the perceived risk to commercial contracts. The third approach was to allow all offenders time to pay fines. This was an extensive problem, it was estimated that more than half of those committed to prison were fine defaulters (Churchill, R., 1967). The principle of 'time to pay' had been introduced on a discretionary basis under the Summary Jurisdiction Act in 1879, and some local courts had been practicing this for some time. This was eventually introduced under the Administration of Justice Act 1914 and had a dramatic impact with the numbers imprisoned for fine default falling from 95,686 in 1908–9 to 5,264 a decade later (Radzinowicz and Hood, 1990). His fourth proposal was that any sentence of less than one month be 'suspensory in character' (Churchill, R., 1969: 1202), meaning that it would only take effect if further offences were committed. This also quickly fell by the wayside following criticism that it was allowing offences to be committed on credit.

As can be seen from these proposals, Churchill was keen to develop meaningful alternatives to imprisonment. This included the reformed fine and the 'suspensory' sentence. He also sought to develop his ideas for a 'defaulters' drill' to replace short-term imprisonment for young offenders. He frequently justified this approach by arguing that petty misbehaviour by the young poor resulted in imprisonment whilst that of the rich went unpunished. However, this did not lead him to conclude that such punishment should be abolished merely that the worst excesses be ameliorated, thus exposing the limits of his liberalism. He saw the drill not in terms of a diverting activity like the then new scouting movement, but saw it as a disciplinary and punitive sentence, which he wrote to the King would be 'v[er]y healthy, v[er]y disagreeable' (Churchill, R., 1969: 1189). This single reform encapsulates the limits of Churchill's radicalism and the dynamic conflict with his own sense of a conservative world order; for him, reform would mean amelioration, not transformation.

Another issue that exposes these limits and tensions is his approach to the Suffragettes. Although he had expressed some sympathy with their cause, he was not willing to rush through any reform, and in the face of their self-assertion, was determined to put them in their place. This went as far as him belligerently arguing in Cabinet that they should 'proceed to lock up Suff[ragette]s wholesale' (Churchill, R., 1969: 1158). Whilst he was keen for power to be exercised humanely by a benign establishment, he was opposed to any kind of self-determination that threatened that order.

There were many other areas within the sentencing system that required reform, but would be left to Churchill's successors. For example, a third of prisoners in 1908–9 were there for drunkenness (Churchill, R., 1967), but this was not effectively tackled until the Great War, mental health provision was not subject to legislation until 1913, and the criminalisation of vagrancy remained a problem.

Churchill entered the Home Office when the prison population was starting to decline, he energetically built on this and capitalised on it. His most effective ideas built upon established areas of reform, in particular diverting young people from custody and making 'time to pay' fines mandatory. Here he embraced the aims of the new Liberal agenda. However, his own ideas, particularly the defaulters' drill betray the conflict between liberalism and conservatism, between reform and punishment that were the ideological battleground both in the development of criminal justice generally, and in Churchill's own personal, political development. His personal interventions in the criminal justice system showed that he had a keen sense of justice but these also reinforced the existing power structure, playing the role of benign patriarch, and confirmed Churchill's instinct to maintain the legitimacy of the ruling class to which he belonged.

Prison staff

Prison staff have been described as 'The Other Prisoners' (Hawkins, 1976: 81), who experience deprivations as a result of their employment. Following the reforms that started in 1895, prison staff felt that they were not participants in the reforms, and there were also recurring tensions between the Prison Commission and the uniformed grades because of the working conditions such as long hours, poor pay and severe discipline (Forsythe, 1990). It has been argued that:

> Churchill's reformative enthusiasm on behalf of the prisoners had no counterpart in the handling of staff affairs. His wish to improve the conditions of the one, and his refusal to do the same for the other was, for staff, the most typical and most depressing feature of Home Office Rule after 1906 (Thomas, 1972: 143).

However, such a sweeping judgement obscures as much as it reveals. The argument regarding Churchill's neglect largely rests upon his response to a parliamentary question on 16 February 1911 regarding collective representation (Thomas, 1972). Asked whether standing orders could be modified to allow prison officers to hold one general meeting a year, and also to give more opportunity for subordinate staff to present grievances he replied that they already had ample opportunity to do so. He stated that prison officers were like police, soldiers and sailors and therefore it was inappropriate for them to form a union. As a result, collective activity went underground, with the production of an unauthorised and unofficial Prison Officers' Magazine. That such a position was taken by

Churchill at that time was unsurprising. His time at the Home Office was dominated by three major industrial disputes involving the Newport transport workers, Rhondda valley miners, and a national strike of railway workers. These were violent and controversial events, including the notorious use of troops at Tonypandy. This was also the era in which the courts had limited the power of unions, the Taff Vale case of 1901 had ruled that trade unions were liable for damages arising from strike action, and the Osbourne judgement of 1909 restrained unions from funding political parties (Pelling, 1976). These judgements curtailed the power and influence of trade unions in an era where they faced a hostile establishment.

Where Churchill did intervene in favour of staff was in individual disciplinary cases. In one case, he was asked to confirm the recommendation that two officers would have their services dispensed with after they took a prisoner to a public house during an escorted absence. In the face of resistance from officials, Churchill ignored protocol to have the punishment reduced to a suspension and reprimand. He also insisted that future cases involving termination of employment should be referred to him personally (Churchill, R., 1969).

In the management of staff, Churchill's conservatism is clearly on show. He was willing to intervene to dispense mercy as a benign patriarch, but resisted the exercise of self-determination by workers through unionisation. Although this may have been in line with the values of the establishment of the age, a true radical, David Lloyd George, was willing to challenge this, seeking to negotiate with unions and legitimise their role (Taylor, 1969). While it is untrue to say that Churchill did nothing for prison staff, his approach to them is telling about his political limits.

Conclusion

Churchill's prison reforms are amongst the most acclaimed work he carried out before his premiership. At the time, Churchill himself commented to Asquith, 'I have never yet launched anything which has commanded such cordial and almost unbroken approval from all sections of the press...and I have heard the same from members of all parties in the House' (Churchill, R., 1969: 1198). His official biographer described that his achievements, 'were to shine for years and to serve as milestones and signposts for future reformers' (Churchill, R., 1967: 393), and a more critical biographer has also described that, 'His ambitious programme of penal reform, though never completed, marked the pinnacle of his achievement in social policy' (Addison, 1992: 110). The praise has not been restricted to historians, criminologists have also claimed that he '...left behind a momentum for reforming legislation...[and] played a crucial role in creating the political climate for change' (Rutherford, 1984: 125) and that he brought 'an energy and independence which was entirely different from his predecessors' (Forsythe, 1990: 38). As has been described above, these celebrated achievements have been wrapped up in the romantic myth of Churchill's personal experience of imprisonment. However, Churchill himself was uneasy about the praise he received, not simply as an act of false modesty, but recognising that his work was not a dramatic departure, but was rooted in the developments of the time. He wrote to Galsworthy confessing; 'I have always felt uncomfortable at receiving the easily-won applauses which come to the heads of great departments whenever they have ploughed with borrowed oxen and reaped where they have not sown' (Churchill, R., 1969: 1190). From his own pen, Churchill hinted that beyond the accumulated mass of praise there is a less neat, more subtle story to be found. That is the story of a time of change, both social and personal.

Churchill's time at the Home Office took place during a period of change in the role of imprisonment. The late-Victorian era had marked a decline in the view that offenders were evil and dangerous and that prisons should be harsh institutions, instead, a view started to emerge that offenders were often the victims of circumstances and those that society had failed, as a result, compassion replaced condemnation and the ideas of a welfarist approach started to grow. This emerging approach was given official sanction in the Gladstone Report of 1895, but the changes still had to be practically realised and this report also ensured that the purpose of imprisonment would remain contentious. The years up to 1910 saw some amelioration of the harshness of prison life, the creation of alternatives to prison through probation and borstal, and the start of decarceration, particularly in relation to children. Churchill entered the fray and built on this, working within the same general direction. His reforms including improving aftercare, continuing to improve conditions, and in preparing legislation that contributed towards the reduction of the prison population, all continued this liberalisation. However, this was not all one way, many still clung to the disciplinary approaches of the past and Churchill's reforming work was criticised by both criminal justice professionals and the press (Forsythe, 1990). Some of his reforms also reflected a more conservative approach. He accepted that prison and punishment should maintain a central disciplinary function as can be seen in his retention of separation and corporal punishment, and in his plans for the defaulters drill. Rather than adopting any particular pure criminological philosophy (Bailey, 1985), Churchill's policies reflect a tension; a desire to both punish the offender and reform them, or even an uncertainty as to which should prevail. His approach reflects the contested and fragmentary nature of criminal justice reform at the time. Churchill's achievement was to embody the time and to powerfully articulate its hopes and aspirations.

As an individual, this has been described as Churchill's most radical period. He had crossed the House to join the Liberal party and was seen as one of the most progressive exponent of new Liberalism. Some of his reforms were illustrative and at heart Churchill displayed a desire to improve the lot of people at the bottom of the social ladder. However, this period also exposed the limits of his radicalism. Whilst he was keen to dispense mercy and justice as a benign patriarch, he was not willing to change the fundamental social structure. This is most vividly seen in his resistance to attempts to exercise self-determination by prison officers and Suffragettes, although it also underlines his whole approach which was based on amelioration rather than transformation. Churchill himself recognised that he had reached his limits, his colleague, Charles Masterman recorded;

> Late one evening when he had become confidential he solemnly announced, 'the fact is David [he always calls L.G. David when something portentous is coming], the fact is, David, I am a *Tory*' (Masterman, 1964: 827 emphasis in original).

Following his period in the Home Office, particularly as a result of his repression of the strikes, Churchill lost his reputation as a radical (Taylor, 1969). By 1924 he had rejoined the Conservative party. By the time he was next in a position to play a role in penal policy, as opposition leader and Prime Minister after the Second World War, there was no sense of radicalism and his most important contribution to criminal justice was to oppose the abolition of the death penalty (Jenkins, 2001).

Beyond the romance and mythology, Churchill's time at the Home Office is an important period in which there was played out the ideological battle about the approach to crime and justice, and a personal battle in which Churchill wrestled with his own political beliefs. The era marked a fork in the road. The prison system went on to its most radical and golden age, with a limited prison population and a commitment to humane and therapeutic treatment based on the welfarist model, and for Churchill it marked the discovery that he had reached the limits of his radicalism and re-established his commitment to preserving and maintaining the existing social order.

6

The Paradox of the 'Respectable Offender': Responding to the Problem of White-Collar Crime in Victorian and Edwardian England

John P. Locker

> Things are not always what they seem. We all know that. We all frequently forget it. Nature is full of examples of creatures pretending to be what they are not. Hover-flies pretend to be wasps. Stick-insects pretend to be twigs. The examples are almost endless. Still we insist on judging by appearances. Every confidence trickster knows that, if you wish to cash a dud cheque, you should be well groomed and wear an expensive suit. We all know that. But still we are deceived by appearances. It is always dangerous to assume that because a man seems to be respectable and acts as if he is respectable, then he is respectable (Piper, 1991: 11).

Introduction

Traditional crime discourses highlighted the association between class and delinquency. For nineteenth-century contemporaries the relationship between lower-class status and crime was firmly entrenched, and while commentators observed that not everyone from the lower classes was a criminal, it was nevertheless supposed that the main criminal threat resided within lower-class communities. In contrast, although not all 'respectable' people were law-abiding, respectability (and its component features) was considered to be a fundamental determinant of honesty. As such, the widespread and unprecedented emergence of the 'respectable criminal' during the nineteenth century presented a paradox for Victorian society. As growing numbers of respectable offenders appeared before the courts, this new criminal type posed important, yet difficult, questions about how such offenders could be reconciled alongside established crime discourses, and what responses were appropriate.

This chapter examines the challenges faced, by courtroom officials and society more broadly, in managing the respectable criminal. The chapter is divided into two parts: part one examines the parameters of nineteenth-century knowledge of 'the criminal' and non-criminal, and the importance of the concept of respectability in setting the boundaries of this knowledge. Furthermore, it illustrates the ideological problems posed by the widespread emergence of a respectable criminal type within an environment governed by ingrained notions of the 'normal' and the 'deviant'. Part two explores the centrality of nineteenth-century perceptions about the nature and dynamics of criminality in understanding social responses to the emerging figure of the respectable criminal. And, using popular and courtroom narratives of (typically) middle-class, white-collar offenders, it considers the impact of such perceptions on the treatment, management, and punishment of respectable offenders.

In doing so the intention of the chapter is not to debate the pragmatics of respectable justice, or whether there was greater leniency towards this offender type within sentencing decisions: as a number of criminologists have noted, research of this nature is problematic for various reasons (Levi, 1989: 95–6). Rather, its purpose is to examine the ways in which court cases and punitive discourses involving middle-class, white-collar offenders operated as important tools in resolving the paradox of 'the respectable criminal', by rebuilding the symbolic divide between criminal and non-criminal (or respectable and non-respectable), bolstering traditional ideologies of criminality, and restoring a picture of criminality that fitted within established axioms.

A number of caveats should be noted at the outset. First, following Sutherland's (1949) definition of 'white-collar crime' and use of 'respectability' as a concept through which to identify such behaviours, it has been widely noted that these terms are problematic owing to uncertainties about their specific meaning and scope. While acknowledging this criticism, respectability was a key term used within nineteenth-century crime discourses to differentiate criminal and non-criminal, and, within the courtroom, to establish the character and status of various white-collar defendants. Respectability was therefore a key concept through which penal discourses filtered. As such, its incorporation within this chapter is critical to an understanding of punitive responses to white-collar offenders, and should be understood in this context rather than as reflecting a naïve attempt to link together nebulous social groups.

Second, while the chapter refers to white-collar and respectable offending, its main empirical focus is on the offence of embezzlement: there are a number of reasons for this. In particular, embezzlement was one of the most notable emerging white-collar offences within the Victorian commercial arena; indeed, the public face of embezzlement expanded considerably after the mid-nineteenth century, and was particularly well represented in the public record. Moreover, the offence captured a range of typically middle (to lower-middle) class, white-collar offenders whose social status was frequently deemed to confer respectability.

Third, to date those who have investigated the historical parameters of white-collar offending have focused principally on either the most financially spectacular (yet numerically insignificant) cases of misbehaviour, or the acts of high-status company employees (Morier Evans, 1859; Robb, 1992; Wilson, 2000, 2003). In contrast, they have fixed only momentarily on respectable middle (to lower-middle) class, trusted employee groups (such as the clerk) who were central to the expansion of the trust environment in which white-collar offending was perpetrated, and who were most heavily represented in key white-collar delinquencies, like embezzlement. Such groups are crucially important to the widespread emergence of white-collar criminality at this time, and are consequently a central focus within this chapter.

The widespread emergence of respectable criminals

The Victorian period gave rise to the widespread emergence of new forms of delinquent behaviour associated with the workplace, which implicated respectable, middle-class, white-collar groups (Robb, 1992: 3). As increasing numbers of such offenders appeared before the courts and in the columns of the popular media, the respectable criminal became an increasingly familiar figure within the public psyche, and Victorian contemporaries became widely recognisant of, if not entirely comfortable with, the relationship between respectability and criminality (Wiener, 1990: 244).

The apparently unyielding growth of various forms of respectable delinquency, together with its peculiarity, served to assure these offending behaviours a prominent place in crime discourses, making them a subject of considerable interest, debate, and concern. For example, in his 1859 compendium, *Facts, Failures and Frauds*, David Morier Evans documented in meticulous detail the growing extent and sheer diversity of the sharp practices, 'which have of late so frequently startled the commercial community from their propriety' (1859: iv; Laing, 1866). Likewise, commenting on the last quarter of the nineteenth century, police court missionary, Thomas Holmes, claimed to have observed notable differences in the nature of offending behaviour.

> Crime has changed in some respects. There are fewer crimes of violence; there is less brutality, less debauchery, less drinking; but – and I would like to write it very large – there is more dishonesty, which is a more insidious evil ... I am afraid of this growing dishonesty, for I have seen something of its consequences. Sneaking peculations, small acts of dishonesty, miserable embezzlements, falsified accounts, and contemptible frauds, have damned the lives of thousands (1908: 26–30; see also Holmes, 1912: 37–8; Stutfield, 1898: 79–80; Barrett, 1895; Du Cane, 1876: 273; Train, 1907: 20–1).

Yet, while the prevalence of respectable, white-collar crime encouraged widespread attention (Robb, 1992: 4), this offender did not fit easily (if at all) into established crime discourses. Indeed, in spite of a growing familiarity with middle-class crime, traditional assumptions about deviancy were enduring, and consequently the process of reconciling this new criminal threat remained problematic. As noted by Emsley, while contemporaries came to recognise 'that men of wealth and social standing committed offences ... such offenders, however common in fiction, newspaper accounts, and journal literature, were not perceived as members of a criminal class and were categorised as 'criminal' with some difficulty' (2005b: 57).

The challenge of respectable crime

The late nineteenth century witnessed a paradigm shift in understandings and interpretations of 'the criminal', away from moral and towards more 'scientific' notions of their nature and existence (Wiener, 1990; Garland, 1985; Leps, 1992; Pick, 1996; Horn, 2003). However, notwithstanding this development, there were a number of popularly held traditional perceptions about criminality that prevailed throughout (and beyond) the Victorian period.

Most fundamentally, discourses about the criminal focused largely – if not quite exclusively – on the lower- or working-class offender (Emsley, 2005b: 173–82; Bailey, 1993: 254). A lower-class background was undoubtedly the most characteristic identifier of the lawbreaker, and while many commentators were eager to note that not all members of the working-class population were offenders, the main criminal threat or 'criminal army' (Du Cane, 1876: 279; Anon, 1844: 12) was perceived to have emerged from amongst the least privileged sections of the community. Thus, in 1874, the Rev. Thomas Hutton repeated a well-trodden axiom when stating, it is 'the lowest strata of society from which our criminals generally come' (1874: 311–12; see also Beggs, 1869: 342; Beames, 1852: 130; Anon, 1844: 12).

The law, the efforts of the criminal justice system, and public attention were firmly fixed upon the delinquencies of the lowest social strata, and the varieties of lawbreaking in which they featured most heavily. Thus, contemporary discussion about illegality centred upon the street, which, as The Times noted in 1855, 'swarms with crime'.[1] This perception was reinforced through the writings of a variety of social anthropologists, whose forays into lower-class communities in search of the 'criminal underworld' reiterated the presumed association between the criminal and working classes (Mayhew, 1861; Beames, 1852; Campbell *et al.*, 1895).

Criminality was defined in opposition to respectability, and came to denote everything that the respectable person was not; thus, while respectability was characterised by qualities such as self-regulation, integrity, temperance, honest labour, and family values, most social commentators identified the main causes of crime as 'moral weakness, luxury, idleness, corrupting literature, parental neglect, and lack of education' (Emsley, 2005b: 58; see also Leps, 1992: 26, 31).

The class status and associated characteristics of the typical white-collar employee challenged the possibility of their involvement in criminal activity. While crime was perceived to emanate from within society's lower classes, the middle- (or lower-middle) class standing of even the most junior embezzling clerk immediately set them apart from the 'social debris' where the main criminal threat was believed to reside; even more so in the case of men of very high social standing who were increasingly notable for their criminal proclivities (Robb, 1992). Those charged with fraudulence were commonly assigned all the outward characteristics of moral decency associated with their class position, being depicted as properly educated, morally upright, and pleasant. They were repeatedly represented as valuable members of their communities, pillars of society, philanthropists and regular churchgoers, who had always previously borne exemplary characters (Best, 1985: 282–4).

The apparently respectable backgrounds of such men made their offences even more inconceivable, shocking and unusual. For instance, in 1890 when Arthur Frederick John Standish was charged with embezzlement, his case was reported to have 'excited considerable interest, for the prisoner is well known and highly respected. He was secretary of a dissenting chapel, and took a prominent part in temperance advocacy'.[2] James Bellamy, a bank cashier charged with peculations of almost £4,000 was described as a man who 'lived in a quiet manner, had earned the confidence of a large number of friends', and was a regular attendee at his local church where he acted as organist.[3] Similarly, the news of Joseph Mitchell's arrest for fraudulence in 1891 was said to have 'caused considerable sensation at Hill Top [his home], where [he and his] family is well known and respected'.[4] Indeed, the lifestyles of many white-collar delinquents were so compatible with the moral fortitude and righteousness of the respectable classes, that Victorian contemporaries found considerable difficulty in reconciling such behaviours alongside their criminality. Thus, following the discovery and proof of Leopold Redpath's huge frauds of more than £240,000, and in the face of wide media acknowledgement of his extravagant use of these funds, for some, Redpath's reputation for philanthropic endeavour undermined the very possibility that he might be guilty. As one commentator noted:

> He left no stone unturned to be talked of as a kind-hearted, benevolent, charitable gentleman whose hand, heart and purse were open to all-comers … indeed, so many benefited from his munificence that when the whole of his swindling transactions were exposed to the broad light of day, there were still plenty to be found who declined to believe that so good and charitable a gentleman could have been so great a rogue (Horler, 1931: 78–82).

The respectable, middle-class, white-collar offender was also particularly difficult to reconcile and comprehend since they did not, in any way, conform to popular stereotypes about the physical appearance and characteristics of the criminal that pervaded the Victorian and Edwardian periods. For many, physical characteristics were deemed to be key identifiers of the criminal. Popular writers argued that the criminal classes of England could be recognised by sight, through appearance, mannerisms, and even by the distinctive language or 'cant' that they used (Anon, 1860; Horlsey, 1887; McGowen, 1990). The perceived synonymy between lower and criminal classes ensured that depictions of the offender's physical appearance typically echoed those of the poor more generally. Thus, images of destitution, penury, raggedness, and dirt, were regularly revisited in the popular descriptions of England's lawless populations, with writers frequently commenting on the gaunt exterior, dissipated looks, or shabby clothing of many such men, women and children.

Such depictions of the delinquent were increasingly intermixed within a growing body of thought that further identified the criminal through innate physical and mental characteristics. Thus, particularly during the latter decades of the nineteenth century, the association between environmental factors, biological failings, and criminal activity became increasingly noted, as contemporaries distinguished the bodily stigmata from which criminality could be gleaned. For instance, prison chaplain J. W. Horsley suggested that, 'dangerous criminals have a type of face which would warn the innocent or the unsuspecting' (1913: 35). Given the social biases inherent in traditional mores, such pronouncements were heavily class-specific.

Dominant discourses of criminality involved the middle classes only insofar as to serve as information and warning about how to avoid victimisation at the hands of such criminals. Respectable offenders were not implicated or incorporated within popular cultural portrayals of the criminal's physical distinctiveness. In their physical appearance middle-class delinquents were often the very antithesis of the criminals portrayed in such writing. Indeed, social pressures dictated that white-collar staff adhere to proscribed standards of respectable dress and decorum within their working and social lives (Best, 1985: 284; Newsome, 1997: 75; Simmons, 1974: 14–20). While this often placed a heavy burden on those at the lower end of the business spectrum (and ironically has been cited as a determining factor in the peculations of some men) it ensured that the appearance of the embezzler, fraudster, or swindler, when alluded to, was typically described as one of propriety and respectability. For instance, in 1880, when Giovanni Lusatte was tried for embezzling £2,350 from his employers, he was described as a 'gentlemanly-looking man',[5] while Thomas Smarwaite was referred to in court as 'respectable-looking'.[6] Likewise, arch swindler Leopold Redpath was depicted as 'highly moral in his external character [and] was regarded as a model man' (Horler, 1931: 77–8). Indeed, describing the scene at Redpath's trial before the Central Criminal Court in 1857, one writer noted of the fraudster:

> He was generally considered rather a noticeable man, but now that he attained notoriety through the commission of a serious crime, his appearance was more strictly scanned with a pardonable inquisitiveness. A rather tall, fresh-looking man of forty, slightly bald, but with a profusion of hair under the chin, he possessed a thoroughly English look. He might have been supposed to be a country squire or justice,

'his belly with fat capon lined', retaining a family seat in the church-warden's pew, delighting in a conservatory, and keeping a good balance at his bankers. *There was little of the criminal about him* ... and some, indeed, seemed to think he was somewhat out of place in the felon's dock (Horler, 1931: 86, emphasis added).

Such sentiments were ceaselessly reiterated. For example, in 1869, James Greenwood noted the importance attached to appearance and the difficulty with which members of the public combined a respectable façade with a criminal character, stating, 'I have heard it remarked more than once, by persons whose curiosity has led them to a criminal court when a trial of more than ordinary interest is proceeding, that really this prisoner or that did not look like a thief, or a forger, or stabber, as the case might be' (1981: 77). Even at the turn of the century (by which time the respectable delinquent was a very familiar figure) contemporaries continued to find difficulty in reconciling criminality with external notions of respectability. Such was evidenced by Thomas Holmes, in documenting a case of petty theft before the London Police Courts:

Only a short time back an exceedingly well-dressed man stood in the dock at North London charged with stealing a watch from a jeweller's shop. He was of middle age, and quite intellectual in appearance. His frock-coat with silk facings, his silk hat, gloves etc., all combined to make him as unlike a criminal as possible (1902: 134).

A further central defining feature of Victorian crime discourses was the ingrained association between illegality and unemployment, particularly in the case of serious and habitual criminals. Honest toil was taken as an indicator of individual decency, and it was primarily amongst those who did not have regular work that criminality was thought to be at its most virulent.

Work was an absolute necessity. Without it there was no hope of achieving ... respectability. Hence, parents and preachers, writers and lecturers, proclaimed as with a single voice that man was created to work, that everyone had his [sic] appointed calling in which he was to labour ... [and] that idleness was a moral and social sin (Houghton, 1957: 189).

Within heavily moralistic Victorian crime discourses, habitual offenders were perceived to prefer criminality to steady work because of ethical failings which encouraged indolence and greed. Thus, in 1855 *The Times* commented that, 'it is idleness, or want of regular occupation, that drives the poor to crime',[7] while, for Victorians like Henry Mayhew it was those who did not work – the voluntarily unemployed – who offered the most serious criminal threat (1861: 29–35; see also Mayhew and Binny, 1862: 84). Such claims were widespread and made repeatedly throughout the period. In 1869, James Greenwood noted of the 'thieving classes': 'they will tell you plainly that they do not intend to work hard for a pound a week, when they can earn five times as much by thieving in less time' (1981: 64; Lettsom Elliot, 1869: 334; Morrison, 1891: 85–6; Bosanquet, 1899: 69). Indeed, in the view of one commentator, the indolence of the criminal population was so entrenched that it encouraged some criminals to go to extreme lengths to avoid any form of honest labour. Thus, commenting on an 'epidemic' of self-injury amongst convict prisoners in 1876, E. F. Du Cane stated that 'the probable object of those who began self-mutilations, and of most of those who followed them, was to evade labour' (1876: 303–4).

In contrast, employment was perceived to have a positive moralising influence on those so engaged, discouraging laziness and deviance, and promoting virtues of decency and propriety (Houghton, 1957: 189). 'Work itself was seen as a therapy that made for human rectitude or, at the very least, for keeping the working man from mischief' (Briggs *et al.*, 2001: 127). Thus, by the very virtue of their employment status, the white-collar worker was immediately considered to be morally decent. In fact, within the work environment trusted, middle-class, white-collar servants were seen to be particularly honest and reliable since these attributes were demanded by the nature of their roles. Their trusted position within the workplace meant that they enjoyed the complete confidence of employers, and were relied upon to handle money to which they had no personal claim. Instances of fraud and embezzlement by such men were therefore seen to be both incompatible with the Victorian work ethic, and also with their respectable persona.

Reconciling and responding to the respectable criminal

The increasing public presence of the respectable offender undeniably called into question traditional presumptions about the nature of crime, the characteristics of the offending population, and the social and geographical spaces from which criminals were drawn. In particular, it became apparent that crime was not solely a feature of lower-class life; that respectability was not necessarily a foil for criminality; that at least some varieties of serious crime were perpetrated by seemingly decent members of society; and that the workplace, rather than being the panacea of crime, was increasingly vulnerable to new forms of dishonest behaviour. While crime was a continual source of social anxiety, the widespread emergence of the respectable offender potentially exacerbated such anxieties by blurring the boundaries between the respectable and the criminal. For the first time it was not immediately possible to discern criminal from non-criminal, good from bad, respectable from disreputable. Indeed, as one Victorian commentator noted, 'all the received tests of respectability seemed to be of no avail and people literally could not tell whom they might trust' (Morier Evans, 1859: 3–4).

Not surprisingly, given their apparent opposition to (and ability to unseat), established claims about crime and criminality, the respectable offender was a source of considerable social interest and debate. A central aspect of such debate was the tension between respectability and criminality, and one of the key sites in which this was played out was the courtroom. As increasing numbers of respectable white-collar offenders appeared before the courts charged with various delinquencies, criminal justice officials were faced with the challenge of responding to these offenders.

Details of the offender, their background, and their motivations, were key aspects of the courtroom process. By providing knowledge of the individual, this information steered official judgements of the offender and their treatment by the court; and such details and judgements were debated and interpreted within a framework of established traditional axioms about the nature of crime. For instance, within a system that aligned criminality with idleness and profligacy, reports of the unemployed status of the lower-class defendant accused of petty theft could easily invoke (and give credence to) notions that their behaviour had been a consequence of immorality. Lower-class offenders, whose criminality was easily explainable through traditional moral discourses, were unproblematic when defined in such ways. However, the respectable offender, whose social status and characteristics challenged the very tenets of this knowledge, presented a far greater challenge.

The question of how the courtroom (and Victorian society more broadly) responded to and reconciled such challenges is fundamental to understanding the treatment, management and punishment of the respectable offender. Writing generically about respectable offenders before the Victorian courts, Conley has argued that this group could be dealt with in three possible ways: first, by denying that the person, by nature of their respectability, could have committed the alleged offence;

second, (and most frequently) by distinguishing between the actions of the respectable offender and those of 'real' criminals; or third, by stripping the respectable offender of their respectability (1991: 173–4). Nineteenth-century penal discourses relating to respectable, white-collar offenders can be meaningfully interpreted in such a context. In responding to the paradox of the respectable criminal, courtroom (and other social) discourses worked to deconstruct and reconstruct this offender type, either in the form of 'the unrespectable offender' or 'the respectable non-offender'. In instances of the former, such discourses served to deny the truly respectable status of the accused, thereby removing them from the remit of respectability (a process of estrangement); in cases of the latter, they conversely sought to downplay the significance of their criminal actions by highlighting the offender's respectability (a process of exoneration). These dual strategies of 'estrangement' and 'exoneration', and their meanings, are explored below.

Estrangement and the unrespectable offender

Nineteenth-century penal discourses were peppered with reminders about the importance of respectability, the responsibilities that it conferred, and the consequences of ignoring its guiding principles. For example, in 1870 Herbert Norton, a stationmaster with the Midland Railway Company, was called to account for embezzling two small sums of money. While Norton received 'excellent character' references from various respectable persons, in summing up the case the judge pronounced:

> You were placed in a position of responsibility, and you abused your trust. Although the sums you are charged with having embezzled are small, yet the offence is a very serious one, considering the situation in which you were placed. The jury have recommended you to mercy on account of your good character, but it was on account of that good character that you were placed in a good position.[8]

Similarly, in 1890, when a sub-postmaster was charged with nine counts of systematic embezzlement, the man was admonished by the judge for hiding behind a respectable façade in order to perpetrate his offending:

> This was a very serious offence committed by a principal officer in the post office of the district. The prisoner belonged to a most estimable religious persuasion, and had maintained a high position and character among them by what he must call most scandalous

hypocrisy, whilst all the while he was carrying on an atrocious system of fraud.[9]

Apparently respectable persons who did not take notice of reminders to act according to their status, and who subsequently found themselves before the court, could be portrayed very negatively. Such condemnation was especially observable within aetiological narratives. Understanding the offender's motivation was a key part of the courtroom process, since it informed mitigatory pleas, penal judgements and sentences. Furthermore, owing to difficulties in fully conceptualising the external features of the respectable criminal, there was often a particular interest in gaining insights into the underlying causes and motivations of their behaviours.

Traditional aetiological narratives typically sat in opposition to notions of what it meant to be respectable. Respectability derived from behaviours such as 'frugality, saving, sobriety – even teetotalism ... clean and tidy clothes and houses ... education, religion, rigid sexual propriety and family-centred values and social life' (Morris, 1979: 65–6). Yet many of the aetiological discourses about respectable workplace offenders echoed widely used mitigatory pleas, which operated in opposition to these values, such as the 'evil' effects of intemperance, gambling, and bad company, or the desire for quick wealth without proper labour. For instance, in cases of embezzlement, the claim that offenders 'had been extensively engaged in betting transactions',[10] or 'had disposed of the money in gambling and betting',[11] were regularly made. Thus, in a typical pronouncement, following his arrest for embezzlement in 1880, Edwin Henry Harris was reported to have confessed, 'I am very sorry; I have been very foolish ... betting has done it for me, but I intend to leave off now'.[12] Similarly, Midlands railway clerk, Adam Bunce, reportedly stated that his motivation had been 'Wolverhampton races and betting'.[13] Magistrates often concurred; for example, one London justice highlighted, very clearly, 'the directness of the path from betting to bondage [and] from Epsom to the Old Bailey', noting, in 'recent years he had hardly ever had a case of embezzlement before him which was not connected, either directly or *au fond*, with betting. Nor would he admit that this plea of betting was merely an excuse put forward without real cause. On the contrary, very careful inquiry into the cases proved conclusively that the plea was a true one' (Horsley, 1905: 85–8).

On the subject of intemperance, police-court missionary, Thomas Holmes (1902: 35) stated that drink was one of 'the chief factors in the downfall' of the embezzler, while Henry Mayhew similarly noted that,

alongside gambling, 'the habit of drinking [was one of] the chief induce-
ments' that led to embezzlement (Quennell, 1983: 326). Offenders regularly cemented this supposition by citing drink as a prevailing cause of
offending. For instance, in 1870 William Graham was reported to have
admitted that his embezzlements were 'caused by his giving way to
drink'.[14] Likewise, in 1850 when John Macarthy absconded with fifty
pounds, he shortly afterwards 'gave himself into custody at the [police]
station', reportedly, 'in a state of intoxication', having spent the money
on alcohol.[15]

Aetiological explanations of this nature were not specific to white-
collar offending behaviours, or even to the nineteenth-century courtroom, but were instead longstanding and widely used axioms applied
across the spectrum of criminal offending. Indeed, such motivations
were more regularly applied to the offences of the lower/criminal-class
offender than those of respectable standing. Given their apparent conflict with accepted standards of respectability (Clapson, 1992: 2), and
the widely noted importance of these standards as benchmarks of a
respectable persona, the use of such traditional aetiological narratives
in the case of respectable offenders is therefore of interest.

As noted by Benson (1985), in part, the use of such narratives by
respectable offenders can be understood through the need to employ
explanations that were familiar and acceptable. However, the use of such
traditional explanations also served a number of other important functions. As older mechanisms of control had become outmoded within the
industrial world of the nineteenth century, the ability to know, see, and
label criminals played an increasingly important role in the management
of that group, and also in assuaging middle-class fears about the criminal
threat. One of the key identifiers of 'the criminal' was their lack of res-
ectability. Therefore, in an environment where respectability and criminality were incompatible, these discourses acted as a lever for their
separation, re-establishing the distance between the two concepts. This
leverage was applied both in proactive and reactive ways. In a proactive
sense, aetiologies about intemperance, gambling, immoral associations,
and the desire for quick wealth, challenged the core tenets of respectability – 'hard work, thrift, and self-denial' (Clapson, 1992: 2) – and their
use in courtroom narratives of white-collar offending served to continually highlight and warn against the ramifications of moral slippage. However, where such warnings were not heeded the use of these aetiologies
also acted as reactive measures, dissolving the distinction between respectable and other offenders. In cases where the respectable criminal and
their offence could be seen as similar to (and driven by the same base

moral instincts as) those of other (more familiar) criminal types, their respectability was called into question. The effect of doing so was to symbolically lower the respectable criminal by challenging their claim to respectability: respectability was something else entirely to that seen in such cases, and the relevance of traditional aetiologies to the apparently respectable offender confirmed this. This reassessment of the respectable offender as not truly respectable enabled such individuals to be reclassified simply as criminals. Interpreted in this way, the respectable offender did not challenge established knowledge claims about the criminal but rather confirmed them. As Henry Mayhew noted:

> Many of these [respectable criminals] formerly belonged to the ranks of the honest and industrious middle-classes, and not a few of them are well connected, and have lived in fashionable society. By improvidence, extravagance, or dissipation they have squandered their means, and have now basely adopted a course of systematic dishonesty rather than lead an industrious life. Some of them have led a fast life in the metropolis, and are persons of ruined fortune. Others are indolent in disposition, and carry on a subtle system of public robbery than pursue some honest occupation or calling (1861: 276).

The pervasiveness of this view led some to argue that, given the similarity of respectable and other types of crime, no distinction could or should be made between them. Thus, in some cases white-collar offences were downgraded and compared with other varieties of property offending – such as robbery, burglary, or petty theft. In 1895, for example, A. R. Barrett purposely incorporated the offences of fraud and embezzlement within broader theft terminology arguing that, for ideological reasons, there was no justification for the separation of what were essentially behaviours of the same type:

> I speak of these acts as 'robberies', for I believe in calling them by their true name. Whatever may be the social position of a man, when he makes illegal use of the funds ... entrusted to his care ... he becomes a thief, just as much as the man who at night blows open the safe and takes what he can find (1895: 196).

Likewise, noting the essential similarity of all varieties of thievery, Arthur Train claimed, 'there is no practical distinction between a man who gets all of a poor living dishonestly and one who gets part of an exceedingly good living dishonestly' (Train, 1907: 24). By separating the truly respectable from those who maintained its appearance to perpetrate immoral acts of theft, such discourses served as an important device through which the dichotomy between respectable and criminal could be rebuilt and popular fears about new types of criminal alleviated.

Beyond their symbolic functions these narratives also had practical utility. While respectable offenders were difficult to identify using most traditional prompts, through the application of familiar aetiological narratives the visibility of this offender was increased, enabling them to be better known. This knowledge subsequently enabled and encouraged new strategies of protection. For instance, companies were warned to be wary of staff who displayed such qualities. Thus, A. R. Barrett claimed that, 'no man who gambles in any way, or patronizes the horse races or pool rooms, should be allowed to fill any position in a financial institution' (1895: 198). Some companies clearly acted on such advice in attempts to protect themselves from staff fraudulence. In 1852, for example, upon learning about the involvement of one of its stationmasters in gambling activities, the directors of the Midland Railway Company severely sanctioned the man for spending his leisure hours 'betting upon horse races'. Furthermore, the board noted its 'strong displeasure' at his choice of pastime and warned that he would only be retained in the company's service upon 'promising that he would not in future indulge in such practices and give the earliest information to the directors should he hear of anyone belonging to the company doing so'. Indeed, so concerned were the directors about the impact of gambling upon their business that following this case they resolved to dismiss 'any servant of the company who shall hereafter be found guilty of betting'.[16]

Exoneration and the respectable non-offender

As evidenced within courtroom and media discourses, traditional images of criminality could be (and were) used to portray respectable offenders in a negative light, to denounce their behaviours, and, crucially, to question their claims to respectability. In some cases, the respectable offender could be viewed as doubly (even trebly) deviant, for betraying legal, contractual, and moral/class-based obligations. However, the opposite could also be true. In other instances the same types of respectable offender, using the same explanations, were portrayed with empathy, and traditional aetiological narratives were used to mitigate, or even justify, their actions.

Again, such responses were grounded in the desire to separate the concepts of respectability and criminality. Thus, while acknowledging the emerging respectable criminal, some contemporaries went to considerable lengths to minimise the seriousness of such offending, and to redirect attention towards the 'real' threat: the lower-class, dangerous-class, or criminal-class. For instance, in his characterisation of 'the criminal' George Woodyatt Hastings paid only momentary attention to the respectable fraudster or embezzler, simply highlighting that they belonged to the 'casual', rather than 'habitual' class of offender and were not therefore 'ordinary criminals' (1875: 120). Likewise, writing in 1862, Mayhew and Binny felt the need to distinguish between the 'habitual' and the 'casual' criminal, noting that the former category included 'those who indulge in dishonest practices as a regular means of living', while the latter incorporated 'those who are dishonest from some *accidental* cause', and who could neither 'make a trade or profession' from their crime, 'or resort to them as a regular means of subsistence' (1862: 87–8, emphasis added). Offences associated with the white-collar classes were typically incorporated into this latter category.

Similar mitigatory techniques operated within the courtroom; here traditional aetiological discourses were used to explain away behaviour by distinguishing the respectable offender from the 'true criminal'. For example, ignoring for a moment the most financially significant yet untypical acts of white-collar offending, aetiological claims founded on notions of financial difficulty were often made by respectable middle/lower-middle class employees. In a climate where key elements of the respectable, white-collar workforce (for instance, clerks) could be paid relatively low wages (Harrison, 1990: 59–63), the associations between respectability, financial need, and white-collar delinquency were noted with some regularity. Thus, defendants who were described as respectable, or from respectable backgrounds, continually explained their behaviours as products of their inability to support large and dependent families, or sick relatives, on existing salaries. In 1865, for instance, in a typical case, the respectable Frederick William de Poidevin explained his fraudulent appropriation of £1,600 by stating that 'a falling off in the amount of his salary and the fact of his having to bring up a large family had led him to commit acts of which he was now heartily ashamed'.[17] Likewise, in accounting for a small embezzlement, Thomas Easton stated 'that he had used the money through distress. He had buried his wife and one child, and had seven children, one of them subject to fits, dependent on him'.[18] Of course, such pleas were often dismissed, particularly in cases where a defendant's wage level, actions, or apparent extravagance seemed to undermine claims of need; however, some respectable offenders could find mitigation in these explanations. In such cases, employers could be partly blamed for encouraging fraudulence by underpaying staff. Thus, in 1895 one contemporary claimed that employers who paid low wages had to accept some culpability for subsequent acts of fraud and embezzlement, as these were a foreseeable consequence of such policies (Barrett, 1895: 201; Anderson, 1976: 39–40). In the case of Robert Blagdon, before the courts in 1880, the man's employers were admonished by the magistrate for paying inadequate wages, thereby forcing him into thievery. In these circumstances, owing to his reduced level of culpability, Blagdon was noted to have received the sympathy of the court and a lenient sentence.[19]

Linked to aetiological claims of financial difficulty, the struggle to achieve the facets of a respectable lifestyle was seen to bear particularly heavily on lower-middle class sections of the workforce – particularly young clerks (Anderson, 1976: 52). In consequence, it was believed that some were pressured to spend beyond their financial means in order to 'keep up appearances', a path argued to lead many into debt, corruption, and ultimately peculation (Quennell, 1983: 328–9).

While some respectable offenders could utilise the well-trodden explanation of financial need to account for their thefts, as Conley has noted, such explanations were typically met with less sympathy when the defendant was of a lower social status (and the theft offence of a more traditional nature): 'ironically, while the poor were being told it was more respectable to starve than beg or steal, similar behaviours by middle-class members of the community could be excused on the grounds of distress' (1991: 176).

It was not simply need that could be used as mitigation for respectable, white-collar offending: other familiar narratives could also generate understanding and alleviate blame. For instance, while respectable offenders who claimed to have been drawn into embezzlement by 'slow horses and fast women' (Peterson, 1947: 98) could be denounced as immoral, they could also be portrayed as accidental criminals or unfortunate dupes in a wider immoral environment that encouraged 'low' forms of entertainment. Defendants often claimed to have been 'induced' into gambling and subsequently forced into fraudulence to pay off debts;[20] and such explanations could encourage sentiments of condemnation towards those shadowy figures who had led the respectable astray. Thus, in 1880, commenting on the case of a respectable gentleman embezzler, one magistrate claimed 'with regard to the system of betting, that he regretted *those who led young men into it* and so onto ruin could not be punished'.[21] The influence of low company (more broadly) could similarly be used in mitigation of fraudulence, by deflecting responsibility from the respectable perpetrator towards invisible others. Thus, in summing up the case of Albert Napoleon Dunn, charged with embezzlement in 1880, the magistrate lamented that he, 'like many other young men, had got into bad company, had been *led astray* and *induced* to spend more money than he had'.[22]

While particular immoral influences within society could be held liable for leading the industrious into fraudulence, it was similarly argued that a more pervasive decline in business morals had a similar effect on staff (Carter, 1893; Holland and Carter, 1905). For some, the 'acquisitive spirit of the age' (Robb, 1992: 135), reified the importance of material wealth and financial success at all costs, and had corrupted the morals of the whole business community by making greed, covetousness, and extravagance the guiding principles of industry. In this climate the desire to get rich quick had taken precedence over the more morally-sound principles of integrity, honesty and hard work (as the watchwords of business practice), and the consequence was thought to be widespread dishonesty (Morier Evans, 1859: 1; Van Oss, 1898: 738). Thus, detailing the new atmosphere of fraudulence that was seen to pervade the business world, Morier Evans noted, 'the standard of commercial morality' was so much changed from what it had been formerly that, 'many men perpetrated deeds they would have blushed even to contemplate a few years previously' (1859: 3; see also Laing, 1866: 393; Smalley, 1890: 438–41; Stutfield, 1898: 77). In consequence, staff from all levels of the respectable working world were thought to have been brought low and corrupted by this deficient moral atmosphere (Locker, 2004).

If respectable offenders could not always claim that their offences had been forced upon them by others or by their environment, they could, at least plead that they were a momentary lapse, or accident, in an otherwise respectable life. Thus, narratives about the stability of their lifestyle or their involvement in various community organisations were often incorporated within courtroom accounts. For example, in 1870, when James Bellamy was charged with embezzling more than £3,500 from his employer, the Hereford Bank, he explained that he 'was a married man, with seven young children ... [that he] acted as organist at St Nicholas Church [and that] he lived in a most quiet manner, and had earned the confidence of a large number of friends'. However, in 'an unfortunate moment', that was totally out of character with his respectable lifestyle, he took to gambling 'and so *was led* into his present position'.[23] Even in the face of evidence to the contrary, the enduring appeal of respectability as a central tenet of honesty, together with the ability of such figures to demonstrate their general compliance with a respectable lifestyle, certainly placed them in a stronger position to make this case than the typical lower-class thief.

Just as narratives of financial need, acquisitiveness, intoxication, or undesirable associations could be used to denounce the respectable offender, conversely, they could also provide opportunities to explain their behaviour. While not always successful, in some cases respectable offenders could benefit from a variety of explanatory frameworks (often rooted in traditional aetiological discourses) which served to partially mitigate their offending and divert blame to other sites of culpability – for example, social and economic pressures, miserly employers, deviant others, and the corrupting social or business environment. Through such mitigation, the restricted culpability afforded respectable offenders was used to limit or even bring into question their status as a criminal. Instead, their respectable status was often reified, while their criminality was nullified. Such depictions inevitably served to deflect the main thrust of societal concern away from respectable offenders and towards more familiar sites of perceived criminality. In so doing, these discourses undoubtedly contributed to the appeasement of middle-class public concerns about the growing incidence of respectable crime, and cemented more traditional images of crime and criminality.

Of course, respectable criminals were not the only ones who were able to utilise traditional aetiologies or benefit from them; however, their social status, together with ingrained class-specific views about criminality and respectability gave some such defendants tools with which to exploit these aetiologies to a greater degree than others.

Conclusion

On the surface nineteenth-century discourses of the respectable offender appear to offer a farrago of opposing and contradictory messages about social attitudes towards such behaviours. Traditionally this variation has been used to debate whether or not respectable offenders were/are treated less punitively than other offenders when before the courts. In contrast, this chapter has argued that, more fundamentally, nineteenth-century courtroom discourses pertaining to the respectable offender were charged with important symbolic meaning about 'the offender', 'the respectable', and 'the respectable offender'. Respectability was a lynchpin of middle-class moral values; furthermore, adherence to this lifestyle (and all it implied) was a key mechanism of control and social discipline that increasingly pervaded Victorian society. However, the proliferation of middle and lower-middle class, white-collar offenders before the courts, threatened to undermine the concept of respectability by those social groups who proscribed its importance. In responding to this threat, courtroom and other social discourses about the respectable offender were important devices for counteracting the paradox of the respectable criminal. Through the dual processes of 'estrangement' and 'exoneration', respectable criminals were portrayed either as 'respectable' or 'criminal' but rarely as respectable and criminal. In consequence, traditional knowledge about the offender was reaffirmed (even cemented), the distinction between respectability and criminality was reinforced, and the established social order remained intact.

Notes

1 *The Times*, 13 January 1855: 6.
2 *Ibid.*, 10 March 1890: 3.
3 *Ibid.*, 6 August 1870: 12.
4 *The Staffordshire Advertiser*, 18 April 1891: 3.
5 *The Times*, 17 September 1880: 9.
6 *Ibid.*, 20 March 1850: 7.
7 *Ibid.*, 13 January 1855: 7.
8 *Ibid.*, 28 February 1870: 11.
9 *Ibid.*, 19 July 1890: 13.
10 *The Times*, 11 July 1870: 5; for similar see *ibid.*, 10 September 1850: 7; *ibid.*, 7 March 1865: 11; *ibid.*, 1 and 15 February 1870: 9; *ibid.*, 1 July 1880: 14; *ibid.*, 2 July 1870: 11; *ibid.*, 16 September 1880: 9.
11 *The Times*, 1 March 1870: 11.
12 *Ibid.*, 11 October 1880: 12.
13 *The Staffordshire Advertiser*, 1 October 1870: 7.
14 *The Times*, 2 July 1870: 11.
15 *Ibid.*, 18 February 1850: 7.
16 Midland Railway, Directors' Minutes, 1 December 1852, min. no.3069, NA, Rail 491/17.
17 *The Times*, 2 February 1865: 11. See also, the case of John Laming, *ibid.*, 3 November 1880: 4; James Holmes, *ibid.*, 18 March 1890: 3.
18 *The Times*, 6 March 1880: 12. See also, the case of Thomas Isherwood, *ibid.*, 27 April 1835: 4; John Henry Rawlings, *ibid.*, 4 January 1870: 9.
19 *The Times*, 29 September 1880: 9.
20 For example, the case of James Brown, *The Times*, 1 February 1870: 9; Paul Cocks, *ibid.*, 7 March 1865: 11; Walter Bunn, *The Staffordshire Advertiser*, 24 September 1870: 3, 22 October 1870: 7; George Baker, *The Times*, 1 July 1880: 14.
21 *The Times*, 18 October 1880: 12 (emphasis added). For similar, see the cases of William M'Swiney, *The Times*, 3 December 1880: 11; Lewis Jones, *ibid.*, 26 November 1890: 3.
22 *The Times*, 29 January 1880: 11 (emphasis added).
23 *Ibid.*, 6 August 1870: 12 (emphasis added).

7
Controlling the 'Hopeless': Re-Visioning the History of Female Inebriate Institutions c. 1870–1920

Bronwyn Morrison

During the last quarter of the nineteenth century, the Inebriates Acts 1879 to 1898[1] created an alternative system of inebriate institutions in England. Collectively these Acts enabled judges to sentence recidivist drunkards, who had hitherto received short prison sentences, to compulsory treatment in a private, certified, or state inebriate reformatory for up to three years. Between 1879 and 1923 (when the last inebriate institution closed) over 3,500 people were confined within such institutions.[2]

For the duration of the time the system was in operation, women represented the minority of those apprehended for drunkenness offences, and were significantly less likely than their male counterparts to be officially defined as 'habitual drunkards'. Despite this, women were vastly over-represented within inebriates' institutions. The highly gendered nature of these institutions, however, has frequently been overlooked in historical and criminological accounts (see, for example, Garland, 1985; Wiener, 1990; Radzinowicz and Hood, 1990; MacLeod, 1967), and, where acknowledged, has often been dismissed as an unintended consequence of an ill-conceived system (Johnstone, 1996a, 1996b; Zedner, 1991; Hall, G., 2002).

While the skewed gender composition of inebriate institutions has been frequently obscured, scholars have nonetheless identified the arrival of this system as a pivotal moment in English penal history. It has been alleged that the creation of these institutions represented a significant departure from traditional forms of punishment, based on classical notions of individual responsibility, offender rationality, retribution, and determinate sentencing. In contrast, it has been argued that inebriate institutions signalled the beginning of a new, welfarist penology, underpinned by notions of offender irrationality and irresponsibility, rehabilitation, and indeterminate sentencing (Garland, 1985, 2002; Zedner, 1991; Radzinowicz and Hood, 1990; Wiener, 1990). Within the welfare framework, the prison was decentred, becoming a sanction of last resort, while punitive and deterrent measures more generally were increasingly perceived as 'unpleasant but unavoidable evils, out of keeping with the general tenor of the system' (Garland, 1985: 27). The emergence of the welfare paradigm, it has been further claimed, saw reform become the guiding principle of punishment, with the relationship between the state and the offender re-conceptualised as a 'positive attempt to produce reform and normalisation for the benefit of the individual as well as the state' (Garland, 1985: 31).

Within such accounts, inebriate institutions have been constructed in opposition to the punitive modes of punishment concomitant with the prison, with the relationship between inebriates and the state recast as 'positive' and 'productive', rather than negative and non-productive. Whereas the aims of deterrence, control and retribution dominated the Victorian prison, reform has been identified as the governing force behind the development and operation of inebriate institutions. The general portrait painted of inebriate reformatories has therefore been one of curative treatment shorn of all the punitive aspects evident in the prison regime. As Zedner noted in her study of inebriate institutions, 'the overall impression is more akin to a jolly girls' school than a reformatory supposedly for the worst incorrigibles of London's prisons' (1991: 243).

Utilising empirical evidence obtained from institutional records, contemporary social discourse, and government reports, this chapter re-examines the history of inebriate institutions.[3] In doing so, it challenges the contention that the gendered nature of this system was somehow accidental, and questions the degree to which inebriate institutions marked a significant departure from traditional modes of punishment. The first part of the chapter explores the emergence of the inebriate system, investigating the contradictory motivations behind its creation and gendered implementation. The remainder of the chapter provides an alternative account of inebriate institutions. Using empirical data predominantly drawn from the institutional records of Langho Reformatory (the largest women's inebriate reformatory in England) and official reports from the Inspector under the Inebriate Acts, it argues that the reformatory regime was strongly reminiscent of that of the prison, and in many ways represented 'an appendage and extension' (Dobash and McLaughlin, 1992: 68) of existing penal arrangements rather than a radical departure from them.

Gendering the drink problem in Victorian England

Drunkenness was a dominant cultural preoccupation of Victorian society. By the second half of the century drunkenness was the largest category of crime in England and Wales, and by 1870 accounted for almost one-quarter of all recorded crime.[4] Over the later part of the century, concerns surrounding drunkenness underwent a metamorphosis, as the perception of habitual drunkenness as a disease gradually gained credence among medical experts (Radzinowicz and Hood, 1990: 289). At this time, public anxieties and legislative efforts became focused on the habitual drunkard, who lacked sufficient willpower to curb their own alcohol consumption (Peddie, 1861: 539). By 1870, it was estimated that there were 600,000 habitual drunkards in Britain, who were collectively perceived to represent a significant barrier to national progress (Dalrymple, 1870: 281). Crucially, however, this re-conceptualisation of the drunkard coincided with the gendering of the drink problem, as the habitual drunkard became typically conceived of as female, and women's drinking assumed an increasingly prominent position within contemporary discourses about drunkenness.

From the 1860s onwards, while it was widely recognised that drunkenness had diminished amongst men, female drunkenness was believed to be growing progressively worse. Available statistical 'evidence' reinforced this perception. For example, judicial statistics demonstrated a 62% increase in the number of women apprehended for drunkenness offences between 1870 and 1903, from 32,928 to 53,383.[5] Prison data appeared to confirm this alarming trend. For example, *The Times* noted in 1893 that 80 to 85% of female prison committals were alcohol-related, compared to only 60 to 65% of male committals.[6] Contemporary discourses also increasingly represented the hardened, recidivist drunkard as female, and, over the latter decades of the century the media frequently reported the escalating conviction tallies of habitual female drunkards. For instance, in 1871 *The Times* reported that Ellen Shute had appeared at Bristol police court 251 times charged with drunken and disorderly behaviour,[7] and in 1888 reported on the case of Annie Gregory after she amassed a total of 300 convictions for drunkenness.[8] As the *British Medical Journal* noted in 1896, 'women keep up their reputation for excelling men, even in such matters as recorded convictions for drunkenness' (Anon, 1896: 959). This view was reinforced by prison data. For example, statistics from Liverpool Borough Gaol revealed that while less than half of all male offenders in prison for drunkenness had previously been convicted of drunkenness, almost 80% of women imprisoned for drunkenness had at least one prior conviction for this offence (Dalrymple, 1870: 281).

Admittedly the evidence used to support claims of women's escalating drunkenness was prone to liberal interpretation. For instance, a review of the available judicial statistics reveals that the rate of female apprehensions for drunkenness was actually declining from 1876 onwards, and continued to do so well into the twentieth century (Wilson, 1940).[9] Moreover, far from confirming that female drunkards were more prone to be recidivist offenders, the official statistics demonstrated that men were substantially more likely to qualify as habitual drunkards, accounting for almost 75% of those officially labelled as 'habitual drunkards' between 1870 and 1895.[10] However, despite the existence of evidence to the contrary, late Victorian society nonetheless increasingly conceptualised habitual drunkenness as a gendered problem principally associated with women. This, in turn, had significant implications for legislative developments pertaining to the habitual drunkard and the subsequent implementation of that legislation.

The motivations behind the Inebriates Acts 1879–1898

As high profile cases of recidivist female drunkards attested, the existing system of pecuniary fines and short terms of imprisonment repeatedly failed to deter, reform, or, more importantly, control, habitually drunken women. By the 1890s, anxieties about the legal and penal treatment of female habitual drunkards experienced a watershed as contemporaries began to blame the traditional system of magisterial fines and short prison sentences for the manufacture of recidivist female drunkards, who were increasingly seen to reside beyond the limits of state control. The persistent failure of the prison to reform inebriate women offered a highly visible example of its inability to fulfil the general objectives of deterrence and reform, and contributed to a more fundamental crisis in penal legitimacy at this time (Garland, 1985, 2002; Pratt, 1997).

Under the Licensing Act 1872[11] persons found drunk and incapable in public could be fined up to 40 shillings, and in default of payment were liable to between seven and 14 days' imprisonment. In cases where drunkenness was accompanied by 'riotous and disorderly' behaviour, offenders were liable to a fine not exceeding 40 shillings and/or imprisonment (with or without hard labour) for a period not exceeding one month. This traditional system of punishing drunkards was widely deemed inadequate, as it failed to effectively control or reform drunken women, and was increasingly considered to contribute to the production of recidivism amongst this group.

The practice of fining drunken women was typically criticised because it failed to prevent re-offending. For example, Ann Blade was arrested three times in three days in 1871 for being drunk and disorderly. Having being fined for the first two offences, the presiding magistrate noted that 'there was absolutely no use in fining such a person', and sentenced her to seven days' imprisonment.[12] Magistrates were also reluctant to fine drunken women because the financial burden of payment often fell to husbands. For example, in the case of Mary-Ann Mycock, the magistrate refused to impose a fine on the basis that this would only punish her children and husband, 'who was a hard-working and respectable man'.[13] The fact that husbands would simply pay a fine on their wives' behalf, magistrates argued, allowed married women to continue as drunkards without fear of punishment.

The system of short prison sentences was equally problematic. Following the nationalisation of local prisons in 1877, the failures of the prison could no longer be ascribed to a lack of uniformity within the system, and the prison itself was increasingly condemned as inflexible, inefficient, and unduly repressive (Zedner, 1991; Garland, 1985; Wiener, 1990). Against this backdrop, the repeated imprisonment of drunken women offered stark evidence of the manifest failings of the prison system to control or prevent crime. Medical authorities, government discourses, and the press regularly relayed the extensive conviction tallies of female inebriates as irrefutable evidence of the prison's fundamental shortcomings. For example, in 1895 the Lord Chancellor quoted the case of a female drunkard who had spent an average of one day in every two in prison over a 20-month period.[14] Similarly, Dr Dalrymple, a dominant figure in the medical campaign for the compulsory treatment of habitual drunkards, offered the case of Christiana M'Taggart, who spent 3,215 days in prison over 20 years for drunkenness offences, as evidence of the utter futility of traditional modes of punishment for combating drunkenness (1870: 278).

Contemporaries criticised the imposition of short prison sentences on drunken women on two main fronts. First, many argued that it was inhumane to punish what were effectively 'diseased' persons, and second, it was held that short sentences failed to provide sufficient levels of control over drunken women. As Wiener has argued, by the 1890s cultural attitudes towards recidivist offenders had fundamentally altered, as repeat offenders were increasingly viewed less as moral actors operating through free will, and more as inadequate individuals determined by social and biological forces beyond their control (1990: 237). During the second half of the nineteenth century, habitual drunkenness was increasingly defined as a medical condition and/or disease, which led to the suspension of individual willpower, especially in the case of women. For example, in describing dipsomania (the medical term applied to extreme alcoholism), Dr Alexander Peddie noted that:

> There is, however – especially in persons of a nervous or sanguine temperament, *and more readily in women than men* – a condition in which mere vice is transformed into a disease, and the mere vicious habit into an insane impulsive propensity, and then the drunkard becomes a dipsomaniac (1861: 539, emphasis added).

Short sentences were therefore criticised because they amounted to punishing the female drunkard for a condition over which she was considered to have little or no control. For this reason, proponents of this view stated that the current system was inhumane and unjust (Horsley, 1887: 195). It was argued that the female inebriate was a deficient character in need of 'care and control on looser lines'.[15] As Dr Norman Kerr, the founder and first president of the British Society for the Study and Cure of Inebriety, implored in 1880:

> Is it not madness to punish [a drunken woman] as a criminal without any hope of reformation, when if she was treated as a diseased person in an inebriate retreat there would be a fair opportunity of curative treatment? (1880: 23).

As well as being inhumane in principle, short prison sentences were considered physically, mentally, and morally detrimental to the female drunkard in practice. Periods of short imprisonment were thought to provide insufficient time for the reformation of habitual drunkards. In addition, it was widely held that the sudden temporary withdrawal from alcohol on a regular basis could cause irreparable damage to a person's mental condition.[16] This was particularly true in the case of the female drunkard, who was considered more susceptible to the negative influences of prison life than her male counterpart. As Lady Henry Somerset, a temperance advocate and the proprietor of Duxhurst Women's Inebriate Retreat, stated in 1901:

> Sending inebriates to prison is worse than useless for it renders the offenders hard and callous, and saps every vestige of self-respect that

may be left. Women have been sent to prison as many as two or three hundred times for being drunk and disorderly, and far from being cured have gone from bad to worse ... this kind of treatment is irrational and unscientific (quoted in Tooley, 1901: 23).

Similarly, when London magistrate, Mr Bridge, asked habitual drunkard Margaret Hearn if she had anything she would like to say to the court, she stated in a loud and excited voice:

All I have to say is this, I am a victim ... the first time I met you, you gave me eight months, now, I have never insulted you Mr Bridge, but imprisonment never did me any good, and I don't suppose it ever will; in fact, it makes me worse.[17]

Other criticisms were less motivated by humanitarian concern. For example, a number of contemporary 'experts' believed that the local prison provided a temporary sanatorium for drunken women: a place where they could recuperate and regain their health in order to continue their lives of drinking and vice with renewed vigour on release. As the police-court missionary, Thomas Holmes, observed, the 'unfortunate result' was that 'the lives of those constantly committed were considerably lengthened'. Indeed, far from damaging their health, short terms of imprisonment, he argued, helped to maintain it and enabled drunken women to 'live beyond their virtuous and industrious sisters' (1908: 73–4).

Inside prison, drunken women were often highly disruptive and posed a considerable control problem for prison officials. As Zedner (1991: 143) noted in her historical analysis of women in local prisons, during the second half of the nineteenth century drunken women represented the largest section of the female prison population, with most only serving sentences of between seven and 14 days. The high turnover of female drunkards presented a number of problems for prison staff. First, it created an administrative burden, which occupied a large proportion of staff time. Second, because many women were admitted to prison while still intoxicated, they required ongoing medical attention (Zedner, 1991: 231). Third, drunken women often refused to, or were incapable of, co-operating with the prison regime. As Alfred Reynolds, a visiting justice to Holloway prison, observed in 1900:

It is a common occurrence to find women in bed for twenty-four hours after admission sodden with drink, and only fit to do labour when the time of their discharge has come. How can this state of things be either a punishment or a deterrent?[18]

Drunken women also had a reputation for unsettling other prisoners, and often assaulted prison staff as well as other inmates. Certainly, there was little incentive to behave well as they would normally be released in a matter of days, or at most weeks, were already on the minimum dietary scale, and lacked any opportunity to accrue institutional privileges during their short stay (Zedner, 1991: 341).

Short prison sentences, it was alleged, also failed to provide adequate protection for the community. The fact that habitually drunken women were only imprisoned for short terms meant that they frequently enjoyed brief periods of liberty between sentences, when, it was argued, they could cause considerable physical damage to property, as well as moral damage to their families, young associates, and the community at large. As Holmes wrote in a letter to the editor of *The Times* in 1907:

> Short periods of liberty to these women ... only enable them to follow the most terrible of lives to which humans can subject themselves, and which involve gross scandal to the community, and great dangers to the state.[19]

Of more concern to many contemporaries was the fact that habitually drunken women had the opportunity to become pregnant during their brief periods of freedom between prison sentences, in turn, contributing to the degeneration of the national stock. As Mary Gordon, the first inspector of women's prisons in England (and subsequently the assistant inspector of inebriate institutions) argued, the prison aided female drunkards in this task:

> The very protection they derive from their frequent detention ... contributes to the prolongation of their lives, and helps preserve their ability, if not their fitness, to reproduce their kind (1914: 100–1).

The prison, Gordon (1914) argued, also provided more favourable prenatal and postnatal conditions for babies of drunken mothers than were available to these women outside the prison. Consequently, children of drunken women had a greater chance of survival than those born to sober women of a similar social position outside the prison walls. In this sense, the short imprisonment of drunken women was perceived to upset the dynamics of natural selection, which would otherwise have ensured that such children rarely survived infancy. Finally, contemporaries complained about the economic burden associated with the regular imprisonment of drunken women. Maintenance in police cells, the cost of police surgeons, accommodation in prison (often for a sizeable proportion of each year), the extensive cost of servicing a police force that dealt primarily with drunken persons, the damage caused to both people and property, as well as the cost of repeated transportation from the court to the prison, cumulatively added up to what many perceived as an unacceptable drain on public resources.[20]

In summary, the traditional system of small fines and short prison sentences was deemed inhumane and unnecessarily penal, while conversely considered too costly and not sufficiently penal, as it failed to deter, punish or provide adequate levels of control over the female drunkard. If the Inebriates Acts were to answer these problems, they were paradoxically required to provide both more control in order to protect the community and prevent drunken women from reproducing, as well as less control – or at least 'care and control on looser lines' – in order to appease public sensibilities and medical campaigners, who demanded a gentler, more humane method of treating habitually-drunken women. The motivation for an alternative system of inebriates' institutions thus sprang from two divergent rationales, with what initially appeared to be opposing objectives. Both rationales, however, were premised on arguments that were gender specific. For example, fines were considered problematic principally because women lacked independent material resources. Moreover, it was the reproductive capacities and moral contagion of drunken women (not men) that were considered a 'danger to the state'.

Developing inebriate institutions: a gendered system of control

The Habitual Drunkards Act 1879 and later the Inebriates Act 1888 attempted to answer the inadequacies of existing modes of punishment through the provision of an alternative system for the treatment of habitual drunkards in licensed homes. Under section three of the Habitual Drunkards Act, a habitual drunkard was defined as:

> Any person who, not being amenable to any jurisdiction in lunacy, is notwithstanding, by reason of habitual intemperate drinking of

intoxicating liquor, at times dangerous to himself or herself or to others, or incapable of managing himself or herself, or his or her affairs. [21]

These Acts, however, only permitted the voluntary committal of habitual drunkards who could afford to pay for their treatment, and only for periods not exceeding one year. The result was the rather *ad hoc* development of a diverse collection of small-scale, government-licensed, privately-managed homes for inebriates, known as inebriate retreats. Admission to a retreat could be obtained voluntarily by a drunkard signing an admission form before two magistrates, or alternatively through private agreement between the drunkard and the retreat licensee. Crucially, although neither Act was explicitly gendered, women significantly outnumbered men in inebriate retreats, and by 1906 accounted for well over half of the total number of voluntary committals and 70% of private committals.[22] As admission was 'voluntary' and the ability to pay for treatment was a prerequisite of admission, retreats principally catered for the well-to-do inebriate to the exclusion of working-class or criminal inebriates. Consequently, the Acts failed to answer the problem of the habitual female drunkard, who rotated repeatedly between the street, the police court, and the local prison.

A second Inebriates Act was passed in 1898 to remedy the class bias of the previous Acts and make provision for criminal inebriates. While keeping the provisions pertaining to the voluntary admission of non-criminal inebriates, the new Act allowed for the compulsory treatment of criminal inebriates, as well as police-court recidivist inebriates. Under the Act, these types of inebriate could be compulsorily committed in two new types of institution (certified inebriate reformatories and state inebriate reformatories) for up to three years. Under section one of the Act, any person who qualified as a habitual drunkard under the 1879 Act, and had committed an indictable offence under the influence of alcohol (or where drunkenness was proven to be a contributory factor to the offence), could be detained in a state inebriate reformatory for one to three years in substitution of, or in addition to, any other sentence imposed by the court. Under section two of the Act, any person convicted four times of drunkenness under the Licensing Act 1872 within a 12 month period, could be sent to a certified inebriate reformatory for between one and three years.

Importantly, then, in the case of the recidivist drunkard, the reformatory did not represent a true alternative to the traditional system of fines and short-term imprisonment, as four convictions (accompanied by fines and/or short periods of imprisonment) were required within a single year before a person qualified for entrance into a reformatory. The second Inebriates Act also increased the maximum period of detention for non-criminal inebriates from one to two years, and perceptively lowered the standard of proof required to gain admission. Across all categories of inebriates, therefore, this Act led to both an intensification and extension of state control.

The passage of the second Inebriates Act saw a sharp increase in the proportion of women confined in inebriate institutions. By 1904, although women accounted for only 20% of police apprehensions for drunkenness, they represented 91% of those confined in certified inebriate reformatories, and of the 3,636 persons committed to these institutions between 1899 and 1910, 84% were female.[23] Thus, by the early years of the twentieth century, the system of inebriate institutions was a profoundly gendered one, with the certified reformatory, in particular, overwhelmingly populated by women. This was not simply accidental, for by 1906 nine out of the 11 certified reformatories in operation were licensed to receive female inebriates only.[24] The inebriate reformatory, then, was always destined to be a gendered institution as there was never an equivalent level of reformatory accommodation made available for inebriate men. Moreover, the objective of control, far from arising in response to subsequent system failures, was clearly a key motive underpinning the initial development of these institutions.

Explaining the gendered system

The basic deficiency in institutional accommodation for inebriate men and the marked overrepresentation of women was generally accepted as 'natural' and obvious, and, consequently, went largely unquestioned by contemporaries (Hunt *et al.*, 1989: 247). As the inspector of inebriate institutions commented in 1909, 'the predominance in the number of women over the number of men committed to reformatories is obvious'.[25] Indeed, so obvious was this disparity that it rarely warranted any explanation at all. It was naturally assumed that drunken women were 'worse' than their male counterparts, and the few available contemporary explanations were often tautological. Thus, one of the principal reasons provided for the gender imbalance in inebriate institutions was the lack of institutions available for men: women thus dominated reformatories because there were more institutions for women. As the inspector stated, this disproportionality arose 'on account that few men would be dealt with under the Act'.[26] Magistrates reaffirmed this tautology. As a London magistrate explained to habitual drunkard, Henry Walker, after the latter requested to be sent to an inebriate reformatory:

> There is nowhere for you to go. Provision ... has been made for women in your position, and I agree that the proportion of men requiring treatment is scanty compared to women, probably not more than one in thirty.[27]

Underlying the deficit of accommodation for inebriate men was a belief that drunken women were somehow 'naturally' in greater need of institutionalisation, despite the fact that women accounted for only a small proportion of those apprehended for drunkenness and labelled 'habitual drunkards' under the Acts. There are several possible explanations for the gendered development of inebriate accommodation.

First, there was often a reluctance to sentence drunken men, still presumed to be the primary family breadwinners, for extended periods of incarceration that would, in turn, leave their families to become a burden on local rates (Souttar, 1904: 232; Price, 1914: 101; see also Harding and Wilkin, 1988: 199; Hunt *et al.*, 1989: 250). The same barrier, however, did not exist for women, who were generally perceived as existing beyond familial controls and, if wives and mothers, were already deemed an economic (and moral) burden on their families. It was further felt that sending a man to an inebriate institution would irreversibly damage his reputation and ruin his future prospects. Because women were not considered the primary breadwinner, their loss of respectability was not considered to be as damaging (Souttar, 1904).

Second, institutional treatment was not deemed to be as necessary in the case of the male drunkard. Male inebriety was often considered a 'disease of the will' (Valverde, 1998), and because men were believed to be 'naturally' endowed with greater willpower than women, compulsory treatment was not perceived to be as appropriate for male alcoholics, as such men could effectively cure themselves. In contrast, women *per se* were considered 'naturally' passive and lacking sufficient willpower to self-cure. Women's general passivity, moreover, meant they were more susceptible to external moral influences. As the inspector observed of inebriate women in 1905:

> These creatures, poor wretches, are like rudderless ships, buffeted by the waves and pushed hither and thither by every wind that blows. They are mere bodies, acting in accordance with every animal

instinct they possess, at the mercy of any stray influence that comes along.[28]

Third, drunken women were widely considered more troublesome and difficult than their male counterparts owing to their innate biological and psychological weaknesses. As the inspector stated in 1909, 'the most cogent of all reasons why more women than men find their way into inebriate reformatories is the different effect of alcohol upon the two sexes'.[29] According to the inspector, drunken women were more inclined to become overemotional and get into trouble with the police, whereas 'hysterical frenzy' was the exception rather than the rule in the case of the male drunkard who, 'usually plods and struggles homewards with dogged determination ... more often than not inoffensive if left alone'[30] (see also Price, 1914: 101). Drunken women, therefore, were perceived as 'naturally' more difficult and in need of institutional control.

Female drunkards were also more vulnerable to institutionalisation within inebriate reformatories due to the unequal distribution of legal power between spouses in Victorian and Edwardian England. Under section five of the Licensing Act 1902,[31] a husband could apply for a judicial separation from his wife on the basis that she was a habitual drunkard. He was no longer obliged to cohabit with an alcoholic wife as long as he agreed to pay a sum not exceeding two pounds to her each week. Wives abandoned in this manner often became destitute, and as a result were more likely to come to official attention.[32] Husbands were also provided with the additional option of having their wives committed (with their consent) to inebriate retreats under this Act: an option not available to wives. As legal commentator, Robert Souttar, observed, husbands often used the threat of separation to coerce women into 'voluntarily' admitting themselves into retreats. Consequently, the number of women who freely and voluntarily admitted themselves into inebriate retreats was actually extremely small (1904: 216).

Finally, during the early decades of the twentieth century, the National Society for the Prevention of Cruelty to Children (NSPCC) became active in securing the institutionalisation of habitually drunken mothers under section one of the Inebriates Act. By 1909, 78% of section one committals were women convicted of cruelty towards and/or neglect of their children.[33] According to Robert Parr (Director of the NSPCC), between January 1901 and March 1908, 358 inebriate mothers had been committed to inebriate reformatories, with the result that a total of 1,253 children had been 'saved' from the pains of drunken motherhood (1908: 80). By institutionalising drunken mothers, the NSPCC had two main objectives: 'to give the children freedom from misery for [three years] at least', while, at the same time, reforming inebriate mothers and educating them in the arts of mother-craft (Parr, 1908: 80). The activities of the NSPCC were undeniably premised on androcentric assumptions about women's 'place' and their 'natural' maternal role: a contention evidenced by the fact that scarcely any fathers were committed to reformatories under section one of the 1898 Act.

In summary, far from being an unanticipated 'accident' of implementation, the Inebriates Acts presented an institutional response to an already highly gendered problem. The fact that the female drunkard, rather than the male drunkard, became constructed as the key problem in need of correction and, most importantly, control, enabled the gendered implementation of the Act to be viewed as obvious and natural.

Having demonstrated that a strong impetus for better modes of controlling female drunkards underpinned the development of inebriate institutions, the remainder of the chapter will examine the aims, regime and clientele of the certified inebriate reformatory. In doing so, it will reassess the degree to which this institution truly represented a fundamental departure from existing penal arrangements, and question the extent to which it actually represented a 'positive attempt' to reform drunken women.

Life inside the reformatory: the question of reform

The aim of reform frequently dominated contemporary discourses surrounding inebriate institutions. With this object in mind, many recommended that reformatories should be as little like the prison as possible; as the inspector noted in 1885, 'everything should be done, as far as possible, to avoid penal measures'.[34] Life within inebriate institutions, he later asserted, should be 'as natural and untrammelled as circumstances permit', and the regime 'as cheerful as discipline allows'.[35] While discipline was still considered a vital component of reformatory life, it was agreed that this should be 'the discipline of a regular well-ordered life, the routine of an army barracks, not of a prison' (Tod, 1881: 249). The Departmental Committee on the Treatment of Inebriates reiterated this point in 1898, stating that the principle of reformation, not punishment, should act as the guiding force within inebriate institutions.[36]

Despite this insistence, however, as the remainder of this chapter will demonstrate, inebriate reformatories, particularly the certified reformatory, had much in common with the local prison, and the principles of containment and control often supplanted reform within these institutions. This is not to deny that the object of reform was also ultimately underpinned by the desire for better modes of control, but rather to suggest that the degree to which the reformatory marked a significant departure from existing penal arrangements has often been overstated. The reformatory diet is a case in point. At first glance the reformatory diet appears to have been superior to that available in the local prison. However, medical experts insisted that inebriates required a 'simple, non-stimulating diet' and recommended a vegetarian diet for inebriate women, as meat was believed to catalyse immoral desires (Kerr, 1880: 323). In practice, the dietary was therefore often not qualitatively different to that served in local prisons. Furthermore, as occurred within prisons, the reformatory diet was regularly adapted for penal purposes and was a key mechanism for disciplining refractory women (Mellor *et al.*, 1986: 200). Interestingly, other than recommending enforced vegetarianism and treating the women's general ailments and health problems, there is little evidence within surviving institutional records that any significant medical treatment aimed at curing alcoholism was ever undertaken inside inebriate institutions. Thus, despite the rhetoric of reformers, as in the case of the prison regime, moral rather than medical treatment remained the core means of exacting 'reform'.

Life inside the reformatory was often considered harsher than the local prison. Thus, although the reformatory regime engaged women in a variety of occupations, ranging from embroidery to dairy farming,[37] residents of certified reformatories were frequently required to work much longer hours than in the local prison system. Reformatory inmates were expected to rise at six o'clock, eat breakfast at seven, and then participate in compulsory physical drills and chapel services until work commenced at half past eight. Dinner was at noon, before work resumed until half past four.[38] Reformatory officials often boasted that the work carried out in reformatories was more intensive and longer in duration than that carried out in the local prison. As the inspector stated in 1901:

> A great deal more work is already done in reformatories than in prisons, and we intend to have more done still. During the current

year some of the worst inmates have given constant trouble, with the intent to compel managers to send them to prison so that they might 'have an easier time'.[39]

The impression that the discipline and regime of the reformatory was harsher than the prison appears to have been held by at least some inebriate women who, as well as causing trouble in the hope of being transferred to prison, often refused to enter retreats and begged magistrates not to send them to reformatories, stating a preference for the local prison. For example, when Mary Louise Strainforth appeared before a London magistrate after escaping from an inebriate retreat, she stated that, '[it was] impossible to remain at an institution where she was a slave from morning to night ... It was a horrid place – worse that the prison'.[40] By 1906, the inspector noted that not only were inebriate women aware of the penal aspect of reformatories, but they believed these institutions represented a much greater punishment than the prison:

> The attitude of the persons now under detention makes it very clear that a two or three year sentence in a Reformatory is considered far more severe than the twelve or eighteen months' prison sentence they would have otherwise received.[41]

Thus, from the perspective of the women confined within them, inebriate institutions did not always represent a 'positive' alternative to the local prison. Indeed, institutional records reveal a number of women went to some lengths (some successfully) to escape from reformatories, again suggesting that the reformatory milieu appeared to be less mutually beneficial from the perspective of those contained within its walls. Indeed, following the successful escape of a woman from Langho in 1910, the director ordered a triple row of barbed wire projecting inwards to be placed around the top of the reformatory fence, 'to ensure the further safe custody of the inmates'.[42] Far from making life as 'natural and untrammelled' as possible, therefore, such decisions ensured that reformatory life increasingly echoed the more coercive aspects of the prison.

Furthermore, despite managerial insistence that the principal advantage of employment was for the women's personal benefit, considerable emphasis was placed on the financial importance of their labour. As the Department Committee noted in 1899, 'every inmate should be encouraged to exercise [her] time as remuneratively as possible'.[43]

The inspector echoed this sentiment in 1901, when he cited the importance of developing 'efficient industries' within reformatories to help contribute to institutional maintenance costs.[44] Thus, although the reformative value of the washtub had been heavily criticised by reformers and had been identified as a dominant cause of female inebriety (Booth, 1971: 267; Tooley, 1901: 25), the large profits obtained from reformatory laundries meant that this continued to be a principal form of employment.[45]

Controlling the 'hopeless': punishment and containment

Regardless of their ability to reform drunken women, reformatories potentially offered a key mechanism for controlling a wide range of troublesome women who existed beyond the boundaries of appropriate femininity and state control. Indeed, the second Inebriates Act was passed explicitly to control recidivist police-court drunkards, who were regularly stated to be beyond the reach of reform. For this reason alone, the control function of the reformatory should not be perceived as some accidental by-product of the inebriate institutions caused by inadequate administration or ill-fitted clientele, as authors such as Radzinowicz and Hood (1990), Zedner (1991), and Hall, G. (2002) have suggested, but rather represented one of the original motivations for this system.

A review of the remaining demographic information about the women contained within reformatories supports this contention, and calls into question the degree to which reform was ever considered the principal objective of inebriate reformatories. For instance, unlike many other semi-penal institutions emerging at this time, which targeted delinquent girls and wayward young women, women sent to inebriate reformatories were typically much older and deemed less amenable to reform strategies (Dodge, 2002; Barton, 2000, 2005; Rafter, 1983; Brenzel, 1980). For example, between 1899 and 1910, almost 80% of the women sent to reformatories were over 30 years old, with a quarter aged between 40 and 50 years.[46] In 1905, the inspector noted that 55 of the women committed to reformatories that year were over 60 years old, while the eldest was 82.[47] That these women were viewed as eligible candidates for moral reform seems highly unlikely.

All the women admitted to Langho reformatory had a criminal history, with each woman having an average of 26 convictions prior to admission.[48] A significant proportion also had multiple convictions for other types of offences, including larceny, violence against person or property, and cruelty to children. By the second decade of the twentieth century, a number of women at Langho were undergoing their second or third sentence in the reformatory, while the Patient Charge Registers reveal that many women had previously resided in other custodial institutions before arriving at Langho. For example, women were frequently sent to Langho from HM Prisons at Liverpool and Manchester. They also often arrived directly from other semi-penal institutions, including borstals and reformatory schools for wayward girls, as well as Magdalene homes and poor-law institutions.[49]

The fact that a large number of women were sent to inebriate reformatories from penal and semi-penal institutions suggests that many were already considered reform failures before they entered inebriate reformatories, and further implies that the reformatory was often used to try and control women who had proved unmanageable in less coercive settings. Dr Gill (the director of Langho reformatory) freely acknowledged this in 1906, when he commented on the case of a woman entering Langho with 106 previous convictions for drunkenness:

> Now it is reasonable to suppose that the court in committing a woman with 106 convictions did so, not so much for her own good, as for the benefit to be conferred on the community, thereby – in plain language, to get rid of her; and there is no doubt that the object of the Court in this respect has been obtained.[50]

If nothing else, the reformatory effectively 'got rid' of inebriate women for a period of three years. By 1906, only two years after Langho Reformatory had opened, Gill stated that it was 'perfectly justifiable for courts to commit cases which are, humanely speaking, "hopeless"'.[51] In dealing with such cases, he noted, it was important to keep the main objective for committing these women in mind: 'namely control rather than reformation should be kept in view'.[52] This belief was not restricted to Langho: as the inspector of inebriate institutions announced in his Annual Report for 1905, 'it has become necessary to set apart some of our institutions as little better than moral refuse heaps, for the detention of the hopelessly defective, at the lowest possible cost to the country'.[53] Just one year later, he decried that the word 'reformatory' had ever been applied to inebriate institutions.[54]

Within official discourses a sharp distinction was drawn between retreats and reformatories, with the latter seen to necessarily require greater levels of coercion and control because the women sent there were typically police-court recidivist drunkards or criminal inebriates incarcerated against their will. This bifurcation was officially recognised by 1901 (just two years after the second Inebriates Act came into force), when the inspector observed that reformatory discipline required 'something much more far-reaching and of a sterner character'.[55] Thus, despite the humanitarian rhetoric of reformers, who suggested the principle of reform should outweigh penal motives in the treatment of inebriates, the penal aspect remained a staple feature of the reformatory milieu.

Reformers fully recognised that the reformatory was harsher than the prison and was intended to serve a more overtly penal function. As the Inspector noted in 1901:

> ... inmates of reformatories thoroughly realise that, although under different conditions, they are nevertheless deprived of personal liberty. Two or three years of such deprivation, under reformatory conditions, is equivalent to a fairly long sentence of prison discipline ...[56]

Reformers also intended that the reformatory should fulfil a deterrent function, which necessarily meant that its regime and internal conditions maintained some of the punitive elements evident in the prison. Dr Gill, for example, observed with satisfaction that evidence from police courts in the Lancashire area demonstrated that the vigorous sentencing of local women to Langho had exercised a deterrent effect on their late associates.[57]

Finally, an overriding purpose of the reformatory was to segregate and contain drunken women to prevent them from reproducing. The arrival of the emerging science of 'eugenics' in the 1880s, saw alcoholism re-conceptualised as a hereditary problem linked to the development of degeneracy in future generations (Valverde, 1998; see also Pick, 1996; Bland, 1995; Rafter, 1997). Crucially, within eugenic discourses, women were considered the primary transmitter of hereditary traits (Bland, 1995: 230). Consequently, the female alcoholic was believed to produce degenerate children and contribute to the degeneration of the national stock (Chesser, 1909: 188). Drunken women were also considered highly promiscuous, and although it was widely accepted that a number of babies born to alcoholic mothers died in infancy, it was generally agreed that female inebriates reproduced at a far greater rate than their sober sisters and thus represented a significant eugenic concern. As the inspector noted in 1905, 92 women held in reformatories were responsible for the birth of 850 children.[58] As he concluded in 1909, 'alcoholism does not check fertility. On the contrary, it seems to favour it'.[59]

The reformatory controlled these women by containing their bodies for extended periods of time. As Dr Gill noted in 1908, 'If inebriate reformatories do nothing else than prevent the reproduction of the species, they have done much to justify their existence'.[60] Buffeted by the new 'scientific' knowledge about inebriety, infant mortality rates, and the hereditary nature of maternal feeblemindedness, many argued that the principal aim of inebriate reformatories should be the containment of drunken women in the short-term, with an eye to preventing drunkenness and degeneracy in future generations. As Harcourt Clare, the chairman of the Lancashire Inebriates' Acts Board, stated in 1908, 'I think it is better to try and improve the rising generation than to reform the existing generation that have gone too far'.[61]

Conclusion: the decline of the inebriate reformatory

By 1921 all inebriate reformatories in England had closed. Scholars have offered numerous explanations for the demise of these institutions. Radzinowicz and Hood (1990), Zedner (1991) and Hall, G. (2002) argue that the system ultimately 'failed' because the curable subject envisioned by the Inebriates Acts simply did not exist in reality. The failure of inebriate institutions to medically or morally 'cure' drunken women, they purport, led to a widespread disillusionment amongst reformers, which undermined the humanitarian zeal that provided the initial impetus for these institutions.

As this chapter has demonstrated, however, such accounts are flawed insofar as they ignore that the reformatory was designed with a custodial purpose in mind. The control function was not simply an unfortunate, unanticipated by-product of the inebriate system, attributable to an ill-fitted clientele or poor administration of the Act. Rather, this function was fully anticipated to be one of the core objectives of inebriate reformatories. As the reports of the inspector and institutional managers attest, reformatories were always intended to punish, segregate, and contain drunken women.

Nor do official discourses reveal evidence of widespread disillusionment over the failure to cure or rehabilitate drunken women. On the contrary, as this chapter has argued, reformatory managers and administrators readily accepted that many women committed were beyond reform. Consequently, any cases of reform were typically heralded as evidence of institutional success.[62] Indeed, the failure of the reformatory to reform drunken women had been officially recognised since 1900 (just two years after these institutions were legislated into existence);

yet, despite this realisation, reformatories continued to operate for a further 20 years.[63] Arguments that claim the system failed due to the decline of the ideal of reform, thus fail to sufficiently explain why the reformatory system persisted for two decades following this realisation. While acknowledging that a number of practical administrative problems contributed to the decline of the inebriate system (see Morrison, 2005; Radzinowicz and Hood, 1990; Mellor *et al.*, 1986; Harding and Wilkin, 1988), it is also likely that the reformatory ultimately 'failed' because it did not adequately fulfil its custodial function insofar as it did not effectively control habitually drunken women. Contemporary evidence supports this contention, revealing a widespread frustration that the Acts did not allow sufficient control to be exercised over female drunkards. For example, by 1910 less than one third of the 227 women discharged from Langho were 'doing well' or 'improved'.[64] Magistrates blamed institutional managers for this lack of control because they released women on licence after serving only nine months, while also bemoaning the lengthy re-admission procedures, which required women to receive a further four convictions for drunkenness in 12 months before qualifying for re-admission to a reformatory.[65] Collectively, they argued that greater state control was necessary. This control was granted with the arrival of the Mental Deficiency Act in 1913.[66] Under this Act, inebriates could be directly transferred from inebriate institutions into asylums for the mentally deficient without the provision of a medical certificate. The Act also enabled non-criminal inebriates to be compulsorily detained in institutions for mental defectives. Once inside, they could be held indefinitely until a medical 'expert' declared them fit to be at liberty. In this sense, the inebriates system did not 'fail' in the true sense of the term, but merely became irrelevant as the expansive scope of the Mental Deficiency Act offered a more pervasive means of controlling recidivist female drunkards.

Notes

1 *The Habitual Drunkards Act 1879* (42 & 43 Vict. c. 19); *The Inebriates Act 1888* (51 & 52 Vict. c. 19); *The Inebriates Act 1898* (61 & 62 Vict. c. 60).
2 *Report of the Inspector under the Inebriates Acts* (hereafter RIIA) 1910, PP, 1912–13 Cd. 6166. xxix. 497.
3 The empirical research on which this chapter is based was funded as part of the Bright Future Scholarship Scheme. The author would like to thank the Foundation of Research, Science and Technology in New Zealand (now the Ministry of Research, Science and Technology) for their support.

4 Judicial Returns for England and Wales (hereafter JR) 1870, PP, 1871 [c. 442] LXIV.1.
5 JR 1870; JR 1905, PP, 1907 Cd. 3315. xcviii.1.
6 *The Times*, 6 December 1893: 3.
7 *Ibid.*, 23 January 1871: 5.
8 *Ibid.*, 17 November 1888: 5.
9 JR 1885, PP, 1886 [c. 4808] LXXII.1; JR 1925, PP, 1927 Cd 2811. xxv. 201.
10 JR 1870; JR 1875, PP, 1876 [c. 1595] LXXIX.1; JR 1885; JR 1895, PP, 1897 [c. 8352, c. 8536] C. 1.
11 35 & 36 Vict. c. 94, s. 12.
12 *The Times*, 13 February 1871: 11.
13 *The Staffordshire Advertiser*, 2 October 1880: 7.
14 *The Times*, 22 June 1895: 10.
15 RIIA 1905, PP, 1906 Cd. 3246. xvi. 1: 19.
16 RIIA 1905: 16.
17 *The Times*, 22 February 1890: 15.
18 *Ibid.*, 11 June 1900: 4.
19 *Ibid.*, 23 September 1907: 4.
20 RIIA 1906, PP, 1907 Cd. 3685. x. 589: 13; Annual Director's Report to the Lancashire Inebriates Act Board (hereafter ADRLIAB) 1910, *HRBC 1/5: 1910–1911*: 17.
21 42 & 43 Vict. c. 19, s.3.
22 RIIA 1906.
23 RIIA 1910: 497.
24 RIIA 1906.
25 RIIA 1909, PP, 1911 Cd. 5799. xxix. Part I. 11: 17.
26 RIIA 1909: 17.
27 *The Times*, 19 December 1900: 15.
28 RIIA 1905: 16.
29 RIIA 1909:17.
30 *Ibid.*, 15.
31 2 Edw 7. c. 28.
32 *The Times*, 23 September 1907: 4.
33 RIIA 1909: 14.
34 *Report of the Inspector of Retreats under the Habitual Drunkards Act 1879* (hereafter RIHDA) 1885, PP, 1886 [c. 4822] XIV. 957: 1.
35 RIIA 1898, PP, 1899 [c. 8997]: 3.
36 *Report of the Departmental Committee appointed to Advise as to the Regulations for Inebriate Reformatories to be made under the Inebriates Act 1898* (hereafter RDCRIR), PP, 1899 [c. 9112] XII. 749: 3.
37 See, for example, RIHDA 1880, PP, 1881 [c. 354] XXIII. 501; RIIA 1901, PP, 1902 Cd. 1381. xii. 697; RIIA 1910; ADRLIAB 1906, *HRBC 1/1: 1906–1907*; ADRLIAB 1909, *HRBC 1/4: 1909–1910*; ADRLIAB 1921, *HRBC 1/12: 1922–1924*.
38 RDCRIR 1898: Appendix VI.
39 RIIA 1901: 56.
40 *The Times*, 16 December 1897: 12.
41 RIIA 1906: 10.

42 Director's Monthly Report to the House Committee of Langho Reformatory, February 10 1910, *HRBC 1/4: 1909–1910*: 7.
43 RDCRIR 1898: 4, italics added.
44 RIIA 1901: 18.
45 ADRLIAB 1908, *HRBC 1/3: 1908–1909*: 11.
46 RIIA 1910.
47 RIIA 1905: 15.
48 ADRLIAB 1906; ADRLIAB 1910; ADRLIAB 1920, *HRBC 1/11: 1919–1921*; ADRLIAB 1921.
49 Patient Charge Registers for Brockhall Asylum 1915–1918 *HRBC 14/1*.
50 ADRLIAB 1906: 20.
51 *Ibid.*
52 *Ibid.*
53 RIIA 1905: 9.
54 RIIA 1906: 15.
55 RIIA 1901: 47.
56 *Ibid.*, 56.
57 ADRLIAB 1908: 15.
58 RIIA 1905: 7.
59 RIIA 1909: 26.
60 ADRLIAB 1908: 15.
61 *Report of the Departmental Committee as to the Operation of the Law Relating to Inebriates and their Detention in Reformatories and Retreats*, Minutes of Evidence, PP, 1908 Cd. 4438. xii. 817: 78.
62 For example, see ADRLIAB 1906: 19.
63 RIIA 1901: 61.
64 ADRLIAB 1910.
65 For example, see *The Times*, 31 August 1920: 7.
66 3 & 4 Geo. 5 c. 28.

8
Punishment, Reformation, or Welfare: Responses to 'The Problem' of Juvenile Crime in Victorian and Edwardian Britain

Heather Shore

The contours of the modern juvenile justice system were arguably fully formed by the early twentieth century (Garland, 1985: 2). The 1908 Children's Act which established juvenile courts, and the approved school system of 1933, were points of formalisation in a system which had its roots in the late eighteenth and early nineteenth centuries. Thus in 1788, the Philanthropic Society was founded by Robert Young in London, and in its earliest prescriptions it developed the Reform for delinquent children, and the Manufactory for orphan children or children of convicted offenders (Carlebach, 1970: 4–15; Shore, 1999: 6, 99). The later fusing of state and voluntary sector approaches would see the division between the Reform and Manufactory reflected in the evolution of the industrial and reformatory schools. Thus vagrant, vulnerable and semi-delinquent children were to be sent to the industrial school, and children convicted of felony were to be sent to the reformatory school. A series of acts pushed the evolution of these institutions during the second half of the nineteenth century and the early twentieth century. However, evolutions are rarely straightforward, and testament to this is a continual debate about the issue of juvenile delinquency and the particular form that punishment should take throughout our period.

This chapter will focus on two key periods. Firstly the decades leading up to the mid-century juvenile delinquency acts; and secondly the late Victorian and early Edwardian period, when new concerns about delinquency and boy labour were to increasingly shape the experience of punishment encountered by juvenile offenders. In the earlier period a number of strands will be explored, including the role of summary jurisdiction, the relationship between voluntary and state sector approaches to the punishment and/or reformation of young offenders, and the emergence of the Reformatory and Industrial Schools Acts that were rolled out from 1854. The second part of the chapter will consider how the system put in place by the mid-nineteenth century evolved, with a particular emphasis on the late Victorian and Edwardian Acts which tied up the loose ends that remained. For example, the Education Act of 1876 put in place industrial day schools and truant schools; and the first children's court was set up in Birmingham in April 1905 (Radzinowicz and Hood, 1990: 181, 192).

Summary justice

Short, correctional periods of custody for juveniles had been recommended from the early nineteenth century. Even before the redefinition of the Vagrancy Act, and the passage of the Malicious Trespass Act in the 1820s, which Susan Magarey argues effected a greater criminalisation of juveniles, substantial numbers of children were being committed to bridewells and houses of correction on charges of vagrancy and for other misdemeanours (1978: 11–27; Shore, 1999: 29–34). As the century progressed this use of custody for summarily processed juveniles was to be matched by the use of custody for those convicted of more felonious crime. Indeed debate about the punishment of juveniles was increasingly concentrated on those who were prosecuted for indictable crime, hence those who had travelled the extra length into the formal criminal justice system. Before the mid-nineteenth century a variety of strategies to deal with convicted juveniles were tried out with varying success. At the root of these strategies was the recognition that society had a larger constituent body of juveniles in the justice system to deal with – it is clear that the 'great confinement' of this period embraced youth (Ignatieff, 1978: 186–7; Rothman, 1971: 207–8). The extent to which this increased juvenile prison population represented a real rise in juvenile crime is nevertheless difficult to assess. Whilst the rhetoric of contemporaries very much reflected a belief that juvenile crime had increased, analysis of indicted juvenile crime in London suggests a more complex explanation (Magarey, 1978: 16–17; Shore, 1999: 103, 115–17). Hence, from the 1820s, the period in which the language of institutional reformation emerged, the chance of acquittal decreased. Whilst the chance of being acquitted declined for all offenders over the period, younger offenders stood the least chance of being acquitted (King, 2006a: 118–19).

Moreover, the reformation of juvenile offenders was to be located firmly within institutional provision. The issue was what the exact form and function of that custodial punishment should be. The great theme of this period was classification and separation of what were perceived as different groups of convicts (Garland, 1985: 22). Thus boys were to be removed from men, and bad boys were to be removed from those identified as less experienced offenders. The paradox in this situation was how to control the behaviour of both those children already labelled as criminal and those children on the periphery of the criminal justice system: the 'dangerous' and 'perishing' juveniles (Carpenter, 1851: 1–3). Rather more children were now spending time in front of the magistrates, and inside the houses of correction, bridewells, and prisons. Moreover, many of the children who spent time in the voluntary custodial institutions, such as the Refuge for the Destitute, and the School of the Philanthropic Society, were not specifically criminal. Often they were the children of convicts, or were children who had been committed for vagrancy. Consequently there was a drive to find a scheme that could incorporate both groups of children, using the systems of classification which were being recommended in legislation such as the 1823 and 1824 Gaol Acts, engineered by Peel himself.[1] The classification and grading of juveniles was already well established in the institutions of the voluntary sector. As we have seen, as early as the 1790s, the Philanthropic Society had placed delinquent boys into the Reform where they were provided with a moral and social education. Once 'sufficiently reformed' they were transferred to the Manufactory where they were taught practical skills and undertook employment.[2]

Philanthropic strategies

It is arguable that it was the representatives of the voluntary sector that provided much of the momentum for change (Platt, 1969). Whilst the parliamentary debate can be traced through the various 'crime' Select Committees of this period, a considerable number of independent philanthropists and researchers were actually going into the prisons of the metropolis and were clearly unhappy with what they found. The members of the *Committee for Investigating the Causes of the Alarming Increase of Juvenile Delinquency in the Metropolis*, established in 1815, emphasised the necessity for separate juvenile provision (Shore, 1999: 20–1).[3] Moreover, the successor to this committee, the Prison Discipline Society, was the major penal pressure group of this period: a sort of proto-Howard League (Highmore, 1822). During the 1820s and 1830s, a variety of evidence was submitted by such organisations, which illustrated the benefits of separate juvenile provision not only on the crime rates but also on the public purse. Moreover, as a result of time spent visiting children in prison, they stressed the counter-productive effects of traditional forms of custody from the early days of the debate.

As early as 1816, designs had been submitted for a juvenile penitentiary, by Samuel Hoare, the Quaker banker and philanthropist, and the architect James Bevan.[4] Bevan was extremely critical of the present system, and rather derisive about both the recently built penitentiary in Tothill Fields and Bentham's Panopticon.[5] Instead he suggested clock and watch making, cabinet making and mathematical instrument manufacture besides various other skilled occupations.[6] Despite progressing as far as survey, costing, and the selection of a location, the plan disappeared without a trace. This plan had intrinsically conflicted with the tenor of contemporary thought on penality. Thus, whilst it was accepted that the new penality needed to be a reformatory experience, contemporaries were also aware of the need for the preservation of the principle of 'less eligibility' (Garland, 1985: 164). As the Governor of Coldbath Fields House of Correction remarked of juvenile inmates in 1831:

> the punishment of prison is no punishment to them; I do not mean that they would not rather be out of prison than in it, but they are so well able to bear the punishment, and the prison allowance of food is so good, and their spirits so buoyant, that the consequences are most deplorable.[7]

In other words, it would be unwise to make the prison too attractive. Consequently, despite calls for separate juvenile penitentiaries throughout the period, it took until 1838 for the first state-run juvenile institution, the ill-fated Parkhurst to materialise. It was not until the 1850s that the reform and manufactory of the Philanthropic Society were to be echoed in state-controlled institutions.[8] Prior to this attention was concentrated largely on types of punishment and methods of control that could achieve the object of moral reformation.

Emigration schemes were to be adopted both by the voluntary institutions (during the early nineteenth century) and by their state counterparts from the mid-nineteenth century. Various voluntary societies used some form of colonial retraining amongst their roster of improvement strategies (Blackburn, 1993; Bradlow, 1984; Hadley, 1990; Radzinowicz and Hood, 1990: 216; Richards, 2004; Shore, 1999: 110–14). For example, as early as the 1820s, the Refuge for the

Destitute supplied outfits and paid deposits for a number of young men to settle in the Cape (Nash, 1987; King, 2006a: 130).[9] Clearly, this emigration has to be seen alongside the more general trend towards colonial emigration in this period, as well as the use of penal transportation.[10] In the context of juvenile penality, emigration can be problematic. On the one hand, the rhetoric of colonial citizenship presented emigration to New South Wales or the Cape as a means of training the 'youth of the empire' (Brenton, 1837). On the other hand, at least in terms of the early cargoes, such emigration schemes were seen as being little more than forced labour, and had more in common with penal transportation. The Children's Friend Society was amongst the earliest to experiment with child emigration to the colonies. Set up as the Brenton Juvenile Asylum or Academy on the edge of Hackney Marshes in 1830, the first party of children were sent to the Cape of Good Hope in 1832 (Blackburn, 1993). By the late 1830s, the Society had been largely discredited after the *Times* published a series of critical articles, including one editorial on 'Children's Kidnapping Society' published in 1839.[11] The society ceased to exist two years later (Radzinowicz and Hood, 1990: 138).[12]

Colonial emigration in its 'voluntary' form would re-emerge again in the later nineteenth century. Children were sent to Canada in the 1870s, through the auspices of organisations such as the National Children's Homes and Orphanages; the Child Emigration Homes of John T. Middlemore; and in the 1880s from Dr. Barnardo's and The Church of England Waifs and Strays Society (Bean and Melville, 1989). Of course, juveniles had long been punished by transportation, although generally youths were not transported until they were aged sixteen. Until then they would be placed on the hulks (King, 2006a: 129–32). From 1816, attempts were made to separate boy convicts from adults, by fitting up a frigate, the *Bellerophon*, especially for the reception of boys. From 1825, juvenile convicts were transferred to the *Euryalus*, another specially fitted frigate, moored at Chatham (Radzinowicz & Hood, 1990: 142–4; Shore, 1999: 102, 107–8). The criticism of the overcrowded and unsavoury hulks was vociferous, particularly from the 1830s, when the *Euryalus* specifically came under fire from Thomas Wontner, in his book *Old Bailey Experience*, and from the Select Committee evidence of an ex-prisoner who had worked on the frigate. Thomas Dexter, a nurse, described horrifying violence and a subculture of bullying and intimidation (Wontner, 1831).[13] Much of the dissatisfaction with juvenile transportation and juvenile hulks reflected the more general and growing unease about arrangements to punish juvenile offenders (Shore, 2002). It was in this climate, in the next couple of decades, that the Reformatory and Industrial School System would emerge.

The Reformatory and Industrial Schools Acts

Whilst historians and criminologists have tended to date the development of the juvenile justice system from the Children's Act in 1908, in many ways, it could be argued that this act formalised and culminated in the various legislation and experimentation of the previous century (Behlmer, 1982; Garland, 1985: 222). Arguably the presentation of the Children's Act as the 'Children's Charter', has misaligned historians and sociologists focus on this as the key moment in juvenile justice (Davin, 1996: 211–12; Pinchbeck and Hewitt, 1973: 493–4). The Children's Act allowed for the establishment of separate juvenile courts, and re-affirmed the differentiation between the reformatory and industrial schools (although this went against the prevailing climate, since any distinctions were later to be abolished by the Departmental Committee on the Treatment of Young Offenders in 1933, under the Children and Young Persons Act (Bailey, 1987: 93)). Yet a closer examination of the history of the legislation of the mid-to-late nineteenth century reveals instead an *ad hoc* system developing through trial and error, and administered by a combination of voluntary and state sector institutions and individuals. Arguably the slew of acts passed between the 1840s and 1850s were the real watershed in the history of juvenile delinquency. A full history of these acts has yet to be written. However, a number of studies do exist which inform us about their foundation and application in the later nineteenth century (Carlebach, 1970; Grigg, 2002; Hendrick, 2006; Mahood, 1995; Radzinowicz and Hood, 1990).

During the early nineteenth century, as we have already seen, the philanthropic sector was already aware of the need for separate penal provision for juvenile offenders. Nevertheless, the state resisted the formal introduction of separate juvenile provision until the mid-century. Why was this? Whilst the government certainly agreed in principle with the separation of youthful offenders it seems likely that it was thought that reorganisation of the current penal system would provide the answer, rather than raise the expense involved in setting up separate provision (Radzinowicz and Hood, 1990: 145–8). Moreover, the state continued to refer young offenders to voluntary institutions such as the Philanthropic Society and the Refuge for the Destitute, throughout the early nineteenth century. Indeed, as Peter King has pointed out, by the mid-1830s the Refuge was essentially a (partially) state-funded juvenile reformatory (2006a: 161).

The separation and categorisation of juveniles within the prison system was recommended from the eighteen-teens, and practiced during the 1820s and early 30s, in theory through the auspices of Peel's Gaol Act of 1823 which emphasised the separation and classification of prisoners (McConville, 1981: 248–50).[14] The 1820s and 30s were arguably an era of experimentation in terms of penal policy. In reality the 'separation' of young from older offenders was rather limited, and characterised by a lack of uniformity. For example, in Gloucester prison there was no separation or education provision. At Worcester, younger prisoners were separated and received educational instruction for two and a half hours daily (Radzinowicz and Hood, 1990: 145). By the 1830s it was clear that, on the ground at least, the Act was not working particularly well. The 1832 Select Committee on Secondary Punishments concluded:

> The larger prisons, especially those in and near the metropolis, usually contain several hundred prisoners, whose periods of confinement before trial, vary from a few days to several months. It is hardly necessary to remark, that any classification, with the inadequate means provided by the Gaol Act, must be inefficacious.[15]

It was not until the mid-1830s, that the government finally recognised the need for some sort of state juvenile penitentiary. The 1835 Select Committee on Gaols and Houses of Correction had recommended the establishment of a separate juvenile prison (McConville, 1981: 428–9; Penwarden, 1980; Radzinowicz and Hood, 1990; Stack, 1979). Despite two decades of calls for such an institution from the voluntary sector, it was actually a very different atmosphere which created Parkhurst. On the one hand, Parkhurst emerged from a period of punitive penality, and indeed much of the criticism of Parkhurst (most notably from Mary Carpenter) rested on its 'apparent' harshness. On the other hand, the establishment of Parkhurst is closely intertwined with the history of juvenile transportation and emigration. Thus in 1837, the Molesworth Committee regarded transportation of juveniles as unworkable, costly, and a poor form of colonisation.[16] In contrast, Parkhurst was to embrace the ideology of colonial citizenship. Thus, the training element, which would be a key feature of the new penitentiary, would produce better and more useful colonial citizens. Consequently, the majority of Parkhurst prisoners were to be transported. However, the boy's performance whilst he was in the institution would determine the form of his transportation. He could be transported as a free emigrant, or under a conditional pardon, or for a more hardened offender, he could be confined in the colonial penal system (McConville, 1981: 205). The parallel with the history of child emigration can be seen in the early ethos of Parkhurst, when 92 boys were taken to New Zealand as free emigrants and colonial apprentices (Wagner, 1982: 19–23). After the passage of the Parkhurst Act in August 1838, the institution opened its doors to its first young inmates in the following December. The twin goals of reform and deterrence underpinned the regime in the early years, with cautious acknowledgements of the potential difficulties of balancing punishment and reformation:

> ...the utmost care must be taken to avoid any species of discipline which is inconsistent with the habits and the character of youth, or calculated in any degree to harden and degenerate. The second object... [reformation]... can only be effected by a judicious course of moral, religious and industrial training, but the means adopted for this purpose should not be of such a nature as to counteract the wholesome restraints of the corrective discipline...[17]

However, according to Radzinowicz and Hood, up to 1841 (in what has been seen as the first phase of the Parkhurst experiment from 1838 to 1842) 'boys of bad character' were not admitted. Thus the first boys to be sent to Parkhurst were essentially minor offenders, prompting criticism from contemporaries that those boys sent to Parkhurst were arguably those least in need of it (1990: 150). The history of Parkhurst as a juvenile specific penitentiary was to be relatively short-lived; closing its door to juveniles in 1864. Overall, the first juvenile penitentiary has been remembered as a failed experiment. Yet, the decline of Parkhurst has to be assessed alongside the passage of the Reformatory and Industrial Schools Acts. Whilst Parkhurst was subjected to vociferous criticism, particularly in its second and third stages (from the early 1840s to the early 1850s), it also had to compete with the move toward the reformatory school system. Thus from 1854, a number of new reformatory schools would increasingly limit the role of Parkhurst, which was essentially seen as part of the convict prison system.[18]

By the eve of the First World War, as Radzinowicz and Hood pointed out, 'there was a network of 208 schools: 43 reformatories, 132 industrial schools, 21 day industrial schools and 12 truant schools' (1990:

182). The vast majority of these had been certified as a result of the legislation of 1854 and after. The Reformatory and Industrial Schools Inspectors in 1866, reported that there were 65 Reformatory Schools (51 in England and 14 in Scotland) and 50 Industrial Schools (30 in England and 19 in Scotland) in December 1865.[19] Clearly by 1914, there had been a shift from the reformatory to the industrial school. In fact the number of reformatory schools seems to have stayed fairly constant throughout the period. The Report of the Inspectors for 1889 reported that in 1888 there were 56 reformatory schools, but 140 certified industrial schools.[20] Between the 1860s and 1880s then the industrial school was to become the dominant institution to deal with young offenders. In order to explain why, it would be useful to review the distinctions between the two institutions. As it has already been pointed out, to a large extent this was a conscious adoption of the divisions which had already been made in the voluntary system, but also in recent distinctions made by Mary Carpenter between 'perishing' and 'dangerous' juveniles (Carpenter, 1851; May, 1973: 22). Thus reformatory schools were to be reserved for convicted offenders, whilst industrial schools (formally and nationally legislated from 1857) took the potential delinquent and neglected child.

The divisions between the reformatory and industrial schools were also a reflection of the divisions between those reformers who were pushing government for action. Essentially the camp was divided into those who supported a more punitive approach to juvenile delinquency, including the Chaplain of the Philanthropic Society, Sidney Turner (soon to be the first Home Office Inspector of reformatory and industrial schools), Jelinger Symons (Inspector of Schools, and the editor of the Law Magazine) and T. B. Lloyd-Baker (a Gloucestershire magistrate). Advocating a more humanitarian approach were Mary Carpenter and Matthew Davenport Hill amongst others (Stack, 1994). Turner, Symons and Lloyd-Baker supported the requirement that all children sentenced to reformatory schools should initially be sentenced to at least 14 days imprisonment.[21] Indeed, the thrust of their argument during the early years of the Reformatory Schools Act seemed to be that prison and reformatory schools were the only way to deal with 'hardened' juvenile offenders, who they saw as 'the leaders in crime' (Lloyd Baker, 1889: 206–7). They fundamentally disagreed with the debate about criminal discretion, and believed that most criminal children were fully aware of their actions. The political tone of this debate is apparent from an address by Symons to the Royal Society of Arts in 1855, when he attacked 'the belief that juvenile offenders are little errant angels who require little else than fondling' (1855: 416). This was a direct attack on the opposing side of the reformatory debate, which disagreed with any form of child imprisonment, and viewed the reformatory as potentially penal, though supporting them in a modified form. More implicitly, this was an attack on Mary Carpenter, who in her work advocated a rather more compassionate approach to juvenile delinquency (Carpenter, 1851: 321–2). Nevertheless, it would be wrong to over-emphasise this debate, or to reduce it to punitive 'reformatories' versus humanitarian 'industrial schools'. What is clear is that industrial schools would gain the precedence over the reformatory during the following decades. In many ways this was a reflection of the views of the reformers. Thus the pre-imprisonment requirement for reformatory schools remained, and so this tended to be the institution for more 'hardened' offenders. The industrial school then, became essentially a diversionary institution for a variety of delinquent and neglected children.

In the early years the criteria for entrance to the industrial schools was very narrow, essentially focusing on vagrant children. John Watson, reflecting on the development of the system in 1896, noted that, 'In the first Industrial Act the only offence under which a child could be committed was that of "vagrancy," a word of vague import' (1896: 273). The boost to industrial schools was provided in 1861 with an Amendment Act which specified four different categories of children who could be sent to industrial schools: (1) children under 14 who were found begging or receiving alms; (2) children under 14 who were found wandering and had no home or visible means of subsistence, or who frequented the company of reputed thieves; (3) children under 12 who had committed an offence punishable by imprisonment, or some lesser punishment; and (4) children under 14 whose parent (or parents) was unable to control him or her (Stack, 1994: 65).[22] The scope of children to be catered for by the industrial schools was further broadened in 1866, when a new category was added, those, 'in need of care and protection', aimed at children aged under 14, with further provisions for those aged under 12.[23] What is clear is that a large element of discretion characterised this system, thus the wording stipulated those under 12, 'who, having committed an offence punishable by imprisonment or some less punishment, ought nevertheless, in the opinion of the justices, regard being had to his age, and to the circumstances of the case, to be sent to an Industrial School' (May, 1973: 26). This points to the importance of continuity between the industrial schools and the earlier forms of juvenile disciplinary institution. As we saw earlier, local justices were making extensive use of respited judgements to divert young offenders to the Refuge to the Destitute. It seems clear that these practices were incorporated into the Industrial Schools Acts and that essentially the Refuge and like institutions, were the first industrial schools (King, 2006a). Indeed a number of Industrial Schools certified from 1856 had their roots in ragged schools or industrial feeding schools. For example, the Battersea Industrial School had been founded in 1843, and the Industrial School for Boys in York, was originally founded as a Sunday School in 1847, becoming a mixed Ragged School in 1849. Aberdeen had a system of industrial feeding schools, which by 1851 included four schools and a child's asylum (Haythornwaite, 1993: 46–7). John Stack points out that prior to 1857 a local bill had been passed (in 1854), which allowed Middlesex to rate itself in order to establish industrial schools for criminal children below the age of 14, the Middlesex Industrial School opened in 1859 (1994: 64).

According to Radzinowicz and Hood, the key legislation that would enable the expansion of the industrial school was the Consolidation Act of 1866. Within a year of the passage of the act the number of admissions to industrial schools had doubled, 'The number of inmates, a mere 1,668 in 1864, had jumped to 5,738 by 1868, and then by leaps and bounds to nearly 17,000 in 1881 and over 20,000 in 1885' (1990: 181–2). One of the changes may have been in how the schools were funded. In the 1857 and 1861 Acts, funding seems to have come mainly from a combination of private funding, parental contribution, and some public money (but much less than was being given to the reformatories) (Radzinowicz and Hood, 1990: 182–3). The 1866 Act seems to have widened the financial remit by allowing for contributions from counties and boroughs.[24] Moreover, the Act's jurisdiction was extended to Scotland, which had previously been dealt with separately (Mahood, 1995).

Increasingly the distinction between the industrial and reformatory schools was blurred, suggesting that magistrates were, by the later sixties, inclined to use the industrial school for both criminal and destitute children. Thus as well as the categories established by the 1861 Act, it further allowed for the detainment of children, 1) found destitute either being an Orphan or having a surviving parent undergoing penal servitude or imprisonment 2) under 12 charged with an offence punishable by imprisonment or a less punishment, but not a felony 3) under 14 whose parents or step-parents or guardians were unable to control their children, could make representation to a magistrate that 'he desires that the child be sent to an Industrial School' and 4) workhouse or pauper school children under the age of 14, deemed refractory by the Guardians of the Poor (or the child of criminal parents) could be sent to an industrial school.[25] These criteria both built upon and expanded previous criteria, and allowed the magistrates a high level of discretion. It would seem fair to conclude that by the later nineteenth century local government was given a high degree of latitude in dealing with the disorderly children of the working class. Hence, the journey from the reformatory school for juvenile offenders in the mid-nineteenth century seems to have transformed into the industrial school for the refractory working class by the latter part of the century.

This point is underlined if we add to this the day industrial schools and truant schools allowed for under the 1876 Education Act, and further acts passed in the 1880s and 1890s, which extended the state's hand into domestic spaces. Anna Davin argues that a range of social legislation enabled access to working-class houses at this time. She points out that the Industrial Schools Amendment Act 1880 and the Criminal Law Amendment Act 1885 allowed for children found in houses used for 'immoral purposes' to be removed to an industrial school (1996: 163–4). An 1891 Reformatory and Industrial Schools Act[26] allowed discharged children to be apprenticed or sent overseas against their parents wishes; further Reformatory School Acts were passed in 1893 and 1899 and an Industrial Schools Act in 1894.[27] This act allowed discretionary powers to industrial school managers to keep children (who had completed their sentence) in the industrial school to the age of eighteen. However, on the ground, there was opposition both from the government and from parents (Radzinowicz and Hood, 1990: 213–14). For later nineteenth and early twentieth century commentators, the 1866 Act had been an effective means of suppression to 'the wholesale manufacture of pauperism and crime which had been going on' (Bosanquet, 1899: 52–3). John Watson described the web of 'agencies at work towards the elevation and reformation of unfortunate and incorrigible children', including the day industrial schools, truant schools, certified industrial schools, reformatories, and prison 'when all these influences fail'. Ultimately, Watson judged the system a success, concluding that, 'The danger, which menaced society some forty years ago from the hordes of savage children prowling the streets of our large cities to beg, borrow, or steal...has, through their agency, been rooted out and removed' (1896: 275, 306).

Experience and resistance in the industrial and reformatory schools

Whilst the experience of young offenders has started to be explored for the early nineteenth and twentieth centuries, the mid-to-late

Victorian period has eluded detailed investigation (Bennett, 1988: 71–96; Christiaens, 2002: 89–104; Cox, 2003: 107–34; King, 2006b; Shore, 1999; Wills, 2005a). Indeed, whilst on the one hand, large numbers of working-class children were effectively institutionalised by the late nineteenth century (with the respectable working classes catered for by the raft of education legislation from 1870), there is also evidence of substantial resistance. The most visible flouting of the system took place on the various training ships which were moored around the country (Radzinowicz and Hood, 1990: 193–202). These ships proliferated from the mid-nineteenth century, established by a variety of institutions with the intention of training and disciplining young, working-class lads for the navy. Not all were 'reformatory' or 'industrial' institutions, in other words, some were prison ships to which youths could be sentenced by the court. Thus in October 1876, the Liverpool Borough Police Court, sentenced a boy burglar, 'who had been twice before in custody, to ten days' imprison-ment and five years detention on board the Reformatory ship Akbar' in Merseyside.[28] As well as the Akbar, the Clarence was moored at Merseyside, and the Cornwall moored on the Thames (Antrobus, 1875; Evans, 2002; Rimmer, 1986). The line between the reformatory ships and the training ships needs to be considered in the context of the web of institutions that have already been discussed. For example, the Exmouth training ship, moored off Grays in Essex in 1877, was administered by the Metropolitan Asylums Board.

The most notorious outbreak of 'mutiny' was on the Akbar, 25 September, 1887. The breakdown of discipline on the ship was attributed to poor management of the boys, 'the cause may readily be traced to a want of firmness and energy in dealing with a mere handful of vicious and depraved youths'.[29] Essentially, the Inspector of Reformatory Schools argued that the management of the ship had become complacent and were unprepared for trouble, 'The boys got the upper hand for a time, and this they ought never to be allowed to do'.[30] According to this report, the mutiny had broken out whilst the captain had been absent, and a number of lads had broken into the ships stores and the captain's cabin. Seventeen of the ringleaders absconded, but were later re-captured and tried by local magistrates. Boys who gave evidence at the Liverpool Stipendiary Court, blamed each other, but there was also some criticism of the ships' officers. One boy Moffat testified, 'There are three officers in the ship who a re trying to do all they can against me'.[31] Later, ten of the boys who were tried at the Winter Assizes in Liverpool were not subject to punishment by the presiding magistrate, Mr. Justice Day, who was critical of the 'defective' discipline on the ship.[32] Nevertheless, the boys who were returned to the ship were punished with the birch, solitary confinement and a diet of biscuit and water (Rimmer, 1986: 29).

A year earlier, on another of the Merseyside training ships, the Clarence, there had also been trouble, again attributed to poor management. According to the report into the incident, unauthorised punishments and excessive use of the cane had been a cause.[33] In July 1899, the Clarence was completely destroyed by a fire on a day in which the ship was receiving illustrious visitors, including the Bishop of Shrewsbury.[34] At the official inquiry into the fire which opened in Liverpool in August, 1899, Captain Yonge (who had had command of the ship from April 1895), dismissed accusations that the fire had been started by the boys, 'Speaking as a Catholic, I feel quite certain that nothing of the kind has been done, and would never have been done with the Bishop and priest there'.[35] By September, the final report of the inquiry had reached no firm conclusions, though 'There remains the theory that the ship was deliberately fired'.[36]

Concerns about excessive violence used in carrying out punishments, and general poor treatment of the boys were also the subject of an inquiry into the Wellesley Industrial Training Ship moored on the Tyne. Inspections into the ship revealed high levels of absconding boys, and the heavy use of flogging (Radzinowicz and Hood, 1990: 198–9).[37] The problem of ill-treatment on the training ship was more fully revealed in the Akbar 'Scandal' of 1910. By this time the ship was no longer being used, and the school had been transferred to the Nautical Training School at Heswall, in the Wirral. Based on evidence from a former Master and Matron of the School, the magazine *John Bull* published a report detailing cruel treatment which had led to a number of deaths. This resulted in a Home Office internal inquiry, which was developed into a full-blown inquiry by the Home Secretary Winston Churchill, to be carried out by the Under-Secretary of State, C. F. G. Masterman.[38] Arguably, the report was a white-wash, although Radzinowicz and Hood suggest that Churchill was unhappy with the findings, 'The facts...disclose the existence of many serious irregularities. I cannot accept the Report of the Committee as dealing adequately with them' (1990: 201).[39] Despite the outcome of the inquiry, it did lead to a Departmental Committee into reformatory and industrial schools in 1913, which investigated the punishment practices used, and the welfare of the children.[40]

The Legacy of the Reformatory and Industrial Schools: From the Children's Act 1908 to the Children and Young Person's Act 1933

After the report of the 1913 Committee, the next watershed would be the 1933 Children and Young Person's Act, which would effectively call an end to the history of the Victorian Industrial and Reformatory School System. The 1913 committee, meeting shortly after the Akbar affair, focused on problems with administration, control and the public image of certified schools (Carlebach, 1970: 86–7). As a result the final two decades of the system were in many ways the most turbulent, underlined by a move towards the unification of the reformatory and industrial schools in the face of increasing accountability. Arguably it was also a more enlightened period. Certainly, there seems to have been a return to some of the ideals of the early years of the system. Victor Bailey saw a new liberalism in this period, obviously coinciding with the 1906 landslide, but also perhaps as part of the backlash after the Akbar Scandal (1987: 194–8). Undoubtedly in this period, reflecting the influence of the Children's Act, there was a new emphasis on the care and protection of children, as well as new prescriptions for adolescence (Childs, 1990; Springhall, 1986). This was reflected not only in the legislation to deal with delinquent children, but can also be seen in concerns about boy labour and street trading. Indeed, a separate Home Office branch was established to deal specifically with such issues (Carlebach, 1970: 88). It was also in this period that energetic practitioners like Alexander Paterson (later to be associated with Borstal) and Charles Russell emerged. Russell's appointment from 1913 as Chief Inspector of the Reformatory and Industrial Schools did much to shape new ideas about boy welfare and to revive the ailing Boys' Clubs, as well as to improve the reformatory and industrial schools (Russell, 1910; Paterson, 1911). The most liberal example of reform was embodied in the Little Commonwealth, a co-educational community set-up in Dorset and certified as a reformatory school by Russell in 1913. Established by an American called Homer Lane, the school represented a radical departure from the existing institutions:

> The chief point of difference between the Commonwealth and other reformatories and schools is that in the Commonwealth there are no rules and regulations except those made by the boys and girls themselves. All those who are fourteen years of age and over are citizens, having joint responsibility for the regulation of their lives by

the laws and judicial machinery organized and developed by themselves (Lane, 1928: 188–93).

The Little Commonwealth was closed down by Arthur Norris, who had succeeded Russell on his sudden death in 1917 (ostensibly the school was closed due to the impact of the war, however, there was a least a whiff of scandal around the female inmates (Wills, 1964: 20)). Despite the new Chief Inspector sharing Russell's beliefs in reform, the reformatory and industrial school system was increasingly caught between the conflicting ideas about adolescence and delinquency which were to characterise this period. By 1920, committals to the schools had greatly declined and the organ of the system, the *Certified Schools Gazette* was voicing the concerns of its members that they were increasingly under attack.[41] Moreover, that there was a deliberate policy by the Home Office to marginalise the schools.[42] Part of the problem was the new accountability. Hence the schools, which had strong traditions of autonomy, were increasingly open to inspection in the face of a barrage of criticism about methods and administration. The decline in committals to the schools was also explained by the wider use of probation, and the increasing expense of the schools (Bailey, 1987: 53). Moreover, there was something of a backlash against institutionalisation. Whereas the institutional experience had underpinned the Victorian system, and removed children from their families, in the 1920s attention was turned to the home-lives of children (Bailey, 1987: 51). Thus family-life and the home environment of children were increasingly seen as significant to the improvement of a child's character. Of course, this had to be the right sort of family life; indeed the Children's Act had enabled legislation which punished 'wayward' parents (Cox, 2003: 5–6). The conflict between bad home environment and institutional treatment were also highlighted by the controversial psychologist, Cyril Burt, who nevertheless recognised the role that residential training played (Burt, 1925: 195).

The discourses of the post-war period would eventually feed into the Departmental Committee on Young Offenders in 1925.[43] Whilst the Committee gave over much of its time to the discussion of the new Borstal experiment, it did recommend the merging of the reformatory and industrial schools, and their replacement with the Approved Schools (see Chapter 11). The Committee also supported a proposal for more short-term institutional training. Arthur Norris, the Chief Inspector of Certified Schools, recognised that many magistrates were unwilling to commit a child to a reformatory for three years, which they essentially saw as a penal experience (Bailey, 1987: 20). This proposal was supported by the Howard League for Penal Reform, who by this time had become an important voice in the debate about the schools. Ultimately, the Committee was accused of being over-cautious and it had remained undecided on many of the key proposals (Bailey, 1987: 65–6). Nevertheless, whilst the abolition of the distinction between the reformatory and industrial schools would not be fully formalised and codified until the 1933 Act, it was during this Committee that the groundwork was done. Perhaps more importantly, in acting as a vehicle to bring together the many voices, it achieved something very important. Thus it cemented the relationship between the various different pressure groups, reformers, magistrates, and practitioners. As Victor Bailey concludes, 'The strength of the alliance lay in a shared experience of voluntary social work amongst school-children and working-lads, in an interchange of personnel between the voluntary and official spheres of child welfare, and in a like-minded evaluation of the causes and correctives of juvenile delinquency. The way now seemed clear for a new Children Act, some twenty years after the initiatory statute of 1908' (1987: 66).

Notes

1 4 Geo. 4, c. 83. and 5 Geo. 4, c. 85.
2 *An Account of the Present State of the Philanthropic Society* (London, 1804).
3 *Report of the Committee for Investigating the Causes of the Alarming Increase of Juvenile Delinquency in the Metropolis* (Dove, London, 1816).
4 See *Select Committee on State of Police of the Metropolis. Report, Minutes of Evidence, Appendix*, 1816, PP, VI, 520–33.
5 *Ibid.*, evidence of James Bevan, 531.
6 *Ibid.*, 532.
7 *Select Committee on Secondary Punishments. Report, Minutes of Evidence, Appendix, Index*, 1831, PP, VII.519, 33.
8 *Parkhurst Prison Act* (1 & 2 Vict. c. 82).
9 NA: CO48/42, Cape of Good Hope Colony, Original Correspondence.
10 For example both British and Australian officials and philanthropists supported the Family Colonization Loan Society, founded by Mrs Caroline Chisholm in the 1840s, to help emigrate poor families to the colonies.
11 *The Times*, 5 April 1839.
12 The *Reports of the Children's Friend Society*, 1835–39 are held at the Gloucestershire Record Office, Gloucester.
13 For the evidence of Thomas Dexter see *Select Committee of House of Lords on Gaols and Houses of Correction in England and Wales. First Report; Second Report; Third Report; Fourth and Fifth Reports, Minutes of Evidence, Appendices*, PP, 1835, XI.1, 495, XII.1, 57, 323.
14 As McConville points out, the impact of Peel's Act was limited in scope since it included the county prisons but not the majority of prisons, gaols and bridewells in London.

15 *Select Committee on Secondary Punishments. Report, Minutes of Evidence, Appendix, Index*, 1831, PP, VII.519, 5.
16 *Select Committee on Transportation. Report, Minutes of Evidence, Appendix, Index*, 1837, PP, XIX.1, 48–9, 151.
17 *Coms. on State and Management of Parkhurst Prison. First Report from Inspectors of Prisons*, 1839, PP, XXII.645, 1.
18 The raft of legislation passed include the following: 1854: *Reformatory Schools Act*, 17 & 18 Vict. c. 74; *Reformation of Young Offenders Act* (17 & 18 Vict. c. 86), *Middlesex Industrial Schools Act* [Local] (17 & 18 Vict. c. 169); 1855, *Youthful Offenders Amendment Act* (18 & 19 Vict. c. 87); 1856: *Reformatory and Industrial Schools Amendment Act* (19 & 20 Vict. c. 109); 1857: *Industrial Schools Act* (20 & 21 Vict. c. 3); *Reformatory Schools Act* (20 & 21 Vict. c. 55).
19 *9th Report of the Inspector appointed under the provisions of the Act 5/6 Will. 4 c. 36 to Visit the Certified Reformatory and Industrial Schools of Great Britain*, PP, 3686, 305–464 (001–158).
20 *32nd Report for the Year 1888 of the Inspector appointed to visit the Certified Reformatory and Industrial Schools of Great Britain. Under the provisions of the Act 5 & 6 Will IV c. 38*, 1889, PP, XLII.1.
21 This was a requirement of the 1854 *Youthful Offenders (Reformatory Schools) Act*.
22 *An Act for amending and consolidating the Law relating to Industrial Schools*, 24 & 25 Vict. c. 113, s. 9.
23 29 & 30 Vict. c. 118; 25 & 26 Vict. c. 10.
24 29 & 30 Vict. c. 118.
25 *Ibid.*
26 54 & 55 Vict. c. 23.
27 57 & 58 Vict. c. 33.
28 *The Times*, 6 October 1876, 10, col. C.
29 *Inspector of Reformatory Schools of Great Britain, Thirty-first Report, 1888*, PP, [c. 5471), 78.
30 *Ibid.*
31 *The Times*, 4 October 1887, 7.
32 *Inspector of Reformatory Schools, 1888*, p. 78.
33 See NA, HO144/130/A34273B: 'Report of mutiny by boys on Training Ship "Clarence" in the Mersey', 1886; HO144/203/A47878, 'Mutiny on board Reformatory Ship "Akbar" at Liverpool. Judge's report of trial', 1887.
34 There had been previous attempts in November 1880 and January 1884.
35 *The Times*, 5 August 1899, 10.
36 *The Times*, 20 September 1899, 10.
37 NA, HO45/9841/B10830A: The Wellesley. Conduct of the Superintendent.
38 'Reformatory School Horrors – How Boys at Akbar School are Tortured – Several Deaths', *John Bull*, 22 October 1910 and 'Report of Inquiry by Mr. C. F. G. Masterman M.P., into Charges made Concerning the Management of the Heswall Nautical School', (Cd. 5541), PP, 1911, vol. 72.
39 From a memorandum dated 12 October 1910, in NA, HO45/10537/1454472/24, 'Inquiry at Heswall Nautical School'. Further discussion of the 'whitewashing' of the events can be found in the periodical, *The New Age*, 2 March 1911, 411–12.

40 *Report of the Departmental Committee on Reformatory and Industrial Schools,* 1913, PP, XXX1X.1.

41 *First Report Home Office Children's Branch,* HMSO, 1923, 17.

42 *Certified Schools Gazette,* v. 13/8, 1921, 94; v. 14/11, 1922, 299, 310; v. 15/4, 1923, 63.

43 *Report of the Departmental Committee on the Treatment of Young Offenders,* 1927, PP, XII. 959.

Part III

Confinement, Discipline and Resistance

9
Prisoner Memoirs and Their Role in Prison History

Sarah Anderson and John Pratt

The nature and scope of prison historiography has changed dramatically since the publication of Michel Foucault's (1977) *Discipline and Punish*. If, before, prison history was typically represented as one of penal progress, it has since reflected the mirror image of this: penal reform only led to the development of new modalities of social control (see, for example, Garland, 1985). While such revisionism has greatly enriched penological scholarship, it has also meant that prison historiography has tended to be more concerned with the imposition of penal power rather than resistances to it, with the abstract and the theoretical, rather than the lived experience of punishment. In relation to imprisonment, this has meant that prisoners themselves have seldom been given a voice. They are completely absent in Garland (1985) and while Ignatieff (1978: 1) asserted that he was concerned with prisoners' 'resistance', his work rarely demonstrated this. However, as we illustrate in this chapter, it was not the case that 'the model of the prison itself went virtually unchallenged' (Garland, 1985: 60) in the late nineteenth century. Instead, we argue that prisoner accounts played a significant role in contesting the legitimacy of the 'hard bed, hard fare, hard labour' regimes legislated for in the Prison Act 1865, and were instrumental in bringing about prison reform at the end of the nineteenth century, notwithstanding the way in which this also made possible the birth of 'the welfare sanction' (Garland, 1985).

The contested prison

The Prison Acts 1865 and 1877[1] passed the control of prison from local authorities to the central state, establishing a new penal bureaucracy, famously presided over by Sir Edmund Du Cane from 1877 to 1895. Prison regimes became increasingly uniform, calculated and measured.

Their carefully constructed standards and rules were designed to eliminate the arbitrariness and discretion that had previously been characteristic of local prisons (see Chapter 4), making them seem simultaneously too brutal and too lenient; and the supposed luxuries of the new 'palace prisons' that Pentonville – opened in 1842 and the model for much prison building thereafter – represented. Palace prisons, equipped with central heating and flush toilets, fresh air systems and regular meals, seemed to be rewarding criminality by providing their inmates with a substantially better quality of life than many free people experienced, complained a host of critics including Carlyle and Dickens.

It was to counter these concerns that the 'hard bed' regime was introduced. At the same time, the development of a centralised bureaucracy meant that the prison became largely impenetrable to outsiders. Whatever took place in prison would be screened physically and administratively from public view. Although commentators and critics initially had enjoyed largely unfettered access to prisons, the new insularity restricted knowledge and debate on prison life. Furthermore, voices from the prison establishment – doctors, governors and chaplains who previously had exposed the shortcomings of prison policy and had presented their own blueprints for reform – were now silenced, as their respective roles and status were redefined by central, as opposed to local regulations. As a consequence, the unified prison authority would be able to shape, define and communicate the reality of prison life in its increasingly anodyne annual reports.

However, new voices of opposition now emerged in the form of prisoner memoirs, often written anonymously, or with *nom de plumes* such as 'One who has endured it' (a businessman serving a sentence of five years' penal servitude for fraud).[2] At this juncture, convict prisons began to receive 'gentlemen' and political prisoners (see Priestley, 1985: 65–7). Many were well educated and articulate and at the same time dissatisfied with existing political and social arrangements, as well as being sensitive to their own treatment in prison. Furthermore, some, such as the Fenian Michael Davitt and Councillor Frederick Brocklehurst, had supporters beyond the prison ready to press their complaints and provide publicity about the reality of its conditions. As such, their accounts had the potential to provide 'an insurrection of knowledge' (Foucault, 1980: 81), which contested the legitimacy of the new prison regime. As Convict Number 77 argued:

Official programmes, however, do not always represent what actually occurs, and to get at the inner life of a prison one must consult some other authority. No better authority can be made than that of a fair-minded, clear headed ex-convict, who, having passed through the mill himself, is able to give a readable account of his experiences, and who has no interest in misrepresenting facts – whose business is to tell the 'truth, the whole truth, and nothing but the truth (1903: 69–70).

Some caveats must be raised about the use of these sources. We rely here on those of male prisoners because those written by women relate to a different set of prison realities at this time. Those who documented their experiences were usually wealthier and more literate prisoners. Furthermore, Chartists and Fenians had an interest in exploiting these. In addition, we rely solely on commercially published texts which are likely to have been edited and written from memory after the event.

Having said this, what would seem to lend the memoirs authenticity (aside from the fact that they are intermittently confirmed in the memoirs of some governors and guards), is the way in which their recurring themes effectively triangulate each other. Those from some of the key prisoner memoirs of this period, which now follow, relate to essential features of prison life in the aftermath of the 1860s legislation, the way in which these affected the physical and mental wellbeing of prisoners and their relationships with the prison authorities, particularly doctors.

Physical deterioration

(i) Cellular conditions

Austin Bidwell, sentenced to twenty years imprisonment for fraud in 1873, was struck with despair on first entering his cell:

[a] little box with a mixture of curiosity and consternation for the thought smote me with blinding force that for long years that little box – eight feet six inches in length, seven in height and five feet in width, with its floor and roof of stone – would be my only home – would be! must be! and no power could avert my fate (1895: 397).

Similarly, Brocklehurst described his experience of one month's solitary confinement, imposed for election irregularities:

Imagine a blind man denied human intercourse, with power of motion only in a space 14 feet by 7, whose only contact with a limited outside world comes through ceiling, walls and iron door, and you can form a faint idea of what life in prison must be. A prisoner sees nothing beyond the limits of his cell; feels only its discomforts; tastes the prescribed prison fare; hears the limited sounds of his strange environment; and smells little beyond the scent of the creosote as it exhales from the oakum (1898: 29).

Prisoners often remarked on the size of their cells, referring to their cramped conditions in which living space was at a premium (Lee, 1885: 11). According to Davitt, his cell at Millbank measured 'some nine or ten feet long, by about eight wide' (1886: 8). Convict Number 77 found his cell in Portland prison to be 'smaller than the third class compartment of a railway carriage' (1903: 12). In addition, they frequently referred to the poorly lit conditions within them. Some found little, if any, natural light entered their cells: 'daylight never entered, except through an aperture under the door' (*ibid.*: 21). In Dartmoor, 'One Who Has Endured It' recollected how any natural light that did enter the cells was diluted as it filtered through a 'narrow window of thick rough plate glass' (1877: 162). These conditions led to frequent headaches and eye problems (Convict Number 77, 1903: 22). In cells where artificial light was provided the control mechanism was located outside the cell doors, and, with no control over the brightness, discomfort was exacerbated.

The bed was the main item of furniture in the cell. As a result of the recommendations of the Carnarvon Committee 1863, plank beds and coarse mattresses replaced hammocks: 'during short sentences, or the early stages of a long confinement, the prisoners should be made to dispense with the use of a mattress, and should sleep on planks'.[3] The plank bed comprised of two boards 3 feet by 2½ which were supported by four legs of often uneven length, and when 'placed end to end they form[ed] a continuous slope' (Brocklehurst, 1898: 11). The pillow consisted of a board nailed to the head of the plank and a mattress of coarse sacking stuffed about half an inch thick with coconut fibre covering the boards (Rossa, 1872: 87). Prisoners not only experienced sleepless nights as a result but, in addition, they referred to bedclothes having 'a foetid greasy scum' that lingered on the prisoner's body after contact and of 'bedclothes soiled with human soil' (One Who Has Suffered, 1882: 583).

Other furnishings were minimal. McCook Weir (a medical doctor before a prison sentence for fraud) found meagre items for ablutions: 'a coarse towel which hangs on a nail or hook, on the door, and a piece of soap, which rests on a few little squares of soft brown paper' (1885: 59). Some cells, particularly those constructed for separate confinement, contained their own lavatories. In Newgate prison, such facilities consisted of 'a water closet seat in a corner' and 'a bright copper wash basin, burnished like gold, fastened to the wall, with a tap over it' (One Who Has Endured It, 1877: 9). However, these arrangements proved to be a mixed blessing. Prisoners who occupied such cells described the insanitary and ill-maintained conditions of the bathroom fixture: 'the flushing was contemptible and was carried on through the discharge pipe of the wash handbasin in proximity thereto' (McCook Weir, 1885: 139). If cells were not furnished with self-contained lavatories, prisoners had to use buckets as a substitute. The resulting smell of communal sewage sickened them. The stench often intensified because the buckets were not emptied immediately, and sometimes only on alternate days. Davitt, when in Dartmoor, explains how the irregularity of bodily functions often meant enduring periods when excreta was left in cells:

> [I]f a prisoner has a call of nature between eight at night and five in the morning, he is compelled to use a utensil in his cell, and leave it there all night, as prisoners are not allowed out of their cells for any purpose during those hours (1886: 16).

Although the hygiene practices of the palace prisons continued to be lauded by prison officials (see Griffiths, 1904: 240), prisoner memoirs emphasised how stench and stagnant air were the result of the architecture itself. Stale air was trapped in the upper tiers, explained Davitt, because there were no perforations to allow polluted air to escape and clean air to enter:

> The sole provision made for ventilating these cells is an opening of two and a half or three inches left at the bottom of each door. There is no opening into the external air from any of those cells in Dartmoor, and the air admitted into the hall has to traverse the width of the same to enter the hole under the cell doors (1886: 15).

Such conditions were heightened during the summer season when he was forced to lie on the floor of his cell to breathe fresher air from the space between the floor and the bottom of his cell door. In winter, however, the cold became unbearable. For Fenian prisoner Jeremiah Rossa, this often meant 'hours of uneasy slumber, you awoke to shiver and shake, with the prospect of hours more of that before the time came to rise and get back your clothes' (1872: 88). He describes the only too familiar experience of 'the horrible sensation of cold in the morning in those cheerless Pentonville cells' (*ibid.*: 86). Despite a transfer from Pentonville to Millbank, his physical suffering from the cold intensified rather than abated:

> If a man ever felt cold, I felt it those nights. It was about the end of March, and I had no bed or bed clothing but a light rug. I was not allowed to walk about the cell, had to remain prone with this rug around me. When I looked out through the hole in the wall next morning, the rooftops were covered with snow...That cell had no window, but there was a hole about two feet long and three inches wide to admit a little light, and, as my bed-board was under the hole, the snow had drifted in on me all night (*ibid.*: 155).

(ii) Prison diet

The *Report of the Committee on the Dietaries of County and Borough Prisons*, in 1864, stipulated that the prison diet was to be calculated with precision, devoid of any elements which might warrant accusations of 'luxurious living' and set at a level just beyond the minimum limit at which 'loss of health and strength' might result.[4] Nonetheless, the diet became a major source of discontent: 'for the first week I existed on seven pounds of brown-to-black bread and ten and a half pints of "stirabout"[5]. Nothing else, *absolutely nothing!*' (Brocklehurst, 1898: 119, original italics). Others found it impossible to discern any taste in the gruel, especially when no ingredients, not even 'a morsel of sugar', were added to enhance or mask its bland flavour (Dawson, 1887: 81). It was not attractive to any palate when it had 'the consistency of "stickphast" paste' (Brocklehurst, 1898: 119). Lord William Nevill (serving a five year sentence for fraud) described prison food as having 'nothing but sameness, tastelessness, and too often repulsiveness in everything [we] have had to eat for years' (1903: 49). Bidwell insisted he was in a state of perpetual hunger, and that there was 'no vile refuse we would not devour if the chance presented itself' (1895: 184). Potatoes, one of the dietary staples, 'usually consisted of two, or occasionally three, shabby-looking tubers, the dirt still adhering to them, and soft and spongy to the taste' (McCook Weir, 1885: 93). Nevill claimed that for five weeks in a row 'they gave us rotten potatoes' (1903: 116) and embezzler Jabez Balfour (1901: 265) believed that at least half of the potatoes served were inedible.

Prisoners also protested about the lack of vegetables: 'only once in nineteen years' did John Lee (1885: 76), famous as 'the man they could not hang' after three failed attempts at execution, taste them. As a result, they experienced insatiable cravings, as Nevill observed:

> Large quantities of excellent vegetables are grown at Parkhurst, but the prisoners are forbidden to eat the smallest morsel, though their craving for green food is such that I have constantly seen men eat all sorts of green weeds, and if they can secretly get hold of a carrot or onion, they ram it into their mouth, tops, dirt and all (1903: 115).

For many, the hunger led to desperation:

> [F]or years this feeling of hunger never left me, and I could have eaten rats and mice if they had come my way, but there wasn't a spare crumb in any of those cells to induce a rat or a mouse to visit it. I used to creep on my hands and knees from corner to corner of my cell sometimes to see if I could find the smallest crumb that might have fallen when I was eating my previous meal. When I had salt in my cell I would eat that to help me drink water to fill my stomach (Rossa, 1872: 94).

Their hunger became so acute that they would eat almost anything. 'To find black beetles in soup, "skilly", bread, and tea, was quite a common occurrence,' according to Davitt:

> and some idea can be formed how hunger will reconcile a man to look without disgust upon the most filthy objects in nature, when I state as a fact that I have often discovered beetles in my food, and have eaten it after throwing them aside, without experiencing much revulsion of feeling at the sight of such loathsome animals in my victuals (1886: 17).

Rossa, though, had no qualms about eating some of these creatures:

> [I]f when eating my eight ounces of bread I found a beetle or a ciarogue between my teeth, instead of spitting out in disgust what I was chewing, I would chew away with the instinctive knowledge that nature had provided for the carrying away of anything that was

foul and the retaining of what was nutritious from what I swallowed (1872: 95).

Desperate convicts ate 'railway grease' and 'brown paper mingled with ravellings from a hole in the dirty sheet' (One Who Has Suffered, 1882: 18). They ate the paper 'issued weekly from the stores for sanitary purposes' ('No. 7', 1903: 171). Davitt even saw 'bits of candles pulled out of the prison cesspool and eaten, after the human soil was wiped off them!' (1886: 18). At Portland, 'Ticket of Leave Man' ('a gentleman with the reputation of an honourable man' serving seven years' penal servitude for violent offences) came across 'half a dozen men who fed themselves daily upon snails, slugs, and frogs, and they did this not only without any interference on the part of the officer in charge, but to his evident amusement' (1879: 225). In addition, 'it was considered by a certain class of prisoners quite a privilege to be attached to the "cart party", on account of the refuse, food and poultices which could be fished out of the infirmary ashes' (*ibid.*: 226).

Although dietary reforms in 1878 reinstated a quantity of meat (usually bacon) to the prison dietary, this did little to alleviate prisoner anguish: 'now what is the good of three-quarters of an ounce of bacon; let anyone weigh that quantity out and see how much it represents' (One Who Has Tried Them, 1881: I, 154). And 'searching for the bacon among the beans is like looking for a needle in a bundle of hay. And when it is found, it is not a tempting morsel. It is very fat bacon, suitable for greasing engine wheels' (Nicholl, 1897: 5). The whole dish was 'a gruesome and nauseating mixture – apt to cause illness' (Pentonville from Within, 1902: 134).

Inevitably, weight loss ensued. Rossa wrote that 'I had lost eight pounds since I had come to London, but others had fared worse. Cornelius, Kane, Michael O'Regan and a few more had lost as many as thirty pounds' (1872: 108). Brocklehurst 'rapidly lost flesh' (1898: 122); Balfour 'lost two stones in weight' (1901: 75); 'Ticket of Leave Man', 'went down from twelve stone to nine' (1879: 80). On release, Davitt noted that his height had reduced from 'six feet to five feet ten and a half inches and [he] weigh[ed] between eight stone ten and nine stone four pounds' (1886: 22–3).

Chronic ill health was likely to ensue. Balfour suffered from 'a severe and constant form of indigestion' (1901: 265). Nevill observed an 'enormous number of prisoners who were admitted to the infirmary suffering from indigestion in various forms – spots, boils, rashes, and other skin disease' (1903: 114). This would be followed by a dramatic physical deterioration, as 'One who has suffered' described: 'when, by and by, he can eat the unpalatable mess provided, he acquires chronic digestion, dimness of eyesight, *tinnitus aurum*, roarings in the head, gastric spasms, shortness of breath, sickly giddiness and absence of staying power generally' (1882: 48). Bidwell similarly described how his fellow Chatham convicts suffered from 'hunger and torment of mind. The first part visibly affected was the neck. The flesh shrinks, disappears and leaves what look like two artificial props to support the head' (1895: 209). Brocklehurst remembered how a prisoner entered the prison 'sunburnt and healthy' but after only a few days confinement 'this splendid specimen of humanity was crawling round the exercise-yard, with head bent, and with feet scarcely lifting from the ground' (1895: 122).

Overall, the dietary arrangements and cellular conditions led to ruined lives. Far from producing resolute citizens determined never to go back to prison on release, the diet only produced legions of incapable, inadequate beings, likely to return to prison because they had been stripped of the willpower and physical resources to do anything but this.

Mental illness

The memoirs also reveal extensive mental torment, anguish and impairment. While in Millbank, Davitt relates how imprisonment caused a number of his companions to suffer from mental illness: 'Richard Burke and Martin Hanley Carey were for a time oblivious of their sufferings from temporary insanity, and...it was here where Thomas Ahearn first showed symptoms of madness, and was put in dark cells and straitjacket for a 'test' to the reality of these symptoms' (1886: 11).

After ten years' imprisonment and still a prisoner, he noted that Ahearn's 'mind is still tottering on the brink of insanity' (idem). Like many other prisoners, Lee found the period of solitary confinement at the start of a penal servitude sentence the worst, driving him to the point of insanity:

> I can think of nothing more calculated to drive a prisoner mad than eight months of solitude with nothing to think of but his own miseries, with no companion save despair (1885: 53).

After three weeks of a seven week confinement in Wormwood Scrubs, Nevill 'got into such a state of nervous irritation that one day, if the priest had not come to pay me a visit at the critical moment, I firmly believe I should have given way to that violent impulse which often overcomes prisoners, and have destroyed the things in my cell' (1903: 26).

'Pentonville from Within' remarked on the silence of confinement, the absence of any human voice, broken only by the crashing of cell doors and the 'frantic and furious cries' of those who were being flogged (1902: 167). The silence would also be periodically interrupted by agonised howls of torment from prisoners who had succumbed to a breakdown:

> [O]ne morning I heard a sound which thrilled every fibre and chilled me to the bone. An awful shriek rent the silent atmosphere, a shriek followed by a howl as from a soul in mortal terror (Brocklehurst, 1898: 25).

And:

> [S]uddenly [in chapel] a wild heart-bursting cry rang out above the voices of the singers from a convict of some forty five years of age...he rushed towards the altar with piercing shrieks while his eyes and face proclaimed the sudden loss of reason and presence of madness (Davitt, 1886, vol. 1: 173).

Serving a life sentence for a one million pound fraud against the Bank of England, George Bidwell's thoughts would 'surge tumultuously as some picture of the happy past flashed across the mental vision plunged the writhing soul into an agony of remorse' (1895: 504). The long vista that tormented Balfour was almost intolerable:

> [W]hen I looked up at that appalling wall of 3,833 days, it seems that I should never surmount it...I had not sufficient mastery of my thoughts at that time to keep my mind from the interminable reflections that haunt a ruined man. My fear was that I should be overtaken by madness (1901: 48).

For some, it was as if they were experiencing a living death:

> I did not know that the living death I was about to endure was more terrible than anything the grave can inflict. I did not realise what it would be to mount slowly up through all those years, bearing

on my shoulders a weary burden of heart-ache and shame (Lee, 1985: 49).

Similarly, Brocklehurst felt that total exclusion from the outside meant that the prisoner 'is shut out from converse with the world, and is for all practical purposes a dead man in a dead universe' (1898: 21–2). The very prison rules that had been designed to bring about certainty and uniformity, to restrict discretion and prevent indiscriminate brutalities only added to the mental torment. 'Convict Number 77' complained of the monotony that these had imposed:

> they are the same yesterday, today and forever...the human element has no place in these establishments...feelings, temperament, affection have no place in the lifeless code of rules and regulations...the bowels of compassion [are shut up] (1903: 57, 71, 73–4).

Prisoners developed a range of strategies to try and ward off insanity. Some sought to obliterate the past as they tried to come to terms with a long sentence: 'the thoughts that troubled me during the day, I tried to count out of my head by counting the stitches I put into the clothes I was making' (Rossa, 1872: 119). George Bidwell did likewise: 'I adopted the device of counting,' he says, 'and this I found necessary to do every waking moment when I could not see to study' (1895: 405). 'One Who Has Tried Them', 'suffered to such an intense degree' with a 'craving to shout out aloud' that he was obliged to force his handkerchief into his mouth to prevent himself from 'yielding to temptation' (1881, vol.1: 218). A different form of physical activity, a recognised response to captivity, was perceived by Brocklehurst in the 'tramp of numberless feet, as my companions moved to and fro in their narrow compass. Tramp, tramp, tramp they went for hours, speaking of a vacuity of mind, and wretchedness of spirit in tones more eloquent than words' (1898: 31).

The cumulative effects of imprisonment under these conditions were summarised by Convict Number 77:

> It is simply impossible for an ordinary mind to survive the experiences of thirty years of English prison life. I have known many who have served that time in prison, but their mental faculties were more or less affected (1903: 172–3).

Prisoner/doctor relations

The 1865 Prison Act stipulated that an infirmary was to be established in every prison and medical officers would visit prisoners at least once a week. The 1877 Prison Act then gave these doctors the power to pass prisoners fit for hard labour or not, as well as issue additional items of diet, admit inmates to the prison hospital and pronounce them fit or unfit to withstand the imposition of dietary or corporal punishment. However, a daily routine which involved distinguishing the undeserving from deserving cases meant that the doctors themselves became imbued with suspicion. Their professional task changed from dispensing medicine to checking for malingerers, notwithstanding the endemic physical and mental suffering in the prison. After consulting the doctor at Dartmoor about a sore throat, Davitt was told that 'there was a little inflammation, but nothing serious, and he ordered me to be reported for falling out without sufficient reason' (1886: 83). Lee complained of chest pains and 'saw the doctor, but he refused to give me anything. He even wanted to report me' (1885: 69). Balfour observed that prison doctors were 'a peculiarly suspicious race' (1901: 76).

Medical staff might deliberately inflict pain to test the genuineness of prisoners claiming to be paralysed or seeking certification as insane by 'putting on the barmy stick' (Davitt, 1886: 142). Some prisoners complained that their medical treatment was administered according to institutional rules and procedures rather than their needs as patients: 'there were several prisoners desirous of seeing the doctor at the same time as I, and in order to prevent us from "communicating" with each other, we were placed about two yards apart, with our faces turned to the wall' (Brocklehurst 1898: 130). Some felt such helplessness and despair at the attitude of the medical staff that they wagered their permanent health and, in extreme cases, their lives, against the chance of temporary relief by exacerbating their ailments–making them acute rather than simply chronic. It was 'by no means an uncommon practice for men to make a wound in one of their limbs, and scratch it to keep it open until a really bad sore comes, or else tie a string tightly round a limb so as to produce inflammation' (Nevill, 1903: 91).

Generally, the prisoners found medical treatment a dehumanising experience when they assembled for 'sick parade' amongst those who simply queued in search of extra food, others who were 'anxious to be taken off the tread-wheel or hard labour' (A Manchester Merchant, 1880: 36), others still who looked for 'an opportunity of conversing with their "chums"' (*ibid.*: 37) and some who would 'do anything, take anything, or go anywhere for variety' (Ticket of Leave Man, 1879: 81). After deferring a visit to the doctor, and in deteriorating health, Brocklehurst could no longer wait and by 'the end of the third week, tired, feeble, and thin, with throat tickling and burning with fever, with lungs painful and cough troublesome, with my sides incessantly aching, in the day too tired to sit up, and in the night too wearied to sleep, I once more asked for an interview with the doctor. This time I was introduced as "Mr Fussy"' (1898: 130). Much to his disappointment and indignity, he found the doctor was 'excessively rude to me... I might have been a dog, so imperatively and abruptly did he call me to him. He addressed me with a 'Come here'; 'Stand there' (*ibid.*: 131). Balfour reported that, during his medical examination at Parkhurst in 1896, the doctor 'punched and probed me to his heart's content. He seemed truly content that he could find nothing the matter with me' (1901: 62). He returned to his cell feeling that he 'had been turned inside out from top to toe: feet; feet, brains, and soul had been investigated' (*ibid.*: 63). Some, however, made allegations of professional incompetence in regard to both their own and others' treatment. After John Hay had been on the treadwheel for a week he 'petitioned the Governor', complaining that he was 'suffering from sciatica': 'the Doctor ordered me to strip, and, having made me get on the scales, said that I was four pounds heavier than when I entered the prison. I don't know how this showed that I wasn't suffering from sciatica' (1894: 32). 'A Merchant', spending two years in the hospital ward of Surrey Prison due to a disease in his knee which resulted in the amputation of his leg, described weeks of suffering with no improvement and complained of an 'apparent sourness, indifference to, and sometimes cruel neglect, if not positive aggravation of suffering' among the staff. His knee became so sensitive that anyone passing near his bed caused excessive pain. It was finally removed by having 'the flesh cut, and the bone sawn through at the thickest part of the thigh' (1869: 50–2).

In such ways it was as if the doctors deliberately reinforced the prisoners' sense of helplessness:

> This policy of mystery and surprise begets among the high officials – governors and doctors alike – a habit of reserve, duplicity and mental reservation, which it would be very difficult to discriminate among other honourable men from downright lying. It leads prisoners 'to mistrust the veracity of the men' (*ibid.*: 55).

Responses of the prison authorities

Prison officials were compelled to respond to this documentary evidence of excessive severity in a series of investigatory formal inquiries that were convened between 1867 and 1879. They were not allowed to ignore the complaints or simply brush them aside. At this juncture in prison history, prisoners – particularly the gentlemen and the politicals – were not the manifest outsiders, to be dismissed out of hand, that they have since become. At the same time, the prison authorities were not yet sufficiently embedded as an institutional structure of modern society to be seen as above any such criticisms. As a result, the various Commissions of Inquiry documented both the formal accounts of the authorities and the prisoners' own experiences of prison life. A select few prisoners were given the opportunity to present their version of penal events to a number of them and, in most cases, this was duly recorded in the Minutes of Evidence.[6] As well as this, various prison officials, including Du Cane himself, were questioned about the contents of *Five Years in Penal Servitude* by 'One Who Has Endured It' (1877) and *Irish Rebels in English Prisons* by Rossa (1872).[7] Nonetheless, the responses of the Commissions invariably upheld the prison authorities by invoking strategies of:

(i) Denial and refutation

After complaints from Irish political prisoners about ill treatment and inhumane conditions, the Commission of Inquiry concluded that:

> A convict's bread is bitter food at best...the terrible monotony of the life; the stern order, and the instant obedience, constitute a very terrible punishment. [However,] we know that these men have a better diet, sleep in better beds, are more cared for in sickness, have lighter labour that the bulk of the labouring classes ...*and that the stories of their ill-treatment are simple falsehoods.*[8]

(ii) Self-validation

The same report affirmed that prison conditions in which the Irish prisoners were held were 'a perfect model of order, cleanliness and propriety', claiming that it would not be possible for the prison to be 'more perfect in all its arrangements'.[9] Similarly, the *Report of the Commissioners on the Treatment of Treason-Felony Convicts in English Prisons* found that 'from the physical appearance of the convicts, as well as from...their general healthiness, we see no reason to doubt the sufficiency of the existing dietary in quantity'.[10]

(iii) Discreditation

While being prepared to hear complaints from prisoners, the Commissions then tended to invalidate them by painting them as troublemakers or 'precious'. The Kimberley Commission acknowledged that:

> It has been stated in evidence that some prisoners eat candles, but we believe this to arise from a desire to eat more fat than the dietary affords, and not from any deficiency in the quantity or quality of the diet...A few convicts were also mentioned as having eaten refuse of various kinds and of disgusting quality whenever they had the opportunity. Similar cases of depraved voracity are sometimes met with among persons other than prisoners, and notably among persons of weak mind.[11]

(iv) Concessions

The *Report of the Commissioners on the Treatment of Treason-Felony Convicts in English Prisons* did concede minor points to prisoners and recommended minor adjustments to lessen the severity of imprisonment. It acknowledged, for example, that 'the tea supplied to certain classes of the prisoners attracted our attention; it appeared to us to be of inferior character, owing to its being kept in the cauldron before use'.[12] And in one instance the Commission detected 'portions of meat unfit for human use in the supply sent in for the infirmary...when three pieces of mutton of greenish colour in parts and of a very bad smell were pointed out'.[13]

After 'One Who Has Endured It' argued that first time offenders like himself were reputable persons who had been temporarily led astray and should be isolated and treated differently from deliberate and professional career criminals,[14] the Commissioners were prepared to endorse the differential treatment of prisoners who did not fit the image of 'real' (professional, repeat offenders) criminals and to decrease the length of imprisonment for juvenile and first time offenders.

(v) Reassertion

However, the Commission would not consider any changes to the principles and administration of deterrent punishment. It rejected suggestions to lower the minimum sentence for penal servitude, fearing that such a change would weaken 'wholesome dread' this invoked in the public mind.[15] There was no need to change this sentence or its administration:

> After examining a variety of witnesses, we have come to the conclusion that the system of penal servitude at present administered is, on the whole, satisfactory: that it is effective as a punishment, and free from serious abuses.[16]

The prison machine breaks down

An inevitable consequence of these responses was that the prison authorities were legitimated, notwithstanding all the complaints and documentary evidence that the prisoners had produced against them. However, the prisoners *had* forced at least some concessions. Nor were the inquiries sufficient to put an end to the criticisms which continued to discredit everything that the prison authorities claimed to be doing. The series of prisoner memoirs that continued for the rest of the nineteenth century (particularly 'One who has suffered', 1882; Davitt, 1886; Bidwell, 1895; Balfour, 1901) continued to prise open the prison door for public scrutiny and questioning. In addition, during the 1880s, there were reports of suspicious deaths in custody and suicides. Ex-prisoners began public campaigns for prison reform, further publicising the memoirs as evidence of the harshness of prison conditions. Two of them – Michael Davitt and John Burns (a trade union activist who had been imprisoned for unlawful assembly) – became MPs and were then able to establish a broader platform for prison reform (McConville, 1995).

By the early 1890s, the now well established criticisms had provided a platform for the Howard Association, philanthropists and sections of the press to campaign for reform, a central theme being that the methods of centralisation and militarism had produced an inflexible, machine-like system. A series of critical articles in the popular press, particularly *The Daily Chronicle* and written anonymously by prison chaplain W. D. Morrison, gave particular attention to the deleterious effects of imprisonment. The autocracy and secrecy of the central prison administration was 'a thoroughly pernicious bureaucracy' that ran a 'cumbrous, pitiless, obsolete, unchanged' system with prisons 'as clean as the deck of an ironclad' but characterised by 'the gloom, the monotony, the nervous strain of a prisoner's life'.[17] Subsequent articles written by Morrison in *The Nineteenth Century* and *The Fortnightly Review* criticised Du Cane's prison system as 'dictatorial', 'rigid', and 'machine like'.[18] This growing public criticism led to the appointment of a further Departmental Committee of Inquiry chaired by Sir Herbert Gladstone. This was to consider not simply the new series of allegations but, in addition, the principles and practices of the whole penal field.

Unlike its predecessors, the subsequent *Report of the Departmental Committee on Prisons* (1895) now acknowledged that prison had become too much of an uncaring, unyielding machine.[19] Six weeks after its publication, Oscar Wilde was imprisoned. It seems clear from the reaction of the prison authorities to his circumstances that they were worried that further scandal might emanate from this. Almost certainly as a consequence, exceptional concessions were extended to Wilde, otherwise his experiences might have provided further public confirmation and validation of decades of prisoner complaints. Indeed, in the early stages of his imprisonment, his health was reported to be suffering and that he was showing signs of insanity.[20] The Home Office duly responded by sending R. B. Haldane, a lawyer, to visit (Ellmann, 1988: 485). Afterwards, he received the first of many concessions, a selection of books (Haldane, 1929: 166–7).

Nonetheless, his health continued to deteriorate, and after he was moved to Wandsworth Prison Infirmary, the Home Office sent two medical specialists to examine him. While finding him distressed by his situation, they pronounced both his physical and mental health to be in a fit state (Radzinowicz and Hood, 1990: 589). Nevertheless, they recommended his transfer to Reading where he was employed for about three hours a day in the garden and given further reading material. As a result, his health began to improve. He was given permission to write and composed his famous letter to Lord Alfred Douglas, *De Profundis*, (Wilde, 1897) where he referred for the first time to his intention to engage in prison reform. On his release, *The Ballad of Reading Gaol* (Wilde, 1898a) was published to generally favourable reviews (although Wilde authored it with his Reading prison number, C.3.3). This was followed by letters in his own name to *The Daily Chronicle*, where he demanded that various reforms of 'our present stupid and barbarous system' be made. His own experience of prison had been:

[A] fiendish nightmare more horrible that anything I had ever dreamed of...when they made me undress before them and get into some filthy water they called a bath and dry myself with a damp brown rag and put on this livery of shame. The cell was appalling:

I could hardly breathe in it, and the food turned my stomach: the smell of it was enough: I did not eat anything for days and days, I could not even swallow the bread and the rest was uneatable; I lay on the so-called bed and shivered all night long...After some days I got so hungry I had to eat a little, nibble at the outside of the bread, and drink some of the liquid; whether it was tea, coffee, or gruel, I could not tell...it produced violent diarrhoea and I was ill all day and all night. From the beginning I could not sleep, I grew weak and had wild delusions...The hunger made you weak but the inhumanity was the worst of it...I had never dreamt of such cruelties (1898b: 190–6).

It was now as if the machinery that had been meticulously constructed and presided over by Du Cane (who had reluctantly retired in 1895) was beginning to break down. The Gladstone Committee had recognised, and Wilde had been able to reaffirm, that although the line of reasoning prescribed in the Prison Acts of 1865 and 1877 had turned prisons into efficient bureaucratic institutions that prevented arbitrariness, these laws at the same time had led to a robotic imposition of unyielding suffering and deprivation, characteristic of the workings of a remorseless punishing machine.

The remainder of this episode in English prison history is well known. The first of a series of reforms to prison conditions was made in 1901. The penal servitude diet changed from 'stirabout' to porridge for breakfast and variations of bread and potatoes and bread and suet pudding for dinner (Pratt 2002: 70). This was followed by improvements to clothing, arrangements for personal hygiene and general cellular conditions. Subsequent legislation was designed to keep large sections of the criminal classes out of prison in new penal arrangements such as probation, so utterly fearsome had the understandings of prison become in the *weltanschauung* of British society. If this marked the beginnings of the welfare sanction and a new modality of social control, the fact that so many criminals began to be spared the privations of the prison experience is due to a great extent to the impact made by prisoners' memoirs and their accounts of the reality of prison life:

An English prison is a vast machine in which a man counts for just nothing at all. He is to the establishment what a bale of merchandise is to a merchant's warehouse. The prison does not look on him as a man at all. He is merely an object which must move in a certain rut and occupy a certain niche provided for it. There is no room for the smallest sentiment. The vast machine of which he is an item keeps undisturbed on its course. Move with it and all is well. Resist, and you will be crushed as inevitably as the man who plants himself on the railway track when the express is coming. Without passion, without prejudice, but also without pity and without remorse, the machine crushes and passes on. The dead man is carried to his grave and in ten minutes is as much forgotten as though he never existed (Bidwell, 1895: 459–60).

Notes

1 28 & 29 Vict. c. 126; 40 & 41 Vict. c. 21.
2 The term 'prisoner memoirs' is used here to describe the specific auto-biographical observations and experiences of life in prison, recorded by prisoners or ex-prisoners. This phrase is used instead of 'prisoner auto-biography' as the works analysed here focus specifically on the subject's life in prison, rather than on presenting a more general story of the subject's life history or autobiography. To maintain focus on the prisoners' voices, the term 'prison biography' (Priestley, 1985) has not been used, as this is a more general category which also includes the autobiographical accounts and reminiscences of various prison officials.
3 *Report from the Select Committee of the House of Lords on the Present State of Discipline in Gaols and Houses of Correction* [Carnarvon Committee], 1863, PP, IX (499), xi.
4 *Report of the Committee on the Dietaries of County and Borough Prisons*, 1864, PP, XLIX (556), 27.
5 '"Stirabout" consisted of one and half pint servings, consisting of 3 ounces of Indian meal [a bland concoction consisting of half a pint of skimmed milk to every 5 ounces of meal (ground down corn on the cob)], three of oatmeal and the rest water' (Pratt, 1999: 294).
6 *Report of the Commission of Inquiry into the Treatment of certain Treason-Felony Convicts in English Convict Prisons*, 1867, PP, XXX [hereafter TTFC, 1867]; *Report of the Commission of Inquiry into the Treatment of Treason-Felony Convicts in the English Convict Prison*, Minutes of Evidence, 1871, PP, XXXII [hereafter TTFC, 1871]; *Report of the Commissioners Appointed to Inquire into the Working of the Penal Servitude Acts*, [Kimberley Commission], Minutes of Evidence, 1879, PP, 1878–9, XXXVII and XXXXI (1).
7 Kimberley Commission, Minutes of Evidence, 1879.
8 TTFC, 1867, 23, our italics.
9 *Ibid.*, 8.
10 TTFC, 1871, 8.
11 Kimberley Commission, 1879, 38.
12 TTFC, 1871, 8.
13 *Ibid.*, 13.
14 Kimberley Commission, 1879: 29.
15 *Ibid.*, 29.
16 *Ibid.*, 21.

17 *The Daily Chronicle*, 25 January 1894: 5b.
18 *The Nineteenth Century*, 1892: 950–62 and *The Fortnightly Review*, April, 1894: 459–69; 1898: 781–96.
19 *Report of the Departmental Committee on Prisons* [Gladstone Committee], 1895, PP, LVI, (C.7702).
20 *The Daily Chronicle*, 5 June 1895; *The Pall Mall Gazette*, 5 June 1895: 4.

10
Challenging Discipline and Control: A Comparative Analysis of Prison Riots at Chatham (1861) and Dartmoor (1932)

Alyson Brown

Criminologists have analysed the English criminal justice system of the post-war era, but the lack of work on this aspect of the twentieth century pre-1945 leaves an important gap in our knowledge (Emsley, 1996: 78; Emsley, 2005a: 117–38; Davies, 2007: 405). Historians, and indeed criminologists, neglect of the inter-war period is particularly evident. Certainly research into prison disturbances and penal policy, the focus of this chapter, remains largely the domain of criminologists studying post-war events. Taking two of the largest English prison riots of modern times, this paper challenges the notion that exceptional events in prison history tell us little about the every-day working of these institutions. As Sykes pointed out in his early sociological examination of prison life in 1950s America, power 'unexercised is seldom as visible as power that is challenged' (1958: 53). Thus exceptional events can exert pressure and test or expose mechanisms which underpin the everyday working of prisons. In addition, this chapter questions Adams' idea that such complex phenomena as prison riots can be seen as 'simple' (1994: 41–2). Indeed Adams' (1994: 7) own conclusion on prison riots that occurred before the 1950s does not match his observation that such riots are a 'contested concept' and a controversial field of debate.

Official and public discourses in the wake of these riots at Chatham Convict Prison in 1861 and Dartmoor Convict Prison in 1932 operated to construct and utilise an image of a core of hardened convicts who were irredeemable and at war with society. This undermined a narrative in which inmates could have legitimate grievances or justifiable reasons for their disorder. The prisoner lost his voice, one of the 'suspended rights' imposed by modern punishment (Foucault, 1977: 11). These riots were a dramatic and very public signal that contemporary prison systems were far from achieving the acceptance and consent of those subject to them. We need to examine therefore the way in which consideration of any legitimate grievances or protests by prisoners was subsumed beneath efforts to allay public concern, downplay the significance of prison riots, and to protect administrations.

In the period between the two riots examined here, there was a change in the way disciplinary problems were considered and framed. Garland (1985: 60) has identified an increasing focus upon flaws in the prison institution itself rather than in the nature of its administration. One aspect of this shift may be attributed to the cultural importance of idealism from the late nineteenth century and its impact upon the work of social reformers. Idealism highlighted the role of ethical and moral individualism in constituting and shaping society. This embodied an organic vision of society in which individual mutual obligation was a vital component. Idealism has been credited with influencing, for example, the Settlement Movement and approaches to early social work, both of which impressed Alexander Paterson in his early life at Oxford University and through his social work in Bermondsey (Offer, 2006: 3, 96). In his later position as a Prison Commissioner (1922–1946), Paterson placed faith in the power and moral authority of the state as well as voluntary organisations to construct carceral contexts enabling prisoners to reconceptualise and develop themselves and their social participation. The extent to which this was achieved is debatable but it is evident in the discourse on the prison at this time.

Both of the riots considered in detail here occurred in convict prisons and therefore held inmates serving longer prison sentences. In terms of numbers involved, damage caused and public attention generated, these riots were the most serious disturbances between 1860 and the 1930s. According to, Philip Priestley 'nothing like the scale of violence [in Dartmoor in 1932] had been known in an English prison since the upheaval at Chatham convict station in 1861' (1989: 180). Precisely because such large-scale prison riots have been uncommon in England, and because of the considerable media attention generated in response, there is more evidence on these flashpoints than for other kinds of disorder. These two 'mutinies' exposed prison administrations to considerable external scrutiny and criticism. They reflected, defined and questioned penal reform in two important eras and focused opinion on the criminal, specifically the recidivist or habitual criminal. Of course, the definition of what was described as 'reform' meant different things to different people and broadly referred to change that was perceived to be positive, at least to those who had been influential in policy decisions and/or practice. However, the rate of progress was disputed, even by 1939, Mannheim felt able to observe that 'so far we have done little more than sweep away crudities and barbarities' (1939: 8).

In purely legal terms a riot required the active participation of not less than three persons and to have resulted in the alarm of at least one person so that it could be interpreted as disturbing the public peace. Of course, this opens up the researcher to having to consider possibly thousands of prison incidents large and small. Official reluctance to use the word 'riot' exacerbates the problem; even the two large-scale events considered here were often referred to as mutinies, disturbances or outbreaks rather than riots. Indeed, the returns collated following the riot in Chatham Convict Prison in 1861 referred in its title to the 'recent disturbances' and the du Parcq inquiry into the causes of the 1932 Dartmoor riot referred to the 'disorder'.[1] This is partly, as Carrabine (2005: 896) points out, because riot is a pejorative term which suggests 'images of frenzied mob violence' and would reflect badly on any prison administration. However, the issue of definition is a less pressing one in this chapter because, as had been noted, both riots were unquestionably large and significant events in English prison history in terms of numbers of prisoners' involved, physical damage caused and the resulting public and political attention.

To assess the nature and impact of these riots in Chatham and Dartmoor it is necessary to outline what actually happened and the contexts in which they occurred. A basic descriptive account of the process of these riots reveals many similarities. Briefly, these outbreaks in Chatham on 11 February 1861 and in Dartmoor on 24 January 1932 occurred following a series of lesser disturbances so that further trouble in some form was expected.[2] These lesser disturbances included failed escape attempts by what were later claimed to be particularly influential convicts. The stated level of awareness of this build up of tension was undoubtedly imbued with the benefit of hindsight, but later investigations showed that in both prisons specific measures had been taken on the days immediately prior to the riots. In Chatham attempts were made to dispose of 'unsuitable' prison officers while in Dartmoor prison officer's leave was curtailed. In both prisons preparations were made to obtain reinforcements in case of trouble and the actions of a small group of four or five 'desperate' criminals were said to have been instrumental. One or more of these men were supposed to have had extraordinary influence over other prisoners. It was claimed that arrangements had been made with accomplices outside of the institutions to facilitate escape: 'burglars' making contact with 'Jews in Petticoat Lane' prior to the Chatham riot and 'motor bandits' and Communists conspiring with London accomplices before the Dartmoor riot.[3] There is evidence in both cases to suggest that inmate informers forewarned prison staff about planned escapes and disturbances but this failed to head-off the most serious outbreaks.[4]

The main rioting was ignited on both occasions by complaints about food, soup in the former and porridge in the latter, and by concern expressed about the treatment of a small number of specific inmates by prison staff so that some convicts claimed their action was defensive. Significantly, when these riots broke out a member of the Prison Commission was in each of the prisons investigating previous disorder.[5] In the face of concerted action by inmates most prison officers appear to have vacated the institutions quite rapidly. Both riots culminated in prisoners taking over effective control of prison space for about one and a half to two destructive hours. During this time, fires were started and personal and official records were targeted, suggesting an attempt to defy and challenge official judgements and control regarding guilt, status, behaviour and health. For a short period, these riots overturned mechanisms of discipline centred on the distinct control and organisation of space, strict regulation of activity and time, and on classification and surveillance.

Police and/or military reinforcements were required to re-establish control and armed force was used. In neither riot were there any escapes, nor deaths caused by prisoners or staff. There were assaults. The *du Parcq Report*, which investigated the causes of the Dartmoor riot, recorded 23 baton wounds, seven 'shot wounds', nine convicts with general bruising etc and an 'unknown number' of injuries 'inflicted by fellow prisoners'. Most of the violence committed by the prisoners appears to have been against the fabric of the prisons. A large proportion of inmates were implicated in rioting but serious exemplary action was taken against a minority; those perceived to be ringleaders or especially active in the violence. Within a few days of the riot in Chatham, 48 convicts were punished with three-dozen lashes of the military cat-o-nine-tails each. In the aftermath of the Dartmoor riot, criminal charges were brought against 32 convicts and a special assize was established in Princetown (the village in which the prison was located) to try them. Twenty-two prisoners also appeared before Dartmoor's Board of Visitors for lesser offences. Both riots were heralded as revealing serious flaws in contemporary penal systems and were used as part of challenges to the direction of contemporary penal policies. To those who had been opposed to the direction of reforms in both eras, the riots provided the most explicit and public denunciation of the effectiveness of the regimes.

On the face of it, therefore, and despite the 70 or so years that divide them, the processes of these riots share many elements. Of course, their historical contexts were very different. The 1850s and 1860s witnessed the winding down of transportation, the closure of the notorious hulks and the founding of a system of convict penal servitude for those given sentences of over two years (after 1857 three years). Public works prisons were established at Portland (1849), Dartmoor (modernised 1850), Portsmouth (1852) and Chatham (1856). In a system adapted from one in which transportation was a crucial pillar, reform was to be encouraged through the inculcation of the habit of work within a domestic progressive stage system. Although many offenders sentenced to transportation were already serving their time in British prisons, the fact that under the Penal Servitude Act 1853 offenders were by law to be retained in the country caused public alarm. This alarm centred on the potential threat posed by men released on ticket-of-leave (a kind of early release on license) but also the disorder supposedly reckless and desperate long-sentenced convicts would cause in prison.[6] In the public concern following the Chatham riot ticket-of-leave men were cited as committing garotte robberies in London. Evidence of recidivism in these violent street robberies was given as proof of the failures of the penal system to reform and the need for increased severity.[7]

An Act of 1853 substituted for sentences of transportation shorter sentences of penal servitude but, contrary to the best efforts of Colonel Joshua Jebb, Chairman of the Directors of Convict Prisons 1850–1863, without remission. A later Act of 1857, which in theory imposed longer sentences, reintroduced the potential to gain remission but this was not extended to those sentenced under the 1853 Act. The issue of remission created resentment and conflict in Chatham and elsewhere between prisoners in the same prison but sentenced under different legislation (Tomlinson 1981: 132–3). In addition, an account published in 1863 and also evidence before a Parliamentary Commission blamed the riot partly on corrupt warders, 'right screws', transferred from the hulks who were trafficking for prisoners at extortionate rates or keeping money received from prisoner's friends and relatives.[8] According to Jebb, some of these officers had been advised they were to be removed from service but at the time of the riot were still in their posts. Furthermore, Jebb claimed convicts knew that a more disciplined regime was on the way.[9] Some of these convicts had themselves been received from the hulks when Chatham opened and may have believed warders would support them against the administration (Thomas and Pooley, 1980: 5). Since then convicts had also been returned from Bermuda, a number of whom had originally been sent out because they were seen as troublesome (Brown and Maxwell, 2003: 233–55). Moreover, newspapers critical of contemporary penal policy were apparently circulating in the prison.

In the context of wider economic problems, a perceived high crime rate heightened public alarm exacerbated by newspaper accounts of disturbances in the new convict prisons. Such outbreaks, according to *The Times*, constituted a 'strategy of war on our own island' by a criminal class ready to rise up against civil society.[10] The local *Chatham News* warned that if 'daring villains once commence a resistance to authority in a case like this [the Chatham riot], the evil example will spread like wildfire among the dreadful crowd around them, ever prone to mischief and violence'.[11] The supposedly reformatory penal system was according to critics, lax, deferential to convicts at the expense of authority and offered offenders a better standard of living than ordinary labourers and workhouse inmates.[12] Joshua Jebb, the first head of the Directorate of the Convict Prisons, was subjected to a hostile personal press campaign accusing him of being misguided (Manton, 1976: 182–5; Smith, 1982: Jebb Papers; Stockdale, 1976: 164–70). A *Punch* cartoon of December 1862, 'Sir Joshua Jebb's Pen of Pet Lambs', depicted him as an obsequious and snivelling bystander of a penal system in which convicts lived in luxury.[13] Challenges also came from the Deputy Governor of Chatham, Charles Pennell Measor (1861, 1864), who resigned after the riot and then posed as an authority on prison discipline. Measor was amongst those calling for more closely regulated prison and ticket-of-leave systems like those in Ireland, which, it was claimed, were more effective in maintaining order and reforming convicts (Clay, 1862; Crofton, 1863). The minority who asserted that increased deterrence would degrade criminals further were, according to Tomlinson 'shouted down by the majority who feared for themselves' (1978: 71). Condemnation of the Chatham riot was part of the wave of criticism which embattled the system of penal servitude in the early 1860s and of the deliberations of the Penal Servitude Acts Commission 1863. The Commission's conclusions, and the Penal Servitude Act 1864[14] which followed, were instrumental in bringing into being the more deterrent and uniform system of penal servitude that developed thereafter (McConville, 1981; Brown, 2003).

Compared to this penal system in its infancy, that of the 1920s and 1930s was mature and centralised with an established, even entrenched, administrative and disciplinary framework. Since the mid-nineteenth century an ever more confident official discourse had developed and become increasingly accepted and acceptable, drawing a more effective curtain of bureaucratic secrecy across prison administration (Pratt, 2004). Parallel to this greater maturity and self-confidence had come a distinct and widely reported questioning of the prison, of the highly deterrent systems of much of the second half of the nineteenth century, but also of the efficacy of the institution itself; that it was physically and psychologically damaging and could operate to undermine human- itarian reform efforts. However, for many of the prison officials and reformers who spoke publicly in these terms it was a means of pro- moting reform in a direction favoured by influential prison adminis- trators. As Pratt has suggested, one effect of the growth of central bureaucratic control since the mid-nineteenth century was to narrow debate on penal policy, official discourse increasingly spoke with one voice (2004: 79). The fall in the prison population from a daily average of around 18,000 before the First World War to around 10,000 during the inter-war period was important in facilitating flexibility to question the impact of imprisonment, ameliorate discipline and encourage experimentation in particular directions (Thomas, 1972: 172). Much of this concerned penal developments, such as the expansion of borstal, probation and aftercare provision, especially for younger offenders, but did have an, albeit lesser, impact upon adult prison conditions. To give some of the clearest basic examples, in 1921 the broad arrow on prisoner's uniforms was removed, in 1922 the prison crop was no longer imposed and by 1931 separation had finally been abolished (Forsythe, 1990: 175).

Alexander Paterson, a prison commissioner whose influence on inter- war penal policy was considerable,[15] referred to the prison as a 'clumsy piece of social surgery', the 'man who comes in as a criminal is made into a prisoner. All initiative and self-reliance is lost' (Ruck, 1951: 61, 24). Idealist tones could be discerned in the plans made to transform the nature of prisons in order to restore prisoners 'to ordinary standards of citizenship by promoting personal responsibility' (Fox, 1952: 70–1). For Paterson, the greatest moral force in this process was religion, which represented a 'clear-cut system of right and wrong'. The uniformity of nineteenth century prisons, he asserted, conflicted with 'God who made men different' (Ruck, 1951: 26, 28). Prison conditions were not to com- pose punishment, as in Paterson's well-known phrase 'Men come to prison as a punishment not for punishment' (*ibid.*: 23). If the fact of imprisonment was deterrent then it would theoretically be possible to remove internal features designed to intensify deterrence without impairing the impact of prison on the individual (Fox, 1934: 32). The changing ethos was proclaimed in several aspects of the prison structure, for example, prison officers, it was asserted, were better trained and more open to ideas about reform, governorships were no longer reserved for retired army officers and prison industries were reorganised (Ball, 1956: 71).

Yet the vision of prison reform, the well-ordered prison of the 1920s and 1930s with its workshops and industries, libraries and lectures, prison visitors and more refined classification was fragmented in its implementation, wedged into systems and routines that had been developed largely in the first half of the nineteenth century and into buildings just as old (Leigh, 1941; Fry, 1951). One ex-Governor commented in his later autobiography that reform was attempted 'within the limitations of a prison system that [was] itself the prisoner of a civilization that knows no better and would not pay the total bill for it if it did' (Clayton, 1958: 126). At the same time some prisoner autobiographies denounced public complacency over the state of prisons fuelled as it was by 'official pronouncements that the system marches steadily forward from reform to reform.' It was pointed out that 'Unfortunately prisons last very much longer than theories and cost more to create' (Dendrickson and Thomas, 1954: 209, 15; also see Macartney, 1936; Phelan, 1940; Sparks, 1961; "Red Collar Man", 1937). Criticism, even by supporters of reform, revealed that many adult prisons remained large with little constructive labour, little development from the nineteenth century and sanitation in some cases worse (Clayton, 1958: 182–3; Watson, 1939; Calvert and Calvert, 1933: 151). Nevertheless, Paterson was optimistic about what could be achieved and had the support of successive Prison Commission Chairmen and Home Secretaries. Faced with practical difficulties considerable reliance was placed upon prison staff whose 'personality and spirit', it was claimed, overcame 'the anachronism of century-old buildings' (Ruck, 1951: 68). Such bland assurances caused resentment among prison officers, which was interpreted as uncooperative self-interest, lack of commitment to reform and resistance to modernisation (Thomas, 1972: 157, 164).

So the visions and developments promoted by Paterson and the Prison Commission were not unopposed or unproblematic but they did create an effective public image of professional knowledge and humanitarianism. However, for those concerned about the direction that penal policy was taking, the riot at Dartmoor was a disaster waiting to happen. In the House of Commons it was asked whether the 'increase of amenities and relaxation of discipline at Dartmoor was responsible for the outbreak?'[16] Tabloid press reports referred to prisons as 'homes of rest' and 'public schools'.[17] One declared, 'The public requires no report to tell it that there is something radically wrong, with the Dartmoor menage certainly and possibly with our whole system of penal restraint.'[18] From a different political standpoint, the National Executive of the Labour Party, the Parliamentary Labour Party and also the General Council of the TUC called for an 'exhaustive public enquiry'.[19] It was stated in *The Daily Worker* (paper of the Communist Party of Great Britain), rightly as it turned out, that evidence accumulated by the du Parcq inquiry would not be made public. Moreover, the Government was accused of setting up the inquiry to 'whitewash the administration' and that 'wild talk' of plots was 'part and parcel of the scheme to distract attention from the scandalous conduct of British penal establishments, aggravated by the "economies" of the National Government'.[20]

There appears to have been no direct public response to the more radical attacks on the Government over the Dartmoor riot, however in response to criticisms that reform had made the prison system lax, some defenders asserted that Dartmoor, the prison for recidivists, the worst inmates in the system, had remained largely untouched by innovations.[21] Dartmoor, the morose and severe institution dominating the moorland village of Princetown was represented as more a part of the nineteenth century than of modern visions.[22] Most convicts at Dartmoor did not have access to educational classes and visitors, one area specifically criticised as generating informality and encouraging leniency. Reformers like the Calverts argued that it was precisely the lack of progress at Dartmoor that had resulted in disorder there (Calvert and Calvert, 1933: 124–5). The *Howard Journal* (1932) published a piece from an ex-Dartmoor convict outlining the limited and monotonous employment and training at the prison, which, it was claimed, contributed to the riot. In a letter to Herbert Samuel, the Home Secretary, it was stated by the Howard League that the main problem with modern prison administration revealed by the Dartmoor riot 'was not excess of leniency or of severity' but 'stagnation'.[23] This may have represented a slowing down in the pace of change from the 1920s, although even then Victor Bailey has suggested that in adult prisons 'the pace of change remained decidedly halting' (Bailey, 1997: 301, 322). Having experienced the other side of the wall, one ex-Dartmoor inmate concurred, 'No waste words. No chances. No pseudo trust. That is and was the Moor' and the 'code of progress, humanitarianism, reform and modernization [was]...so much waste paper' (Phelan, 1940: 99, 121).

In contrast to the brief returns published relating to the Chatham riot and the private flogging of those identified as ring-leaders, the publication of an eagerly awaited 36 page report of the du Parcq inquiry (but not the evidence) into the Dartmoor riot, and the later trial of 32 convicts gave the press plenty to fill its pages.[24] Exemplary penalties were handed down ranging from six months to 12 years in addition to existing prison sentences. Wilfred Macartney, in prison at the time for spying, believed that the administration panicked and sought to regain face by 'staging' a trial as a kind of camouflage to cover what was wrong with the prison system (Macartney, 1936: 97, 255). Certainly, the decision to take the case to the criminal court appears to have been taken within days of the riot. Barrister and Recorder of Bristol, Herbert du Parcq, was appointed to undertake 'an inquiry into the whole of the circumstances connected with the recent disorder' at Dartmoor. This enquiry was completed in three days. During his investigation none other than Alexander Paterson assisted Du Parcq, indeed they knew each other as undergraduates at Oxford (Ruck, 1951: 12). *The Daily Mail* commented that this was unfortunate as Paterson was 'himself to some considerable extent responsible for the system in force...The public wants the opinion of wholly independent experts upon it.'[25]

Unsurprisingly, given Paterson's close involvement, the du Parcq Report asserted specifically that modern prison conditions, or indeed any recent change to discipline, were not responsible for the mutinous behaviour and depicted the riot primarily as an organised plot with outside help from gangsters and Communists, which had misfired.[26] This echoed Jebb's assertion to the Penal Servitude Acts Commission in 1863 of 'desperate burglars' making contact with 'Jews in Petti-coat Lane' prior to the Chatham riot.[27] In the aftermath of the 1861 riot in Chatham it was the influence of convicts serving long-term sentences that was highlighted. Similarly, du Parcq capitalised on the presence of what was seen as a new kind of more ruthless criminal; gangsters and 'motor-bandits' from the major cities serving longer sentences than usual and who continued their gang conflicts and rivalries within the prison. *The Times* noted the activities of 'the hardened convict of the worst and most desperate type' produced by 'the War, the film, and the motor "who could work up their fellows"'.[28]

The unsuitability of Dartmoor for prisoners of 'the dangerous modern type' was maintained in the du Parcq Report, again reminiscent of Chatham riot, but so were corrupt practices by a small number of prison officers. The du Parcq Report concluded that prisoners had no substantial grievances 'and that such grievances as they had would not have led to any disorder unless a few of the dangerous prisoners, partly by their power of leadership, partly by intimidation, had played on the feelings and the fears of others.' Further echoes of the official stance following the Chatham riot can be discerned. At that time it was asserted that:

It is plain from the recent outrageous conduct of the great body of prisoners, either that they do not understand their real position, and the extreme lenity with which they are treated, or that if they do not understand them, they are so incredibly weak and foolish as to be ready at the call of any designing villain to sacrifice all in the vain attempt to resist authority.[29]

Despite the Dartmoor riot being blamed on convicts, the Governor, Roberts, was transferred because it was felt he should have foreseen trouble and did not have the 'exceptionally strong character which might have been able to quell the growing disorder by the force of his personality'.[30] There appear to be strong class assumptions underlying this conclusion in that Roberts was one of a minority of prison governors at that time who had worked their way up through the ranks. Interestingly, Robert's replacement, Major J. C. Pannall, Governor of Camp Hill Borstal, had been Alexander Paterson's Sergeant-major during service in the First World War (Hawkins, n.d: 13).

In 1932 the Prison Officer's Magazine also blamed Communists and gangsters for the riot but included criticism of Prison Commissioners and 'long-haired, water-drinking' reformers generally.[31] Thomas (1972: 160) points out the magazine ignored du Parcq's adverse comments about staff corruption but in effect so did the Prison Commission and Home Office as no action was taken because, according to the Home Secretary, culpability could not be proven.[32] In a letter to the Home Secretary, editor of the Prison Officer's Magazine, E. R. Ramsay (an assumed name), asserted that inmates were 'pampered' by the 'so-called reformer type' and the 'old and established authority of the officers' had been 'considerably undermined', staff number had been reduced and the action of the Governor and staff constrained

– without a return to a better balance of power between officers and inmates, another Dartmoor was threatened.[33]

Certainly, 29 of a total of 56 prisons had been closed since 1914 and Dartmoor was an 'exceptionally expensive' prison to run.[34] From autumn 1931, economy measures meant prison officers leaving the service were not replaced. At the same time, Chelmsford Prison was reopened specifically for younger convicts under 30 years old re-routed from Dartmoor and from November 1931 men sentenced to terms of penal servitude not exceeding three years were to serve their sentences in local prisons. It was envisaged through these policies that more room could be made at Parkhurst to transfer further convicts from Dartmoor.[35] Cumulatively these developments added up to significant reductions in the inmate population of Dartmoor Prison. There had been no new admissions to Dartmoor Prison since the 19th of November 1931 so that by the time of the riot, there were 442 inmates in a prison with 935 cells.[36]

Those identified as most involved in the riot were, following investigations by the Metropolitan Police, charged with criminal offences and a special assize was set up at Princetown. Significantly, these convicts were not charged with mutiny, which could have been punished by corporal punishment, but with offences under the Malicious Damage Act 1861. The image of a succession of floggings, such as occurred following the Chatham riot, would have been an anathema to contemporary penal philosophy and would have received further extensive media coverage negating work done to promote the prison system as humanitarian. The Prison Commission and Paterson in particular, saw corporal punishment as a last resort and had previously promoted abolition. In addition, pressure from the Howard League for Penal Reform, a body with considerable influence with the Home Office, urged against corporal punishment.[37] Members of this active and articulate organisation were well-connected, especially with the Penal Reform Group in the House of Commons and the Magistrates Association, and it was at this time that they were to establish the political and campaigning influence evident in the post-war period (Morris, 1988: 23–4).

Conclusions

An analysis of the nature and process of riots in Chatham 1861 and Dartmoor 1932 reveals many similarities. Some of these similarities reflected the fundamental character of English penal systems: the tensions that can build within carceral institutions; the ratio of staff to prisoners, which affects the measures that can be taken once serious disorder breaks out; last resort back up provided by the police and military; and the importance of food within disciplined and monotonous regimes. But the different methods used to deal with those identified as ringleaders and the specific groups of prisoners highlighted as being responsible for the riots reflect not only changing penal practices and philosophies but also contemporary social anxieties about crime. By the 1930s corporal punishment was rarely used in English prisons and the image of a succession of floggings, as carried out after the Chatham riot, would have received extensive media coverage and negated much of the work done by that time to promote the prison system as humanitarian. Concerns about immigration during the mid-nineteenth century and the increase in car ownership during the inter-war period both reflected particular fears about the character of crime and its perpetrators. In neither riot did any evidence emerge to support the claim that rioters had organised support from outside.

In the aftermath of both riots, it was claimed that these were atypical prisons, their inmates were the worst criminals led by a small number of especially 'desperate' offenders, the least liable to reform and with the least to lose by rioting. This narrative of unredeemable habitual criminals undermined consideration of any legitimate grievances and leaves historians with an enduring but largely one dimensional and distorted explanation. In one respect this has survived in the form of the toxic mix account of prison disturbances in the 1970s and 1980s, whereby prisoners serving very long sentences were depicted as having nothing left to lose (Cavadino and Dignan, 2002: 17–18).

The repercussions of these two riots differed. During the 1860s there was criticism of convicts but the primary targets in the wake of the Chatham riot became the penal system and the administration of Jebb himself. In the aftermath of the Dartmoor riot, the inmates were deemed culpable and tabloid newspapers were eager to make links between inmates, motor bandits and Communists. There was a backlash against the penal regime after the Dartmoor mutiny, as there had been against the developing penal administration of 1861. Yet, in 1932 the tide of penal policy continued to move against the so-called 'realists' who criticised reformers as 'impractical idealists' who had sacrificed 'good order and discipline on the altar of ideals that can never be realized'.[38] In part this was because while the rhetoric was sometimes expansive, in practice reforms affecting adult prisoners were fragmented and alleviated rather than revolutionised, modified rather

212 Punishment and Control in Historical Perspective

than remodelled regimes. However, as Rose points out, the riot did sharpen the debate between those who thought prison discipline was lax and those who believed in 'constructive training' and treatment (1961: 174–5). While the inter-war penal system was subject to considerable criticism it had influential defenders, including The Howard League and *The Times*.

Some of the rhetoric and press reports following both riots illustrated the tendency when faced with such alarming events to fall back on severity to try and restore public confidence. However, prison administrators in the 1930s were able to wield an image of the deterrent penal system of the second half of the nineteenth century as a dark and failed period in prison history in order to promote inter-war penal policy as progressive and offering a new way with crime. By the 1930s an organised, professional prison administration had developed,[39] in tune with liberal and idealist thought of the time and eager to protect the advances that it claimed had been made. Critics could be dismissed as those who knew nothing about prisons and/or as being out of touch with modern ideas. During the 1860s, the penal system that was being constructed as the alternative for transportation for the first time lacked such strengths. Established administrative authority in 1932 was more able to legitimate itself in terms of general social values. Within a prison system that was generally less at the centre of penal policy, as the use of fines and probation were extended, emphasis on the whole remained on younger offenders enabling the continuation of an optimistic and progressive portrayal of penal reform.

Notes

1 *Return of the Number of Convicts (out of the 850 implicated in the recent Disturbances at Chatham) who were removed from the Hulks to Chatham Prison, with the Dates of Removal*, PP 1861 LII.3 (hereafter *Chatham Returns*); *Report on the Circumstances Connected with the Recent Disorder at Dartmoor Convict Prison*, PP, Cmd.4010, February 1932 (hereafter *The du Parcq Report*).

2 *The Times*, 19 January 1861; Rose, 1961.

3 *Report of the Commissioners appointed to Inquire into the Operation of Acts relating to Transportation and Penal Servitude* BPP 1863 XXI (hereafter Report of the Penal Servitude Acts Commission [RPSAC]), evidence of Col. Jebb, qu.582 and *The du Parcq Report*.

4 Regarding Chatham see RPSAC, evidence of Col. Jebb, qu.582 and *The Times*, 21 January 1861. For Dartmoor see NA, Metropolitan Police 2/4959 for the CID Report into the riot at Dartmoor.

5 Inspector-General of Convict Prisons, Captain Gambier at Chatham and Assistant Commissioner, Colonel Turner in Dartmoor.

6 Bartrip, 1981: 153; Davis, 1980; *Punch*, 20 December 1862; *The Times*, 11 February and 21 January 1861.

7   *The Times*, 28 November 1856, 10 February 1859, 18 July 1862.
8   Anon [H. W. Holland and F. Greenwood] (1863), 644. Also see evidence of the Governor of Chatham, Folliot Powell and Col. Jebb, to RPSAC, qu.576, 387, 1206 and pp.334–61.
9   RPSAC, evidence of Col. Jebb, qu.578 & 579.
10 *The Times*, 23 August 1858.
11 *Chatham News*, 16 February 1861.
12 See Anon [H. Martineau] (1865) 361 & 358; *Chatham News*, 16, 23 February and 23 March 1861; *The Times*, 22 February 1861, 5; THE CONVICT COMMISSION, *Punch*, 17 January 1863 in which fictional character, Mr Toby Cribbercrack noted that he had 'never denied himself any comfort when out of prison' and was 'never denied any when in'.
13 *Punch*, 13 December 1862.
14 27 & 28 Vict. c. 47.
15 Paterson has been described as 'one of the giants of prison reform' (Thomas, 1972: 152). For Mannheim, Paterson was 'one of the greatest English experts in this field' (1939: 16). Also see, G. Hawkins (n.d.). Paterson was appointed as a Prison Commissioner in 1922, he never became Chairman of the Commission but reportedly had great influence on Maurice Waller (Chairman 1922–1928), Alexander Maxwell (Chairman 1928–1932) and Harold Scott (Chairman 1932–1938).
16 Captain North, *Hansards* Vol. 261, 11 Feb 1932 Col. 1056. For more on the riot see Brown (2007).
17 *Daily Mail*, 28 January 1932; *Morning Post*, 27 January 1932.
18 *Evening News*, 1 February 1932.
19 *Manchester Guardian*, 28 January 1932.
20 *Daily Worker*, 28 January & 9 February 1932.
21 For example Calvert and Calvert (1933: 151). This view was also put forward by the Howard League and recorded in the Minutes of the Policy Sub-Committee on 18 January 1932 MSS1613/1/1/1 (The Howard League Archive, University of Warwick).
22 *News Chronicle*, 25 January 1932.
23 NA HO45/18006/29.
24 *Returns relating to the recent Convict Disturbances at Chatham*, PP, 1861 (125), LII.3. With regard to the Dartmoor inquiry report, Home Secretary, Herbert Samuel, stated that the evidence could not be published because the inquiry was administrative not commissioned to try the offenders and should not prejudice future legal proceedings. *Hansards* Vol. 261, February 8 1932, col.501.
25 *The Daily Mail*, 28 January 1932.
26 *The du Parcq Report*, commented that convicts had sung the 'Red Flag', 20; *Daily Mail*, 26 and 27 January 1932; *The Times*, 27 January and 8 February 1932; *Evening News*, 19 March 1932; *News Chronicle*, 25 January 1932. For further see NA HO45/18006/31 *Justice of the Peace and Local Government Review*, 15 Feb 1932, 115, 'Treatment of Motorbandits & Gangsters'.
27 RPSAC, evidence of Col. Jebb, qu.582.
28 *The Times*, 25 & 27 January 1932.
29 Chatham Returns.
30 *Du Parcq Report*.

31 *Prison Officer's Magazine,* March 1932 XXI (1), p. 35 and April 1932 XXI (4), 104.

32 *Hansards* Vol. 26, May 5 1932, col.1911–2.

33 NA HO144/20647/71A, Letter 1 Feb 1932, 'The Dartmoor mutiny Its Causes and a Suggested Remedy'. Also, *Prison Officer's Magazine* June 1932 XXI (6) and November 1939 XXVIII (11), 341 HAVE THE COMMISSIONERS ABDICATED.

34 Home Secretary, *Hansards* 1931–32, Vol. 62, February 25 1932, col.537 and Vol.261, 8 Feb 1932.

35 *Annual Report of the Commissioners of Prisons* 1931–32, PP, Cmd 4151 xii.804–5.

36 *Annual Report of the Commissioners of Prisons* 1932–33, PP, Cmd 4295 xv.463 and *Hansards* 1931–2, Vol. 61, 8 Feb 1932, col.500.

37 NA HO45/18006/29, letter from Cicily Craven to the Home Secretary, 17 February 1932.

38 Lieut. Col. Rich (1932: 17, 46, 277); also see Rich, *Sunday Graphic,* 2 February 1932; *The Times,* 19 August 1932 letter THE MODERN PRISON by Brigadier-General S. Lushington.

39 In April 1933, the Prison Service became an Agency of government, a status which enabled greater autonomy in operational matters, while government retained overall control of policy.

11
Resistance, Identity and Historical Change in Residential Institutions for Juvenile Delinquents, 1950–70

Abigail Wills

From the mid-nineteenth century onwards, children and young people given custodial sentences by the courts in England and Wales were committed to dedicated, age-specific residential institutions. The belief in the diminished responsibility of juvenile delinquents relative to adult criminals meant that such institutions were conceived primarily as reformative environments, aimed at fulfilling the welfare needs of their residents rather than the punitive requirements of 'justice'. Through a combination of education, trade training, religious instruction, physical exercise and wholesome recreation, residential institutions sought to restore errant children from 'unsatisfactory' home backgrounds to productive citizenship (Hyland, 1994; Bailey, 1987). In practice, however, this stated humanitarianism concealed more ambiguous motivations for institutionalising errant children. Historians of the subject have emphasised in particular the power-suffused nature of institutional regimes, and the way in which they sought to inculcate a 'hidden curriculum' of class and gender norms into their working class charges. Mahood argues in her study of the Scottish 'child-saving' movement that institutions constituted a 'social system of domination' creating 'female proletarians to take up distinct positions in the class and gender order' (1995: 3). Cox, in her exploration of girls' delinquency in twentieth-century Britain, similarly speaks of institutional reform as a story of 'highly gendered modern disciplinary power' (2003: 171–2, see also Humphries, 1981; Cale, 1993). The dominant historiographical focus, then, is on the study of how institutions created 'compliant subjects' and 'docile bodies'.

This chapter considers the way in which children and young people experienced and influenced this structure of control within institutions. More specifically, it explores strategies of resistance to institutional authority: what they were, and how they should be conceptualised analytically. Ostensibly, this is a well-worn subject. There are repeated pleas in the historiography for delinquent subjectivity and experience to be taken seriously, and for an exploration of how 'working class youth and their parents reacted to the process by which they were perceived and defined' (Mahood, 1995: 14). Yet in practice, historians' accounts of resistance to institutional control have been constrained in various ways by the analytical framework described above: while authors such as Cox and Mahood stress the contested and ambiguous nature of hegemonic values and practices, they see them as ultimately inescapable. Resistance, in this context, is seen as a rational – and laudable – response to an 'oppressive environment', but ultimately futile. As Cox argues, 'to celebrate ... episodes [of resistance] as examples of girls' power would be to seriously underestimate the power of the schools, and by extension the state, to deal with disruptive elements' (2003: 98). Delinquent agency, then, while not absent, is afforded strictly limited analytical significance; the focus is squarely on how institutional regimes successfully imposed their authority on their charges.

As a number of criminologists have argued recently, this understanding is problematic. In particular, it is in danger of constructing the delinquent as a cipher, with his or her agency reduced to a purely reactive process of resisting oppression. As Carrabine and Bosworth note, characterising resistance as a 'privileged quality of the human spirit' – in effect, as a gut reaction to 'relations of simple inequality' – does not do justice to the complexity of why and how individuals choose to resist. As they note, 'counter-conduct' can be motivated by 'pleasure, play and boredom' as much as by 'anger, rage, exploitation and injustice', and it has meanings for the individual that are separate from its 'objective' effects (2001: 505–15). Responses to institutional power need to be seen as complex and variable, influenced both by the particular nature of specific institutional regimes, and by the individual identities and ideologies of those resisting. The existing historiography on residential institutions, by downplaying the historical significance of resistance, fails to consider this complexity. As a result, its accounts of resistance are empirically thin; there is little detailed consideration of the motivations behind 'oppositional' acts, nor of their multifaceted effects.

The argument which follows sets out to reconsider the analytical significance of delinquent resistance. Without seeking to minimise the coercive and brutal aspects of institutional power, it attempts to construct a more nuanced picture of delinquent agency and identity within residential institutions. The chapter begins by outlining the grievances around which resistance coalesced, and argues that it was discriminating to an extent which has not been appreciated by existing studies of juvenile crime. It cannot be understood as a wholesale rejection of institutional power, but rather represented a specific set of objections to particular features of institutional existence. This argument also questions the degree to which fear should be seen as the governing principle behind the extent and nature of resistance. The second part of the chapter explores the effects of this resistance and in particular its ability to influence the boundaries and terms of institutional control. It suggests that 'top-level' actors were by no means all-powerful in their ability to determine the character of institutional existence. Finally, the chapter suggests a way in which this understanding of delinquent agency can give a new perspective on historical change within the juvenile justice system.

The argument focuses on residential reform schools – Approved Schools, Probation Homes and Probation Hostels – for juvenile delinquents in Britain during the decades after the Second World War. Committal to such institutions was the most severe outcome of a juvenile court appearance, involving compulsory removal from family and society for periods of up to three years in the case of Approved Schools, and a year in the case of Probation Hostels or Homes. They were not, as a rule, 'closed' institutions – there were no bars or locked doors – but all required full-time residence, except in the case of Probation Hostels where residents were employed outside the institution during the day. Committal could be the result either of a criminal offence, or of being deemed 'beyond [parental] control' or 'in need of care and protection' by the juvenile court (Rose, 1967: 18–24). The analysis draws largely on the detailed written records – progress reports, minute books and case notes – of four institutions: Duncroft Approved School, Druids Heath Approved School, High Beech Probation Home and Burford House Probation Hostel.[1]

Historians and criminologists have been deeply suspicious of the possibility that official records such as these can be put to use in recovering subordinate resistance within penal institutions. James Scott, in his *Domination and the Arts of Resistance*, puts forward the idea that because of the risks associated with non-compliance to the dominant order, most resistance – both within penal settings and elsewhere – is located within a 'hidden transcript' which 'makes the autonomous life of the powerless opaque to elites' (1990: 132). As a result, he argues that an analysis based on the 'public transcript', of those in power 'is likely to conclude that subordinate groups endorse the terms of their subordination' (cited in Crewe, 2007: 259). It is certainly the case that the form in which accounts of resistance appear within official records was mediated by authority figures, who often had a vested interest in the institution being portrayed in a positive light. Yet at the same time, as the following argument will demonstrate, strategies of resistance are less opaque within the official record than is assumed by authors such as Scott. From the perspective of 'authority', resistance was deplored, but also – paradoxically – confirmed the *raison-d'etre* of the residential institution. Indeed, oppositional behaviour was the primary reason behind the committal of residents, and dealing with it part of the institution's reformative mission. As a result, the voices and motivations of juvenile delinquents form an intrinsic part of the official record of their passage through the institution, albeit in a highly mediated way. The historian ignores such documents at the cost of missing a highly intimate and detailed record of institutional existence.

Varieties of resistance

Delinquent resistance took place in opposition to a wide variety of aspects of institutional regimes. This began with a questioning of the very terms of institutionalisation, and in particular the perceived inequities of the 'welfare' approach to juvenile justice, in which institutionalisation was governed by the particular circumstances and needs of the individual, rather than by the severity of the crime committed. The Ingleby Committee, set up in the 1960s to consider the workings of the juvenile courts, highlighted the dilemma faced by magistrates in this respect, giving the example of:

> a child being charged with a petty theft or other wrongful act for which most people would say that no great penalty should be imposed, and the case apparently ending in a disproportionate sentence ... The court may determine that the welfare of the child requires some very substantial interference which may amount to taking the child away from his home for a prolonged period. It is common to come across bitter complaints that a child has been sent away from home because he has committed some particular offence which in itself was not at all serious.[2]

This contradiction was felt very keenly by children sent to residential institutions. At Duncroft, for example, it was noted by the managers in 1961 that 'some girls feel that in comparison to the behaviour of other girls, they had done nothing seriously wrong and that once having been committed to an Approved School, they are ... subjected to virtually the same punishment as those girls detained for more serious offences'.[3] This complaint indicates the strength of the 'just deserts' principle in governing delinquents' responses to institutionalisation. There was similar resistance to the idea that behaviour within institutions should be governed by nebulous 'welfare' criteria rather than by an objective, measured response. Katy, for example, was noted by a Duncroft manager to be 'sullen and resentful that she had been "down-graded" for "singing" and she regarded her punishment as unjustified and unfair. ... She complained that another girl involved had not received the same punishment on account of something personal and this had made her angry.'[4] In the same way, there was opposition to the fact that a resident's length of stay in Approved School was not determined from the outset, but was governed both by good behaviour and – worse – by circumstances entirely beyond their control. The Duncroft managers, for example, noted in 1961 that 'most girls are anxious to obtain licence, but some feel there is no object in indulging in good behaviour or working hard during their stay if at the end of it owing to unsuitable home conditions or lack of accommodation, they cannot be granted licence when it would normally be due'.[5] All these examples suggest that for some Approved School residents, punitive responses to misbehaviour had a legitimacy and intelligibility which ostensibly more humane, 'welfare-based' approaches did not possess.

A second axis of delinquent resistance was formed in opposition to the rigid timetabling of institution life, particularly in relation to leisure time. Institutions fought a constant battle against attempts to subvert this order. Osbert was typical in being the subject of a complaint by the High Beech warden, who reported to the managing committee that 'Osbert had several times disobeyed his orders and had gone out or had stayed out late to see a girl friend in the village'.[6] Such behaviour could involve a highly studied and symbolic rejection of 'unreasonable' prohibitions. Olivia, for example, was told by the Burford House warden that she 'must stay in on Saturday', but went out anyway, climbing through the window 'even though the door was open', and 'returned at the correct time wanting to introduce her boyfriend'.[7] Freddie justified her late return from leave in similarly mischievous terms, stating that she had gone to a party and 'did not wish to leave early to get back to the hostel'.[8] Bedtimes were a further flashpoint: the Duncroft headmistress complained of girls being 'quite defiant about settling down at night, even when they have gone to bed at about 10.30'.[9] Collective resistance against such restrictions was frequent. In Burford House, in 1969, when refused permission to watch a late night horror film, the residents 'locked themselves in the

TV room … and stayed in [there] for well over an hour'.[10] Two days later, the girls refused to settle for bed until 'well after 1am'.[11] Such actions suggest a desire to reclaim informal time against the strict terms of institutional management, but within well-defined limits, which were related to residents' own understanding of what constituted 'appropriate' restrictions on their conduct.

Equally strong resistance coalesced against restrictions imposed by institutions on the external social contacts of their residents. In the relatively open environment of probation hostels, this was often a losing battle for institution staff: the Burford House warden complained in 1965 that it was 'virtually impossible to exercise authority over [girls] in their free time away from the hostel'.[12] The tenacity of residents was such that undesirable contacts in some cases ended up being reluctantly tolerated by staff: in 1961, the Burford House warden admitted that 'I have been unable to break Lydia's undesirable liaison with the coloured cafe proprietors'.[13] Even in the more restrictive environment of Approved Schools, residents went to significant lengths to maintain forbidden contacts. Julia, for example, was noted to have attempted to send 'illegal' letters to her boyfriend by addressing them to an imaginary 'aunt and uncle'.[14] The ingenuity and determination demonstrated in such attempts was considerable. In the case of Linda and her friends, a desire to keep a rendezvous with some men met in the local town led to a need to 'find a way to get out as we are not allowed out in the evening. So we found our way out but we were caught (this happened twice) and our clothes were taken from us so we were mad and went in pyjamas'.[15] This incident, with its playful overtones, is suggestive of the fact that many episodes of absconding involved attempts to temporarily escape particularly onerous institutional restraints, rather than a last-ditch and desperate desire to permanently flee intolerable circumstances.

A further aspect of resistance related to the perceived attacks made by institution rules on the personal autonomy, privacy and dignity of delinquents. Letter censorship was a particular source of dissatisfaction, as was compulsory religious observance. Judith, for example, 'refused to stand for grace before the evening meal and so was asked to leave the room, which she did'.[16] The lack of properly 'personal' institutional space was also a significant concern: residents at Duncroft, for example, made repeated requests for the provision of individual lockers for their personal belongings, noting that 'there will always be pilfering and [at present] we have to carry our things about everywhere'.[17] Objections to petty restrictions on personal freedoms were often phrased in terms deliberately designed to appeal to institutional concerns. The Duncroft girls asked a visiting manager: 'why should we not talk after lights out, so long as we don't make a noise, after lights out is the best time for talking, it is often easiest to talk in the dark and solves more problems than seeing a psychiatrist.'[18]

On two infamous occasions, in which serious and collective resistance to institutional regimes took place, this was the result of the strength of feeling surrounding institutional assaults on personal dignity. At Standon Farm Approved School in 1947, the assistant gardening instructor was murdered by boys at the school. The crime was directly motivated by conditions within the school; the government enquiry into the incident noted that the nine boys involved claimed that 'we didn't intend to kill Mr Peter, but were determined to kill the Headmaster, because he was always stopping our money and our licences'.[19] The enquiry concluded that the causes of the incident were principally attributable to 'the cumulative effect of a long-standing regime of limited freedom, collective punishments and the threats of collective fines, the inadequate system of distributing pocket money, the lack of understanding on the part of the Headmaster and the boys' belief in his unfairness'.[20] Similar feelings underlay the uprising at Carlton Approved School in 1959. A collective punishment involving the burning of the boys' belts was believed to have 'wounded the pride and self-respect of these young men' leading them to mass revolt.[21] Ninety-five boys, 'marched out of the school after first breaking windows, beds and furniture' before returning, then escaping again the next day.[22]

However, even such collective – and violent – resistance involved attempts at dialogue. In the case of the Carlton uprising, once the boys had left the school, all 95 of them apparently went to the home of an American writer, Talcott Williams, where they typed a list of complaints about their treatment to be presented to the headmaster.[23] In defence of the boys subsequently charged as a result of the breakout, the defence barrister stated that 'he would like to pay tribute to the pupils because although tempers ran very high it was only at the very last moment that rioting broke out'. He submitted that 'there was no evidence that boys before the court were ringleaders of an undisciplined mutiny against authority'.[24] This challenges the notion of resistance as a wholesale rebellion against a system of class-based oppression. It was rare for delinquents to express outright rejection of all aspects of the institutional regime; resistance even in extreme cases involved an attempt at a discriminating and measured response to particular restrictions and indignities.

Resistance within institutions thus took place along a variety of axes, picking up on the inequities of welfare discourses, on the rigidity and lack of freedom of institutional life, and on the assaults that it inflicted on personal autonomy and dignity. Such complaints can be seen as highly cogent responses to the privations of institutionalisation. It is also clear from the examples given above that this resistance took place using a variety of highly creative methods: from verbal complaint, to disobedience and subversion, to collective rebellion.

The sophistication of these responses bears further consideration. To begin with, it is interesting to note the extent to which complaints were actively and articulately vocalised. Individuals were rarely shy about making direct complaints to the staff and managers of institutions, often – as one Duncroft manager put it – quite 'freely and vigorously'.[25] This contradicts the assumption, widespread across the historical and criminological literature, that fear was necessarily the governing characteristic of inmate responses within penal regimes. It was not the case, unlike in Crewe's example of the 'civilised' modern prison, that 'open defiance [was] considered imprudent and ineffective, leading to an outward appearance of calm and compliance' (2007: 256). In the case of residential institutions for juvenile delinquents, at least in the postwar period, open challenges to authority were ubiquitous; indeed they formed part of the daily fabric of institutional life. By the very fact of their presence in the institution, residents had demonstrated that they were relatively immune to the power of official censure and punishment; many showed little hesitation in engaging in open struggles with authority.

Moreover, where open rebellion *was* felt to be too perilous, delinquents could also be highly adept in making their views known through indirect means – but means which nevertheless made their feelings clear to institutional authorities. The letter censorship system provides one interesting example of this process: Emer's letter, ostensibly written to her mother from Duncroft in 1968, states that:

> These letters are censored as you know. ... About that wool you gave me, I'm afraid that owing to some light fingered people ... some kind person (I know who it is) took it. ... I can't get it back because she is senior to me, and all the girls would absolutely hate me if I told the staff about it. ... Everyone is either leaving or absconding lately. All cigarettes have been stopped indefinitely. I wouldn't be surprised if we don't have a mutiny soon.[26]

Here, the institutional rules on censorship were turned by Emer to her advantage, providing a private channel for airing grievances without risking the censure that a direct complaint might arouse. This argument suggests that Scott's notion of resistance as a predominantly 'hidden transcript' is problematic: even where it was disguised or indirect, resistance often remained relatively transparent, both to authorities at the time and, retrospectively, to the historian.

Beyond this, it is also important to note the extent to which resistance involved an active engagement with wider social-cultural contexts. Delinquents often betrayed a sharp awareness of media and professional understandings of delinquency, and a keen eye for their exploitation. The Carlton uprising is one example of such a process: there is evidence that boys in the school were following in some detail the progress of the enquiry on the affair in the press. Thus *The Times* reported an exchange in the enquiry in which the counsel for the Carlton staff, Mr Gardiner, noted that 'although fully qualified in their own trades, [staff] were not certificated teachers. ... As a result of the way in which [this] had been reported in the press, the boys had spent nearly the whole of the previous day saying to the staff: "yah, you are not qualified to teach us."'[27] This reminder of the attentive ears of delinquents within Carlton coloured the subsequent conduct of the enquiry: at one stage, the testimony of the chairman of the managers was interrupted by the head of the enquiry, Victor Durand, who cautioned that 'the words you are using are being heard by reporters present and it would be prudent, would it not, to avoid giving newspapers words which may get back to the school'.[28] The nefarious consequences of the media literacy of delinquents for institutional regimes were similarly deplored by the Approved School Gazette in 1970: the editorial noted that 'in some cases it would appear that gentlemen of the press have ... [been] quite deliberately encouraging certain boys to abscond. Inevitably the effect of all this is felt (after all, our boys do watch the telly and some even read the newspapers!).'[29]

Some delinquents also displayed a strong interest in, and manipulation of, psychological and psychiatric understandings of delinquency: in 1962, the Duncroft headmistress asked the managing committee of the school for 'guidance on books taken out by girls from the public library. It appeared that they were reading a great deal of advanced psychology at the present time.'[30] Such knowledge was often harnessed, with great creativity, to delinquents' own ends in subverting institutional control. In 1954, Josephine, on holiday at her previous children's home, was said to have told the headmistress there that 'it didn't matter what she said and did as [the Duncroft psychiatrist] would put it all right and straighten her mind out for her on return'.[31] Beyond this naive attempt at 'psychiatric exculpation', there are also examples of far more sophisticated uses of psychiatric discourses. In his account of his committal as a teenager to Grendon psychiatric prison, Christopher Finlay describes his first encounter with the resident psychiatrist:

> I wondered to which [psychiatric] school he belonged. Betting on Freud, for he was the only one whose theories were vaguely known to me, I launched into my Oedipus complex. As a throwaway line I said '[My girlfriend] Tam and my mother could easily be twins'. This was instantly misinterpreted. 'So Tam's a lot older than you?' 'Oh no! I don't mean that.' 'Well, what do you mean?' Silence from me and silence from Dr A. Clearly he was no discipline of Freud's if he didn't know what I meant. ... In the past this line had ... raised more than one psychiatrist's eyebrows. Freud having failed me, 'rejection' was my next gambit. 'You know, doctor, I think my real trouble is a feeling of total rejection, of not being wanted'. I had to make sure we were speaking the same language. We were. A couple of quick nods from Dr A, vigorous enough to displace a twist of short, brown hair.[32]

Such a degree of knowing manipulativeness may have been rare, but the possibility of subversive use of psychiatric knowledge was well recognised by institution staff. In the case of Sabina and Vanessa, for example, it was noted by the Duncroft headmistress that '[they have] been simulating symptoms of mental illness and the grapevine has it that both girls are trying to have themselves sent to mental hospital'.[33]

The fact that many delinquents were fully cognisant of developments within contemporary media and professional discourses is highly significant. Indeed, there is a tendency in the existing historical literature to minimise the links between developments at a 'macro' level, such as discussions about the causes of juvenile crime or media panics, and the subjectivities of delinquents. As I noted in the introduction, the historiography has been in danger of portraying 'subordinate' groups such as delinquents not as fully sentient and complex individuals, but as engaged in a timeless conflict with monolithic structures of social power. Such difficulties are compounded by the methodological tradition which has enforced a sharp separation between 'official' and 'personal' sources, between policy history and 'history from below', with 'official' sources deemed out of bounds for a study of 'subordinate' subjectivity. The above analysis of delinquent resistance in the postwar decades exposes the limitations of such understandings, challenging the notion that professional discourses operated on an entirely separate plane to that inhabited by subordinate groups.

The picture of cogent, measured resistance presented thus far does not suggest that all resistance should be understood in these terms. There is a range of oppositional reactions apparent within the records that cannot be contained within a model of rational resistance. Frustration at institutional restrictions was also expressed in less positive ways, such as through violent and uncontrolled outbursts of anger. Natasha, for example, on being 'asked by other [Burford House] girls to stop playing the piano whilst they had the record player on ... ran hysterically ... out of the hostel. For the next hour and a half she ran about the road evading staff and girls who were trying to persuade her to come back.'[34] Others – particularly girls – resorted to self-harm or attempts at suicide, as with two other Burford House residents: Susan, who in 1968 'cut her arm with a razor blade after being told off by Mrs D', and Kathleen, who in 1951 was found 'unconscious having tried to commit suicide by gas'.[35] While accepting that 'pathological' behaviour as defined by institution staff was in part a normative, socially constructed category, it is clear from these examples that not all delinquents were fully in control of their emotions or their judgments.

Relatedly, the level of intelligence of delinquents was a significant factor in dictating the sophistication of responses to the institutional regime. It was noted by the Duncroft staff, for example, that their role as an institution for more intelligent girls 'was often an embarrassment because the girls were needle sharp to see the weak point and work around'.[36] Similarly, it is clear from the descriptions of group rebellions that certain individuals acted as ringleaders, often intimidating more vulnerable individuals. In the Carlton affair, for example, it was suggested (albeit in the context of the prosecution case at their trial) that the ringleaders' method had involved telling younger boys that 'if you do not join in the riots, you will be smashed'.[37] The chairman of the governors noted during the enquiry that 'we have had to send some eight loyal boys who refused to take part in the "mutiny" away from the district for their own safety'.[38] Such examples point to a further danger of characterising resistance as a homogeneous rejection of structures of class and gender oppression: violence and coercion within the delinquent population were also part of the story. Overall, the above analysis highlights the extent to which delinquents played an active part in interpreting the legitimacy of their committal to residential care. Far from seeing themselves as fated to social subordination within a wholly hostile system, they were discriminating in their response to institutional regimes, and targeted their strategies of resistance to the particular nature and characteristics of such regimes.

The limits of institutional control

The argument now turns to the question of the consequences of this resistance, and in particular to an exploration of Cox's belief that the ultimate power to control remained firmly with the institution. It is certainly the case that the power of the institution should not be underestimated. The latter had an armoury of disciplinary measures at its disposal, including solitary confinement, corporal punishment, and the use of incentive-based 'points' systems which allowed for the withdrawal of privileges such as home leave for poor behaviour. Moreover, staff had the power to return individuals to court for possible reallocation to the 'next stage' of the disciplinary continuum – either to Approved School from a probation hostel or home, to a more strict, 'closed' Approved School from an open Approved School, or from Approved School to Borstal for over 14s. As a result, staff were quick to quash any suggestion on the part of delinquents that the institution did not hold the balance of power. Jacqueline, for example, required to reside in a home for unmarried mothers after leaving Duncroft, asked her probation officer:

> 'What happens if I won't go?' I told her it would be a condition of her licence that she went, to which she replied 'And if I don't keep that the school won't have me back, so I am quite safe'. I replied 'If you break your licence you are, of course, eligible for Borstal and you wouldn't really want the baby being born there'. Jacqueline smiled at me sweetly and said 'Oh, I see – you win'.[39]

Such sanctions could apply regardless of the apparent validity of the motivations for resistance. The 'ringleaders' in the Carlton uprising, for example, were committed to Borstal as a result of their role in 'fomenting the riot', despite the fact that the official inquiry subsequently upheld many of the boys' complaints. The magistrates in the case accepted only that 'the boys believed that they had a genuine grievance against the school and not that the boys did in fact have a genuine grievance'.[40]

However, a more detailed exploration of the operation of institutional power suggests that this picture of absolute control needs revising.

To begin with, managing committees were not always blind to the validity of delinquent complaints. Some committees actively solicited delinquent opinions, acting on those which were felt to have substance. In the case of Duncroft, for example, complaints by the girls in 1964 led to the suspension of letter censorship, compulsory church attendance and arbitrary bedroom inspection. Even in the case of the Carlton uprising, the chairman of the managers admitted to the press that 'this trouble has been boiling up for some time and there may be something in their complaints'.[41] It is clear that some institutions were more open than others in soliciting and acting on residents' grievances, and held the ultimate say in whether or not these were taken seriously. Even in institutions such as Duncroft, where girls had free access to members of the managing committee, complaints were frequently dismissed as mere 'childish hostility'.[42] However, the fact that delinquents' appeals to institution managers could on occasion lead to the revision of rules put in place by institution staff is significant: it suggests that managers did not always uphold staff prerogatives to set unreasonable rules. At Druids Heath in 1971, an incident involving an attack by a boy on a member of staff was deemed to have been a result of the boy being 'subject to some provocation'; his mother was assured that the staff member concerned 'would be dealt with by the managers'.[43]

Moreover, where intra-institutional means of resistance failed, delinquents were not entirely cut off from the possibility of having an impact beyond the confines of the institution. This power was demonstrated most notably at Standon Farm and Carlton. The public inquiries that followed both incidents accepted the validity of some of the grievances of the residents – regardless of the arrest of the ringleaders. In the case of Carlton, despite the assertion by the chairman of the managers that 'I cannot believe that nine-tenths of the staff used one-quarter of the violence which has been stated', several staff were deemed to have broken the rules in this respect, and the headmaster was publicly denounced as having acted in a manner 'unbecoming the dignity of a headmaster and not calculated to set a good example to boys'.[44] The uprising also formed a significant staging post in raising the political and social profile of residential institutions for juvenile delinquents in the late 1950s. The public enquiry made a number of recommendations aimed at modernising the Approved School system as a whole, including increased capital expenditure, increased training for staff, and improved facilities for recreation and psychiatric treatment; all these were accepted unreservedly by the government.[45] Commenting on the significance of the Carlton affair, the permanent under-secretary to the

Home Office stated that 'it cannot be denied that the recent disturbances, ...by focusing attention on many of the stresses and strains to
which the schools were subject, has given impetus to changes and
reforms that would otherwise have taken longer to bring about'.[46]

Less dramatically, there are also a number of examples of individual
delinquents making active use of the opportunities for redress provided
by parents or a court intervention. Julius, for example, made a complaint about High Beech during his appearance at juvenile court;
furthermore, he 'informed his Member of Parliament, through his
parents, that during his time at High Beech he had been bullied and
subjected to unpleasant practices, and the Home Secretary had been
asked by the Member of Parliament to provide an explanation'.[47] These
examples suggest that delinquent resistance could on occasion have
significant national impact, and that the balance of power did not
automatically rest with institution staff in such cases. This point is
significant in the context of a historiography which has laid stress on
the all-encompassing, 'total' character of residential institutions, and
the unremitting isolation imposed by their disciplinary structure.

Beyond the power to appeal to higher authorities, there is also a
much more fundamental way in which delinquents can be argued to
have influenced the principles and practices of institution regimes.
This relates to the extent to which they were prepared to consent to
institutional authority. Transfer of an individual out of the institution
was a last-ditch measure; delinquents therefore had significant power
to 'raise the temperature' of institutional life without crossing the
boundary that would lead to their removal. This power was well recognised by staff: the warden of High Beech, for example, commented in
1955 that 'the unsettlement ... was to some measure due to our
increased rate of growth, and I should be glad if we could return to our
old policy of setting a limit of five new boys in any one month, in
order that they may have a chance to settle down to our established
routine, rather than creating standards of their own choosing'.[48]
The nature of peer group relations within institutions also meant that
even a small number of troublemakers could have significant disruptive effects: the Burford House warden, for example, expressed deep
concern about Monica, who was noted to be 'breaking every rule of
the hostel including smoking in bed and going out after lights
out'. This was deemed highly problematic as 'all the other girls do
exactly what she tells them to'.[49] Delinquents thus had considerable ability to influence the limits within which staff power could
operate.

These points suggest that determining the precise balance of power between the institution and its residents is a complex task. At an individual level, the disciplinary power of the institution was considerable; both in the control exercised over the minutiae of residents' lives, and in the punishments meted out to those failing to conform. The institution also set the terms within which successful 'reform' was defined, leaving limited space for alternative formulations. Nevertheless, institutional power was in no sense total or absolute. At a collective level, residents had the power to effect significant changes in regimes by selectively withholding their consent to authority. The historical importance of this power has rarely been acknowledged or analysed.

Resistance and historical change

This point can be further illustrated by reference to the specific changes taking place within residential institutions for juvenile delinquents in the decades after the Second World War. As I have described elsewhere, this period saw significant transformations in both theorisations of delinquency and in its practical management. Within residential institutions, changes taking place included a relaxation in restrictions on residents' freedom of movement, activity, association and belief; a softening of institutional regimentation and punishment regimes, and a widening of the bounds of what constituted 'acceptable' behaviour (Wills, 2005a). Additionally, committal rates to such institutions declined over the period; increasingly, residential treatment was seen as a suitable option only for those with serious previous criminal records (Wills, 2005b). These transformations took place in the context of a wider transformation in socio-cultural norms, termed the 'permissive shift' within the historiography, which involved amongst other things sexual liberalisation, changes in codes of morality, and the growth of youth cultures (Marwick, 1998; Fisher, 1993).

In the context of the argument made above, it is significant to note that the 'subjects' of the juvenile justice system were by no means passive in the face of such changes; indeed, they were active participants in the process. To begin with, the trend towards admitting more difficult and criminal young people to institutions meant that gaining delinquent consent to institutional authority became increasingly difficult. This was well recognised at the time: in Sir Charles Cunningham's 1960 address to the conference of Approved School Headmasters, Headmistresses and Matrons (AHHMAS), he noted that 'there seems to be no doubt that a larger proportion of more difficult boys and girls are now being committed to the schools'. As a result, he stated the necessity for Approved Schools to 'adapt themselves to the earlier maturity and increasing toughness of a growing proportion of the young adolescents who are sent to them'.[50] In part, this adaptation involved tightening control through the increased provision of secure facilities for particularly troublesome individuals. However, it also involved a move towards meeting the new expectations and standards of young people: as J. N. Newby, an Approved School headmaster, noted in 1967, 'it seems increasingly obvious that youth will overthrow many of our set values. ... Already homosexuality, abortion and suicide have reached a level of social acceptance. We cannot therefore just aim at conformity to the values of the school.'[51] In effect, then, a more 'anti-social and anti-authority' residential population meant an inevitable relaxation in the accepted limits of behaviour, as delinquents' tolerance of highly restrictive practices diminished.

However, the transformation in disciplinary norms was governed by more than simply a greater concentration of more difficult individuals within institutions. Broader developments in prevalent understandings of self-identity over the 1960s, linked to the development of increasingly assertive youth cultures, also had an impact on the way in which delinquents responded to institutionalisation. In particular, desires for an expressive, convention-defying, independent existence were put forward with increasing confidence by many delinquents. Rita, for example, was said by her mother to believe that 'at 18 they should be able to run their own lives. ... She does not want to live a "normal" life, getting up each day and going to work. To her, drug taking is a spiritual experience which she must have.'[52] Intercepted correspondence from Duncroft girls during the later 1960s contains increasingly articulate references to drug-taking and sexual intercourse as 'expressive' experiences – transports to 'a world of bliss, sweet delight and sheer ecstasy'.[53] Such self-confident assertions of independence were also linked to increasing awareness of psychological theories of personality. Writing in 1972, the educationalist A. S. Neill, founder of the self-governing school Summerhill, noted that:

> there is a sophistication in the new generation. The new orientation in youth may stem from the spread of knowledge about psychology. Some of my older pupils ... juggle with terms like inferiority complex, mother fixation etc. If today, at one of our self-government meetings, a boy were charged for destroying books in the library and I made the proposal that he be appointed chief librarian, I am sure

there would be a cry of 'One of Neill's psychological tricks again'. No child would have said that forty-five years ago (1973: 209).

This belief in the changing subjectivity of young people was – again – reflected in official interpretations of the changing nature of delinquent populations. The AHHMAS technical sub-committee's 1969 'study of development' in Approved Schools stated that 'the current problem of the schools is that delinquent patterns are shaped and reinforced by peer groups to an extent that has not been possible in the past. Peer group support is more articulate and delinquent patterns are more explicit.' Their solution to this difficulty again involved positively engaging with this shift: 'depersonalising practices that appear necessary in the interests of control need to be avoided to assist in the child's search for self-identity'.[54]

The notion of permissive transformations as a function of an active relationship between delinquent expectations and 'official' understandings and practices goes well beyond the role allowed to delinquents within the existing historiography: it suggests that delinquents, in creatively resisting the parameters of institutional control, played a central role in the permissive transformations of the juvenile justice system in the postwar period. This was in part due to the increasingly criminal orientation of the individuals admitted to residential institutions, but it was also due to a broader shift in expectations: the above argument has illustrated the ways in which delinquents were fully cognisant of broader trends in national life, and how the resulting vision of what constituted acceptable levels of institutional control fed back into and reinforced transformations in professional ideology and practice.

This chapter has sought to re-think the paradigm set out in the existing historiography on juvenile delinquency, which involved seeing residential institutions as expressions of binding ruling-class social power, and resistance as a monolithic and ultimately futile gesture, driven by anger and fear. It has put forward a contrary model of resistance as imaginative, targeted and actively engaged with wider socio-cultural and professional contexts. As a consequence, juvenile delinquents should not be seen as analytically 'passive' or insignificant in accounts of historical change. Indeed, in the decades after the Second World War, they had a significant role to play in the permissive transformations of the juvenile justice system. Such a conclusion does not deny the reality of structures of power and coercion, which represented very real constraints on the freedom of action of residents within institutions. This was perhaps particularly the case for the Victorian and Edwardian institutions studied by authors such as Mahood, Cale and Cox. Never-theless, their analytical model by definition limits the possibilities for exploring the complexities and ambiguities of resistance. Ultimately, even in the most repressive of regimes – such as that of the Carlton Approved School – there remained a space in which delinquent agency could operate. As the juvenile justice system at the time was well aware, refusal to consent to authority could profoundly disrupt institutional regimes and, by extension, society at large.

Notes

1 Duncroft (1948–1982), run under the auspices of the National Institute for Mental Health, catered for girls aged between 15 and 18, focusing particu-larly on girls of 'good intelligence' deemed to be 'in need of psychiatric oversight'. Its records are held in the Barnardo's Archive, Sydney Jones Library, University of Liverpool, D3/iii/b1 and D3/3c5. Burford House (1951–1970) and High Beech (1949–1978), both overseen by the London Police Court Mission, catered respectively for girls and boys aged between 15 and 18. Its records are held in the Rainer Foundation Collection, Galleries of Justice, Nottingham, boxes 2, 10, 13 and 25. Druids Heath (1940–1980), run by Barnardo's, took in boys aged between 8 and 15. See Barnardo's Archive, Sydney Jones Library, University of Liverpool D3/3a/10. Access to archival material was made possible by kind permission of the Sydney Jones Library, University of Liverpool, by Barnardo's UK, and by the Galleries of Justice, Nottingham. None bear any responsibility for the argument presented in the paper. All names and other identifying details have been altered to protect the anonymity of the individuals concerned. To ensure complete anonymisation, quotations from progress reports are referenced only by month and year in footnotes; the date of entry to the institution of the individual concerned is not given. I am indebted to Beverley Baker and Adrian Allan for outstanding archival access and support.
2 O. P. I. Ingleby, *Report of the committee on children and young persons*, Cmnd. 1191 (London, 1960), p. 26, para. 66.
3 Duncroft Approved School [hereafter Dn], Visiting manager's report, Managing committee meeting minutes [hereafter MCMM], February 1961.
4 Dn, Visiting manager's report, MCMM, August 1962.
5 Dn, *ibid.*, February 1961.
6 High Beech Probation Home [hereafter HB], Managing committee meeting minutes [hereafter MCMM], November 1950.
7 Burford House Probation Hostel [hereafter BH], Progress report, April 1955.
8 BH, *ibid.*, September 1962.
9 Dn, Headmistress's report, MCMM, July 1961.
10 BH, Daily record book entry, December 1969.
11 BH, *ibid.*
12 BH, Warden's report, MCMM, February 1965.

13 BH, Progress report, April 1961.
14 Dn, 'Julia', Letter from headmistress to mother, 1961.
15 Dn, 'Linda', Letter from Linda to parents, 1956.
16 BH, Daily record book entry, August 1966.
17 Dn, Visiting manager's report, MCMM, February 1965.
18 Dn, *ibid*.
19 J. C. Maude, *Report of the committee of enquiry into the conduct of Standon Farm Approved School and the circumstances connected with the murder of a master at the school on 15th February, 1947.*, Cmd. 7150 (London, 1947), 6, para.5.
20 *Ibid.*, 26–7, para. 39.
21 'Master admits "blunder": boys' belts burnt at school', *The Times*, 5 September 1959, 4.
22 '80 [sic] break out of Approved School', *The Times*, 31 August 1959, 8.
23 *Ibid.*
24 'Master admits "blunder": boys' belts burnt at school', *The Times*, 5 September 1959, 4.
25 Dn, Visiting manager's report, MCMM, April 1961.
26 Dn, 'Emer', Letter from Emer to parents, 1968.
27 'Q.C. blames "system" as a cause of Approved School trouble', *The Times*, 6 November 1959, 8.
28 *Ibid.*
29 Editorial, *Approved Schools Gazette*, February 1970, 479.
30 Dn, MCMM, April 1962.
31 Dn, 'Josephine', Letter from children's home to Duncroft', 1954.
32 Christopher's account was transcribed by his mother in Finlay (1971), see also Finlay (1969).
33 Dn, 'Sabina', File note, 1968.
34 BH, Daily record book entry, February 1966.
35 BH, MCMM, July 1951.
36 Dn, Visiting manager's report, MCMM, June 1968.
37 '80 break out of Approved School', *The Times*, 31 August 1959, 8.
38 *Ibid.*
39 Dn, 'Jacqueline', Letter from probation officer to headmistress, 1964.
40 'Disturbance at Approved School', *The Times*, 7 September 1959, 7.
41 '80 break out of Approved School', *The Times*, 31 August 1959, 8.
42 Dn, Visiting manager's report, MCMM, February 1962.
43 Druids Heath, Management committee meeting minutes, November 1971.
44 V. Durand, *Disturbances at the Carlton Approved School on 29th and 30th August, 1959: report of inquiry*, Cmnd. 937 (London, 1960), 24, para. 89.
45 *Ibid.*
46 'Approved School changes coming: impetus given by Carlton affair', *The Times*, 27 May 1960, 6.
47 HB, Warden's report, MCMM, July 1967.
48 HB, *ibid.*, August 1955.
49 BH, Progress report, April 1968.
50 'The address of Sir Charles Cunningham, K.B.E, C.B., C.V.B., at Southport', *Approved Schools Gazette*, June 1960, 99.

51 M. J. N. Newby, 'Social training within the Approved School', *Approved Schools Gazette*, December 1967, 433.
52 Dn, 'Rita', Letter from mother to headmistress, 1970.
53 Dn, 'Frankie', Letter from boyfriend to Frankie, 1970.
54 Association of Headmasters, Headmistresses and Matrons of Approved Schools, *Approved Schools 1969: a study of development*, Technical Sub-Committee; no. 9 (1969), 13.

Concluding Remarks: The 'Punitive Turn': The Shape of Punishment and Control in Contemporary Society

Helen Johnston

In drawing together these historical contributions, this conclusion will discuss the shape of punishment and social control in contemporary society, focusing particularly on what has been described as the 'punitive turn'. This conclusion will examine emerging trends and theoretical concepts that have come to dominate discussions of punishment and control in recent years. The focus of this conclusion will predominantly be on two themes or concepts, namely, mass imprisonment, and the 'new punitiveness'. Where useful, and appropriate, these themes will also be linked back to the historical contributions in this collection. Where necessary, this will identify continuity and change, with regard to punishment and social control. First, a brief context for this discussion will be provided.

At the time of writing, April 2008, the prison population in England and Wales stood at over 82,000, hitting a 'new all-time high' (Prison Reform Trust, 2008a), in recent months, police cells have been used for the 'overflow' and prison overcrowding has become an issue of concern for many commentators. The prison population in England and Wales has grown from 10,000 in 1940 to over 80,000 at the end of 2006 and has doubled in size since 1993 (cited in Jewkes, 2007). In the last 20–30 years, it has often been argued that the prison or penal system in England and Wales is 'in crisis' (various perspectives have been offered, see Cavadino and Dignan, 2002 for overview). Often these discussions have debated whether this is a crisis of the prison system, or a broader crisis of the penal system (sentencing, the courts system etc). Fitzgerald and Sim (1982) maintain that this crisis has been 'perpetual' since the Gladstone Committee in 1895 (see Chapter 5 and Chapter 9).

Whilst this high prison population is significant in England and Wales, we are not alone in the maintenance of a high and expanding prison population, and features of the prison system that commentators regard as disturbing. More people are being sent to prison and more people being sentenced to longer periods of imprisonment in England and Wales. Many Western countries have followed the lead of the United States, and prison rates have increased, yet this does not seem to be related to crime rates, as they have been declining (Pratt, 2007).

Throughout the world, there are more than 9.25 million people held in prison, either as remand (pre-trial detainees) or as sentenced prisoners. Almost half of these are held in three countries; the United States has a prison population of 2.19 million, there are 1.55 million people held in China (plus pre-trial detainees and those held under 'administrative detention') and 0.87 million are imprisoned in Russia (Walmsley, 2006). Whilst the US and Chinese prison populations have been increasing, US by 10%, China by 3%, the Russian prison population has fallen by 22% since 1999 (King, 2007). However, there may be some indications that the prison population in the US is beginning to wane, at least within the state prison system (King, 2007). Prison populations have been growing dramatically in other countries, in England and Wales from 88 per 100,000 population in 1992 to 145 in 2006, in New Zealand, from 128 in 1995 to 189 in 2006 (Pratt, 2007).

As King (2007) observes these countries have different histories, different cultures and different levels of crime and one of the most important differences is the extent to which cellular confinement is practised. The historical origins of this use of panopticism (see Introduction) will be returned to at the end of this concluding piece. It is within this context, across these trends, and other disturbing features of contemporary imprisonment and punishment, (in predominantly Western societies) that sociologists and criminologists have created and utilised the concepts alluded to at the beginning of this chapter.

Mass imprisonment

The term 'mass imprisonment' has recently been used to describe the situation of imprisonment in the United States in recent years. For Garland, mass imprisonment is not just the sheer numbers of people in prison (above historical and comparative norms) but also the 'social concentration of imprisonment's effects' (2001: 6). Garland maintains that 'imprisonment becomes *mass imprisonment* when it ceases to be the incarceration of individual offenders and becomes the systematic imprisonment of whole groups of the population' (2001: 6, original emphasis). The population systematically imprisoned in this way, are young black urban males, for whom imprisonment has become 'normalised', a 'regular, predictable part of experience, rather than a rare and infrequent event' (2001: 2). The Big House prisons of early twentieth century has been replaced by the 'warehousing' of offenders (see Chapter 1) in what has been described as the 'great American carceral boom' (Wacquant, 2005: 5). In understanding the racial disproportionality in US prisons, Wacquant argues that the prison has become part of a 'historical sequence of "peculiar institutions" that have shouldered the task of defining and confining African Americans, alongside slavery, the Jim Crow regime and the ghetto' (2001: 95). The prison and the ghetto have met and meshed as mass incarceration has been adopted to 'discipline the poor and contain the dishonoured, lower-class African Americans [who] dwell not in a society with prisons as their white counterparts do, but in *the first genuine prison society of history*' (Wacquant, 2001: 121, original emphasis).

Although the US is an extreme example, the disproportionate and discriminatory incarceration of minority groups is not geographically bounded. The overrepresentation of minority ethnic or indigenous populations is a concerning feature of imprisonment in England and Wales (Edgar, 2007), and in other countries around the world, such as Australia (Brown, 2005), and New Zealand (Pratt, 2006). The shift from the Big House to the Warehouse prison reveals the ways in which these prisons now rely on 'coercive regimes of total segregation to isolate the most threatening inmates'; increasingly reliant on technology and militarised guards and an interior which, 'no longer reflects any imperative of order other than concentration in space and containment' (Simon, 2000: 228–9).

Within this context, King (1999) argues that one 'of the most dramatic features of the great American experiment with mass imprisonment' is the rise of the use of super-maximum security prisons (supermaxes). These were constructed to deal with disruptive or problematic prisoners that 'normal' maximum security prisons could not hold. The use of the supermax, predominantly in the US, but also reflected in other countries, has escalated since its origins in the early 1980s and they are often significantly over-used. King (1999) indicates that the 'proliferation of supermax' facilities, resulted in an estimated 20,000 prisoners held in such conditions in the US in 1998 (although use varies in different states) and a system in which these prisons are 'significantly and inappropriately over-used'. Under such conditions prisoners are 'locked down in conditions of separate confinement in an environment virtually devoid of stimulation. When they leave their cells, it is only when hand-cuffed, leg-ironed, belly chained and, sometimes, spit-masked, and when accompanied by at least two, sometimes more, officers' (King, 2007: 118). In US states where the death penalty is retained, those on super-max 'death row', live out their time in units which are 'literally trans-forming those waiting to die… into a kind of untouchable toxic waste that need only be securely contained until its final disposal… [and] may well be made more pliable and willing to die as a result' (Lynch, 2005: 79).

Recently in England and Wales, the government has announced its plan to build three 'titan' prisons, holding about 2,500 prisoners in each to tackle the overcrowding crisis. As part of this programme other prisons will be re-configured and the Ministry of Justice is said to be 'actively looking at securing a prison ship'. The intention is to increase prison capacity to 96,000 by 2014 (Dyer, 2007).

The 'new punitiveness'

More recently, theorists have discussed the 'new punitiveness' (Pratt *et al.*, 2005), the idea that this period of the twenty-first century reflects a change in the way that punishment has been delivered in Western society. The features of this new punitiveness are not only an increase in prison populations, and longer sentences across Western societies (although not all societies), but the ways in which imprisonment, sen-tencing policy, and the operation of the penal system in some coun-tries have become more punitive for the increasing numbers of people being confined. For example 'three strikes' laws, mandatory and inde-terminate sentencing, shaming and public humiliation punishments (chain gangs), austere prison regimes, electronic surveillance techno-logies, features which were once 'exceptional …becoming far more central to the penal process as a whole' and which 'seem to abandon long-standing limits to punishment' (Pratt *et al.*, 2005: xii).

Some features of this 'new punitiveness' are clearly reminiscent of features of Victorian imprisonment and penal policy – long hours of isolation (or lockdown), sensory deprivation, deprived and unproduc-tive prison regimes. Here the historical links to the use of the separate and silent systems, and the enduring nature of the use of separation, which remained in England and Wales, until the early twentieth century is obvious. Chapters 4 and 10 research periods in which the use of the separate and silent systems, and deterrent regimes from the 1850s, predominated in local and convict prison respectively.

Additionally, Chapter 9 focuses on the prison experience in the late Victorian period and demonstrates the ways in which prisoner memoirs were instrumental in challenging the severity of such prison practices, but also the physical and mental deterioration experienced by those confined under such conditions.

Yet, the focus on the emergence of the modern penal-welfare complex of the late nineteenth and early twentieth centuries (Garland, 1985), has drawn attention away from the daily realities of imprisonment for the majority of the population. The removal of groups such as young offenders (Chapter 8), those with mental illness, inebriates and the creation of distinct policies to deal with certain types of offenders, (e.g. preventive detention), may appeal to this welfarist or rehabilitative shift, but there are caveats to such an approach. As Chapter 7 observes, female inebriate reformatories were designed for control and containment, and there was widespread disillusionment over the reformatories ability to cure, or rehabilitate these women. It must also be noted that although women were removed from the prison, state controlled and private or charitable semi-penal institutions for women, continued throughout the twentieth century, to regulate women who were regarded as 'deviant', but were not necessarily criminal (Barton, 2005). In addition, the local and convict prison (Chapter 10) regimes which prisoners continued to be subject to should 'give pause to those who insist the Edwardian period witnessed the emergence of a new penal structure' (Bailey, 1997: 302).

Therefore, as Chapter 5 reveals changes in prison conditions and practices in the early twentieth century, continued to be based on the amelioration of excesses of punishment, rather than any transformation of such practices. Isolation, sensory deprivation and deprived penal regimes continued, at least until the 1930s. The inquiry, *English Prisons Today* published in 1922, by Hobhouse and Brockway, notes continued concerns with the deep psychological effects of such regimes on prisoners and the debilitating effects of the prevention of communication. The prevention of communication impacted on prisoners' ability to communicate in later life, affecting the potential for employment and 'reinforcing the criminal as "anti-social" or "other"', lacking the social skills to converse in the wider world (Jewkes and Johnston, 2008). Contemporary parallels with the debilitating effects of preventing communication are also demonstrated in the research on in-cell television. It is often those prisoners least able to engage in social intercourse, the vulnerable or fragile, that become invisible behind cells doors as they tuned into television and 'tuned out' of prison culture (Jewkes, 2002).

In 2004, suspected terrorist detainees held at Belmarsh prison and others in immigration detention centres, were suffering from severe depressive illnesses and forms of institutionalisation. 'One detainee was removed from Belmarsh to Broadmoor after his behaviour deteriorated rapidly. He cut his arms, drank toilet cleaner, set himself on fire' (Jewkes and Johnston, 2008: 6).

However, it is argued that what is 'new', about the new punitiveness, is that these features mark a departure from the prison as a social laboratory producing docile bodies, but rather 'the prison has been reborn as a container for human goods now endlessly recycled through what has become a transcarceral system of control' (Pratt *et al.*, 2005: xiii).

Whilst we can observe the comparisons between, the historical use of punishment and imprisonment, and make observations as to the continuities, or the departures from such penal practices, it appears that features such as isolation, lack of communication and deprived regimes are more enduring. It is also the case that in the UK, thousands of prisoners are locked up for long hours in Victorian prisons (HMP Liverpool is currently the largest prison in Western Europe, closely followed by HMP Wandsworth, both were built in the 1850s); whilst the philosophies of punishment behind their confinement may have been through various changes and developments since their construction, to some extent, the physical and architectural environment remains strikingly similar to the experiences of their nineteenth century counterparts (Jewkes and Johnston, 2007). Many of these, often 'local prisons', are inadequate and overcrowded, 'they have not been consigned to the history books; thousands of prison inmates still live, sleep and work in these monoliths of the Victorian penal imagination' (Jewkes and Johnston, 2007: 191). At the end of March 2008, of the 'top ten' most overcrowded prisons, eight were built in the nineteenth-century; HMP Shrewsbury, originally built in 1793 and altered in the 1880s (Jewkes and Johnston, 2007), is second in the list at 181% overcrowded, but all the Victorian prisons in the list were overcrowded by 157% or more (cited by Prison Reform Trust, 2008b). This list also contains HMP Altcourse, 165% overcrowded, the first purpose built, financed and managed private prison which opened in 1997 and is run by GSL (HM Prison Service, 2008). HMP Pentonville, was also singled out recently when the annual report of the Independent Monitoring Board of the prison highlighted their concerns at the 'endemic squalor and poverty of regime which ought to be a matter of deep shame to Government in twenty-first Britain' (cited by Prison Reform Trust, 2008c).

As noted earlier, in examining international prison rates, King (2007) has usefully argued that what most of the countries, with high prison populations share, is the use of cellular confinement. Predominantly, they are Western societies, with prisons that were historical built on notions of protestant ethic, a feature often overlooked within this debate. He maintains that what is need is a reconsideration of 'panopticism' (see Introduction). Further, it is perhaps this deep 'cultural attachment' to prison that constrains and limits our penal imagination (Jewkes and Johnston, 2006). Thus, it is to the historical origins of the prison, that we must look to understand how and why 'the seeds of the obsession with containment and control' were planted (Fitzgerald and Sim, 1982: 163). However, as Ignatieff observes:

> it is easier to explain the coming of the penitentiary than it is to decide how that history continues to constrain the present and define the future. In one sense Pentonville is gone. Its silence has been broken and its routine has been shattered. In another sense, it is still there, a Victorian carapace of spaces and walls that continues to constrain any attempt at a new start (1978: 215).

Bibliography

A Manchester Merchant (1880) *Kirkdale Gaol: Twelve Months Imprisonment of a Manchester Merchant* (Manchester: Heywood & Son).

A Merchant (1869) *Six Years in the Convict Prisons of England* (London: R. Bentley).

Adams, R. (1994) *Prison Riots in Britain and the USA* (Basingstoke: Macmillan).

Addison, P. (1992) *Churchill on the Home Front 1900–1955* (London: Jonathan Cape).

Allen, H. (1987) *Justice Unbalanced* (Milton Keynes: Open University Press).

Allen, R. L. (1999) 'The socio-spatial making and marking of 'us': toward a critical postmodern spatial theory of difference and community', *Social Identities*, 5 (3): 249–77.

Anderson, G. (1976) *Victorian Clerks* (Manchester: Manchester University Press).

Anon (1844) 'Causes of the Increase of Crime', *Blackwood's Edinburgh Magazine*, 345 (56): 1–14.

Anon (1860) 'Thieves and Thieving', *The Cornhill Magazine*, 2: 326–44.

Anon [H. W. Holland and F. Greenwood] (1863) 'Revelation of Prison Life', *The Cornhill Magazine* 7: 638–48.

Anon [H. Martineau] (1865) 'Life in the Criminal Class', *The Edinburgh Review* 122: 337–70.

Anon (1896) 'License – Not Liberty', *British Medical Journal*, October 3: 959.

Antrobus, E. (1875) *Training Schools and Training Ships* (London: Staunton & Son).

Bailey, V. (1985) 'Churchill as Home Secretary: Reforming the Prison Service', *History Today*, 35 (3): 10–13.

Bailey, V. (1987) *Delinquency and Citizenship: Reclaiming the Young Offender 1914–1948* (Oxford: Clarendon).

Bailey, V. (1993) 'The Fabrication of Deviance: "Dangerous Classes" and "Criminal Classes" in Victorian England', in J. Rule and R. Malcolmson (eds) *Protest and Survival* (London: Merlin).

Bailey, V. (1997) 'English Prisons, Penal Culture, and the Abatement of Imprisonment, 1895–1922', *Journal of British Studies*, 36 (3): 285–324.

Bainbridge, B. (1984) *Watson's Apology* (Harmondsworth: Penguin).

Balfour, J. (1901) *My Prison Life* (London: Chapman & Hall).

Ball, Rev. P. H. (1956) *Prison Was My Parish* (London: Heinemann).

Ballinger, A. (1996) 'The Guilt of the Innocent and the Innocence of the Guilty: The Cases of Marie Fahmy and Ruth Ellis' in A. Myers and S. Wright (eds) *No Angels* (London: Pandora).

Ballinger, A. (2000) *Dead Woman Walking: Executed Women in England & Wales 1900–1955* (Dartmouth: Ashgate).

Ballinger, A. (2005) 'Reasonable Women Who Kill: Re-interpreting and Redefining Women's Responses to Domestic Violence in England and Wales 1900–1965' in *Outlines: Critical Social Studies*, 7 (2): 65–82.

Ballinger, A. (2007) 'Masculinity in the Dock: Legal Responses to Male Violence and Female Retaliation in England and Wales 1900–1965', *Social & Legal Studies*, 16 (4): 459–81.

Ballinger, A. (2008: forthcoming) 'Gender, Power and the State: Same as It Ever Was?' in R. Coleman, J. Sim, S. Tombs and D. Whyte (eds) *State Power Crime* (London: Sage).

Barrett, A. R. (1895) 'The Era of Fraud and Embezzlement: Its Causes and Remedies', *Arena*, 14: 196–204.

Bartky, S. (1990) *Femininity and Domination* (London: Routledge).

Barton, A. (2000) 'Wayward Girls and Wicked Women: Two Centuries of Semi-Penal Institutionalisation on Merseyside', *Liverpool Law Review*, 22: 157–71.

Barton, A. (2005) *Fragile Moralities and Dangerous Sexualities: Two Centuries of Semi-Penal Institutionalisation for Women* (Aldershot: Ashgate).

Bartrip, P. W. J. (1981) 'Public Opinion and Law Enforcement: The Ticket-of-Leave Scares in Mid-Victorian Britain', in V. Bailey (ed.) *Policing and Punishment in Nineteenth Century Britain* (London: Croom Helm).

Bauman, Z. (1995) *Life in Fragments: Essays in Postmodern Morality* (London: Blackwell).

Beames, T. (1852) *The Rookeries of London: Past, Present and Prospective* (London: Bosworth).

Bean, P. and Melville, J. (1989) *Lost Children of the Empire: The Untold Story of Britain's Child Migrants* (London: Unwin Hyman).

Beaumont, G. and Tocqueville, A. De (1833/1979) *On the Penitentiary System in the United States and its Application in France* (Southern Illinois: Southern Illinois University Press).

Behlmer, G. (1982) *Child Abuse and Moral Reform in England, 1870–1908* (Stanford: Stanford University Press).

Beggs, T. (1869) 'On the Same', *TNAPSS*: 338–48.

Benjamin, W. (1936) *The Work of Art in the Age of Mechanical Reproduction* [On-line]: www.marxists.org/reference/subject/philosophy/works/ge/benjamin.htm

Benn, T. (1987) *Out of the Wilderness: Diaries 1963–67* (London: Hutchinson).

Bennett, P. W. (1988) 'Taming "Bad Boys" of the "Dangerous Class": Child Rescue and Restraint at the Victoria Industrial School, 1887–1935', *Histoire Sociale – Social History*, XXI (41): 71–96.

Bentley, J. H. (1996) 'Cross-cultural interaction and periodization in world history', *The American Historical Review*, 101 (3): 749–70.

Benson, M. (1985) 'Denying the guilty mind: accounting for involvement in a white-collar crime', *Criminology*, 23, (4): 583–607.

Berman, M. (1982) *All that is Solid Melts into Air* (London: Verso).

Best, G. (1985) *Mid-Victorian Britain 1851–75* (London: Fontana).

Bidwell, A. (1895) *From Wall Street to Newgate* (London: Forum Press).

Birmingham Justices (1921) 'Clinical Treatment for Defective Offenders', *The Howard Journal*, 1: 78–80.

Blackburn, G. (1993) *The Children's Friend Society: Juvenile Emigrants to Western Australia, South Africa and Canada, 1834–42* (Northbridge, Western Australia: Access).

Bland, L. (1995) *Banishing the Beast: English Feminism and Sexual Morality 1885–1914* (London: Penguin).

Booth, C. (1971) 'Life and Labour of the People in London' in A. Fried and R. Elman (eds) *Charles Booth's London* (London: Penguin, first published 1903).

Bosanquet, B. (1899) *Rich and Poor* (London: Macmillan).

Bosworth, M. and Sparks, R. (2000) 'New directions in prison studies: some introductory comments', *Theoretical Criminology*, 4 (3): 259–64.

Bosworth, M. and Carrabine, E. (2001) 'Reassessing Resistance: Race, Gender and Sexuality in Prison', *Punishment and Society* 3 (4): 501–15.

Bradlow, E. (1984) 'The Children's Friend Society at the Cape of Good Hope', *Victorian Studies*, xxvii: 155–77.

Brenton, E. P. (1837) *The Bible and the Spade, or Captain Brenton's Account of the Rise and Progress of the Children's Friend Society* (London).

Brenzel, B. (1980) 'Domestication as Reform: A Study of the Socialisation of Wayward Girls, 1856–1905', *Howard Educational Review*, 50 (2):196–213.

Briggs, J. Harrison, C. McInnes, A. and Vincent, D. (2001) *Crime and Punishment in England* (London: UCL Press).

Brocklehurst, F. (1898) *I Was in Prison* (London: T. Fisher Unwin).

Brown, A. (2003) *English Society and the Prison: Time, Culture and Politics in the Development of the Modern Prison, 1850–1920* (Woodbridge: The Boydell Press).

Brown, A. (2007) 'The Amazing Mutiny at the Dartmoor Convict Prison', *British Journal of Criminology* 47 (2): 276–92.

Brown, A. and Maxwell, C. (2003) 'A "Receptacle of Our Worst Convicts": Bermuda, the Chatham Prison Riots and the Transportation of Violence', *Journal of Caribbean History* 37 (2): 233–55.

Brown, D. (2005) 'Continuity, rupture, or just more of the 'volatile and contradictory'? Glimpses of New South Wales penal practice behind and through the discursive' in J. Pratt, D. Brown, M. Brown, S. Hallsworth and W. Morrison (eds) *The New Punitiveness: Trends, Theories, Perspectives* (Cullompton: Willan).

Burt, C. (1925) *The Young Delinquent* (London: University of London).

Cairns, D. (1998) *Advocacy and the Making of the Adversarial Criminal Trial, 1800–1865* (Oxford: Clarendon).

Cale, M. (1993) 'Girls and the perception of sexual danger in the Victorian reformatory system', *History*, 78, 201–17.

Calvert. E. and Calvert, T. (1933) *The Lawbreaker: A Critical Study of the Modern Treatment of Crime* (London: George Routledge & Sons).

Campbell, H., Know, T. W. and Byrnes, T. (1895) *Darkness and Daylight* (Connecticut: Hartford).

Carlebach, J. (1970) *Caring for Children in Trouble* (London: Routledge & Kegan Paul).

Carlen, P. (1983) *Women's Imprisonment* (London: Routledge & Kegan Paul).

Carlen, P. (1988) *Women, Crime and Poverty* (Milton Keynes: Open University Press).

Carpenter, M. (1851) *Reformatory Schools for the Perishing and Dangerous Classes and for Juvenile Offenders* (London: C. Gilpin).

Carrabine, E. (2005) 'Prison Riots, Social Order and the Problem of Legitimacy', *British Journal of Criminology*, 45 (6): 896–913.

Carswell, D. (ed.) (1925) *The Trial of Ronald True* (Edinburgh: Hodge & Co).

Carter, J. (1893) 'Commercial Morality', *Economic Review*, 3, (3): 318–47.

Cavadino, M. and Dignan, J. (2002) *The Penal System: An Introduction* (Third Edition) (London: Sage).

Chadwick, R. (1992) *Bureaucratic Mercy: The Home Office and the Treatment of Capital Cases in Victorian England* (New York: Garland).

Cheli, G. (2003) *Images of America: Sing Sing Prison* (Charleston: Arcadia).

Chesser, E. (1909) 'Inebriety Among Women', *British Journal of Inebriety*, 6 (3): 186–9.

Childs, M. J. (1990) 'Boy Labour in Late Victorian and Edwardian England and the Remaking of the working class', *Journal of Social History*, 23 (4): 783–802.

Christiaens, J. (2002) 'Testing the Limits: Redefining Resistance in a Belgian Boys' Prison, 1895–1905', in P. Cox and H. Shore (eds) *Becoming Delinquent: British and European Youth, 1650–1950* (Aldershot: Ashgate).

Churchill, R. (1967) *Winston S. Churchill: Young Statesman 1901–14* (London: Heinemann).

Churchill, R. (1969) *Winston S. Churchill Companion Volume II Part 2 1907–1911* (London: Heinemann).

Churchill, W. (1900) *London to Ladysmith via Pretoria* (London: Longmans Green).

Churchill, W. (1930) *My Early Life* (London: Odhams Press).

Clapson, M. (1992) *A Bit of a Flutter: Popular Gambling and English Society, c.1832–1961* (Manchester: Manchester University Press).

Clark, A. (2000) 'Domesticity and the Problem of Wifebeating in Nineteenth-Century Britain: Working-Class Culture, Law and Politics' in S. D'Cruze (ed.) *Everyday Violence in Britain 1850–1950* (Harlow: Longman).

Clark, M. J. (1982) *'The Data of Alienism': Evolutionary Neurology, Physiological Psychology and the Reconstruction of British Psychiatric Theory, c.1850–c.1900*, Unpublished D. Phil thesis, University of Oxford, UK.

Clarke Hall, W. (1926) *Children's Courts* (London: George Allen & Unwin).

Clay, W. L. (1862) *Our Convict System* (London: Macmillan & Co).

Clayton, G. F. (1958) *The Wall Is Strong* (London: Long).

Cohen, S. and Taylor, L. (1972) *Psychological Survival: The Experience of Long-Term Imprisonment* (Harmondsworth: Penguin).

Cohen, S and Scull, A. (1983) (eds) *Social Control and the State* (Oxford: Martin Robertson).

Cohen, S. (1996) 'The Punitive City' in J. Muncie, E. McLaughlin and M. Langan (eds.) *Criminological Perspectives* (London: Sage).

Collier, R. (1995a) *Masculinity, Law and the Family* (London: Routledge).

Collier, R. (1995b) 'A father's "Normal" Love?: Masculinities, Criminology and the Family' in R. Dobash and R. Dobash (eds) *Gender and Crime* (Cardiff: Cardiff University Press).

Conley, C. (1991) *The Unwritten Law: Criminal Justice in Victorian Kent* (New York: Oxford University Press).

Connell, R. W. (1987) *Gender & Power* (Cambridge: Polity Press).

Connell, R.W. (1996) 'The State, Gender and Sexual Politics: Theory and Appraisal' in H. L. Radtke and H. J. Stam (eds) *Power/Gender: Social Relations in Theory and Practice* (London: Sage).

Conover, T. (2001) *Newjack: Guarding Sing Sing* (New York: Vintage Books).

Convict Number 77 (1903) *The Mark of the Broad Arrow* (London: R. A. Everett).

Cooper, D. (1974) *The Lesson of the Scaffold* (London: Allen Lane).

Cox, L. (1986) 'My impressions of Sing Sing', *The Westchester Historian*, 62 (2): 44–53.

Cox, P. (1996) 'Girls, Deficiency and Delinquency' in D. Wright and A. Digby (eds) *From Idiocy to Mental Deficiency: Historical Perspectives on People with Learning Disabilities* (London: Routledge).

Cox, P. (2003) *Gender, Justice and Welfare: Bad Girls in Britain, 1900–1950* (Basingstoke: Palgrave Macmillan).

Crewe, B. (2007) 'Power, adaptation and resistance in a late-modern men's prison' *British Journal of Criminology*, 47 (2): 256–75.

Crofton, W. (1863) *Convict Systems and Transportation* (London: William Ridgeway).

Dalrymple, D. (1870) 'What Measures May be Adopted with a View to the Repression of Habitual Drunkenness', *TNAPSS*: 276–9.

Davie, N. (2005) *Tracing the Criminal: The Rise of Scientific Criminology in Britain, 1860–1918* (Oxford: Bardwell).

Davies, A. (2007) 'Glasgow's 'Reign of Terror': Street Gangs, Racketeering and Intimidation in the 1920s and 1930s', *Contemporary British History*, 21 (4): 405–27.

Davies, O. (2005) *Murder, Magic, Madness: The Victorian Trials of Dove and Wizard* (Harlow: Pearson Longman).

Davin, A. (1996) *Growing up Poor: Home, School and Street in London, 1870–1914* (London: Rivers Oram Press).

Davis, J. (1980) 'The London Garotting Panic of 1862: A Moral Panic and the Creation of a Criminal Class in Mid-Victorian England', in V. A. C. Gatrell, B. Lenman and G. Parker (eds) *Crime and the Law: The Social History of Crime in Western Europe* (London: Europa).

Davitt, M. (1886) *The Prison Life of Michael Davitt* (Dublin: Lalor).

Dawson, J. (1887) *Imprisoned in the House of Detention for Libel* (London: John & Robert Maxwell).

de Certeau, M. (1988) *The Writing of History* (West Sussex: Columbia University Press).

De Tocqueville, A. (1835/1998) *Democracy in America* (Hertfordshire: Wordsworth Editions).

DeLacy, M. (1981) ''Grinding Men Good?' Lancashire's Prisons at Mid-Century' in V. Bailey (ed.) *Policing and Punishment in the Nineteenth Century* (London: Croom Helm).

Deleuze, G. (1986) *Foucault* (Minneapolis: University of Minnesota Press).

Dendrickson, G. and Thomas, F. (1954) *The Truth About Dartmoor* (London: Victor Gollancz).

Dobash, R. P., Dobash, R. E. and S. Gutteridge (1986) *The Imprisonment of Women* (Oxford: Basil Blackwell).

Dobash, R. P. and McLaughlin, P. (1992) 'The Punishment of Women in Nineteenth-Century Scotland', in E. Breitenbach and E. Gordon (eds) *Women in Scottish Society 1800–1945* (Edinburgh: Edinburgh University Press).

Dodge, L. M. (2002) *'Whores and Thieves of the Very Worst Kind': A Study of Women, Crime and Prisons, 1835–2000* (Dekalb: Northern Illinois University Press).

Donzelot, J. (1979) *The Policing of Families* (London: Hutchinson).

Du Cane, E. F. (1876) 'Repression of Crime', *TNAPSS*: 271–308.

Dumm, T. L. (1987) *Democracy and Punishment: Disciplinary Origins of the United States* (London: University of Wisconsin Press).

Durham, A. M. (1989) 'Newgate of Connecticut: origins and early days of an early American prison', *Justice Quarterly*, 6 (1): 89–116.

Durkheim, E. (1973) *On Morality and Society: Selected Writings* (Chicago: Chicago University Press).

Dyer, C. (2007) 'Three supersize prison housing 2,500 each will be built to tackle overcrowding crisis', *The Guardian*, 6 December.

East, W. N. (1927) *An Introduction to Forensic Psychiatry* (London: J. and A. Churchill).

East, W. N. (1949) *Society and the Criminal* (London: HMSO).

Edgar, K. (2007) 'Black and minority ethnic prisoners' in Y. Jewkes (ed.) *Handbook on Prisons* (Cullompton: Willan).

Eigen, J. (1995) *Witnessing Insanity* (Baltimore: Johns Hopkins University Press).

Eigen, J. (2003) *Unconscious Crime* (Baltimore: Johns Hopkins University Press).

Elias, N. (1978) *The Civilizing Process* (Oxford: Blackwell).

Ellmann, R. (1988) *Oscar Wilde* (New York: Alfred A. Knopf).

Emsley, C. (1996) 'Albion's Felonious Attractions: Reflections upon the History of Crime in England' in C. Emsley and L. A. Knafla (eds) *Crime and Histories of Crime: Studies in the Historiography of Crime and Criminal Justice* (London: Greenwood Press).

Emsley, C. (2005a) 'Crime and Punishment: 10 years of research, Filling in, adding up, moving on: Criminal Justice History in Contemporary Britain', *Crime, Histoire & Sociétés / Crime, History & Societies*, 9 (1): 117–38.

Emsley, C. (2005b) *Crime and Society in England 1750–1900*, Third Edition (Harlow: Pearson Longman).

Evans, B. (2002) *The Training Ships of Liverpool* (Birkenhead: Countywise).

Evans, R. (1982) *The Fabrication of Virtue: English Prison Architecture, 1750–1840* (Cambridge: Cambridge University Press).

Fairfield, C. (1898) *Some Account of George William Wilshere, Baron Bramwell of Hever, and his Opinions* (London: Macmillan).

Fiddler, M. (2006) *The Penal Palimpsest: an exploration of prison spatiality*, Unpublished Ph.D. thesis, Keele University, UK.

Fiddler, M. (2007) 'Projecting the prison: the depiction of the uncanny in 'The Shawshank Redemption'', *Crime Media Culture*, 3 (2): 192–206.

Field, S. (2006) 'State, Citizen and Character in French Criminal Process' *Journal of Law and Society*, 33 (4): 522–46.

Finlay, F. (1969) *A Boy in Blue Jeans: A Woman's Story of her Delinquent Son* (London: Hale).

Finlay, F. (1971) *Boy in Prison: A Young Offender's Story of Grendon* (London: Hale).

Fisher, T. (1993) 'Permissiveness and the politics of morality', *Contemporary Record*, 7 (1): 149–65.

Fitzgerald, M. and Sim, J. (1982) *British Prisons*, Second Edition (Oxford: Basil Blackwell).

Forsythe, B. (1995) 'The Garland Thesis and the Origins of Modern English Prison Discipline: 1835 to 1939', *The Howard Journal*, 34 (3): 259–73.

Forsythe, W. J. (1987) *The Reform of Prisoners 1830–1900* (London: Croom Helm).

Forsythe, W. J. (1990) *Penal Discipline, Reformatory Projects and the English Prison Commission 1895–1939* (Exeter: Exeter University Press).

Foucault, M. (1970) *The Order of Things* (London: Tavistock).

Foucault, M. (1977) *Discipline and Punish: the Birth of the Prison*, trans. A. Sheridan (Harmondsworth: Penguin).

Foucault, M. (1978) 'Tales of Murder' in M. Foucault (ed.) *I, Pierre Rivière, Having Slaughtered my Mother, my Sister and my Brother...* (Harmondsworth: Penguin).

Foucault, M. (1980) 'Truth and Power' in C. Gordon (ed.) *Michel Foucault: Power/Knowledge, Selected Interviews and Other Writings, 1972–1977* (Brighton: Harvester Press).

Foucault, M. (1990) *The History of Sexuality*, trans. R. Hurley (Harmondsworth: Penguin).

Foucault, M. (1993) 'About the beginning of the hermeneutics of the self' (transcription of two lectures in Dartmouth on Nov. 17 and 24, 1980), by M. Blasius (ed.) *Political Theory*, 21 (2): 198–227.

Foucault, M. (2002a) 'Truth and Juridical Forms', in J. D. Faubion (ed.) *Power: Essential Works of Foucault 1954–1984, volume 3* (London: Penguin).

Foucault, M. (2002b) 'The Dangerous Individual', in J. D. Faubion (ed.) *Power: Essential Works of Foucault 1954–1984, volume 3* (London: Penguin).

Foucault, M. (2003) *Abnormal: Lectures at the Collège de France 1974–1975*, trans G. Burchell (New York: Picador).

Foucault, M. (2006) *History of Madness*, trans. J. Murphy and J. Khalfa (London: Routledge).

Fox, L. (1934) *The Modern English Prison* (London: Routledge).

Fox, L. (1952) *The English Prison and Borstal Systems* (London: Routledge & Kegan Paul).

Freedman, E (1981) *Their Sister's Keeper's: Women's Prison Reform in America 1830–1930* (Michigan: University of Michigan).

Fry, M. (1951) *Arms of the Law* (London: Victor Gollancz).

Gado, M. (2004) 'Stone upon stone: Sing Sing prison' [Online]: www.crimelibrary.com/notorious_murders/famous/sing_sing/index.html.

Garland, D. (1985) *Punishment and Welfare: A History of Penal Strategies* (Aldershot: Gower).

Garland, D. (1990) *Punishment and Modern Society* (Oxford: Clarendon Press).

Garland, D. (2001) 'The meaning of mass imprisonment', *Punishment & Society*, 3 (1): 5–7.

Garland, D. (2002) *The Culture of Control: Crime and Social Order in Contemporary Society* (Oxford: Oxford University Press).

Gatrell, V. A. C. (1994) *The Hanging Tree – Execution and the English People 1770–1868* (Oxford: Oxford University Press).

Giddens, A. (1984) *The Constitution of Society: An Outline of the Theory of Structuration* (Cambridge: Polity Press).

Gilbert, M. (1991) *Churchill: A Life* (London: Heinemann).

Godfrey, B. S., Lawrence, P. and Williams, C. A. (2008) *History and Crime* (London: Sage).

Goffman, E. (1961) *Asylums: Essays on the Social Situation of Mental Patients and Other Inmates* (Harmondsworth: Penguin).

Gordon, M. (1914) 'Female Inebriates', *British Journal of Inebriety*, 12 (2): 98–101.

Green, E., Hebron, S. and Woodward, D. (1987) 'Women, Leisure and Social Control' in J. Hanmer and M. Maynard (eds) *Women, Violence and Social Control* (London: Macmillan).

Greenwood, J. (1981) *The Seven Curses of London* (Oxford: Basil Blackwell, originally 1869).

Griffiths, A. (1904) *Fifty Years of Public Service* (London: Cassell).

Grigg, R. (2002) 'Educating Criminal and Destitute Children: Reformatory and Industrial schools in Wales, 1858–1914', *Welsh History Review*, 21 (2): 292–327.

Gura, P. F. (2001) *Buried from the World: Inside the Massachusetts State Prison, 1829–1831, The Memorandum Books of the Rev. Jared Curtis* (Boston: Massachusetts Historical Society).

Hadley, E. (1990) 'Natives in a Strange Land: The Philanthropic Discourse of Juvenile Emigration in Mid-Nineteenth Century England', *Victorian Studies*, xxxiii: 411–37.

Haldane, R. (1929) *Richard Burton Haldane: An Autobiography* (London: Hodder & Soughton).

Hall, G. (2002) 'Disorderly Acts: The Court Disposal of Liverpool's Inebriate Women', in A. Boran (ed.) *Crime: Fear or Fascination?* (Chester: Chester College).

Hall, P. (2002) *Cities of Tomorrow*, Third Edition (London: Blackwell).

Hammerton, A. J. (1992) *Cruelty and Companionship: Conflict in Nineteenth-Century Married Life* (London: Routledge).

Harding, C., Hines, B., Ireland, R. and Rawlings, P. (1985) *Imprisonment in England & Wales: A Concise History* (London: Croom Helm).

Harding, C. and Wilkin, L. (1988) 'The Dream of a Benevolent Mind: The Late Victorian Response to Inebriety', *Criminal Justice History*, 9:189–207.

Harrison, J. F. (2000) *Penal Reform and Prison Administration with Special Reference to the Example of Wakefield Prison, 1865–1895*, Unpublished Ph.D. thesis, University of Leeds, UK.

Harrison, J. F. C. (1990) *Late Victorian Britain 1875–1901* (London: Fontana).

Hastings, G. W. (1875) 'Repression of Crime', *TNAPSS*: 120–31.

Hattersley, R. (2004) *The Edwardians* (London: Little Brown).

Harris, R. (1989) *Murders and Madness: Medicine, Law and Society in the Fin de siècle* (Oxford: Clarendon).

Harris, R. (1994) 'Understanding the Terrorist: Anarchism, Medicine and Politics in Fin-de-siècle France' in M. Clark and C. Crawford (eds) *Legal Medicine in History* (Cambridge: Cambridge University Press).

Hawkins, G. (n.d) *Alec Paterson 20-XI–1884–7-XI–1947: An Appreciation* (Eastbourne: Sumfield & Day Ltd).

Hawkins, G. (1976) *The Prison: Policy and Practice* (Chicago: University of Chicago Press).

Hay, D. (1975) 'Property, authority and the criminal law' in D. Hay, P. Linebaugh, J. G. Rule, E. P. Thompson and C. Winslow (eds) *Albion's Fatal Tree: Crime and Society in Eighteenth Century England* (London: Allen Lane).

Hay, J. (1894) *A Gross Miscarriage of Justice: Seven Years Penal Servitude or the Value of a Royal Pardon* (London: Literary Revision Society).

Haythornwaite, J. A. (1993) *Scotland in the Nineteenth Century: An Analytical Bibliography of Material Relating to Scotland in Parliamentary Papers, 1800–1900* (Aldershot: Scholar Press).

Haywood, C. and Mac an Ghaill, M. (1996) 'Schooling Masculinities' in M. Mac an Ghaill (ed.) Understanding *Masculinities* (Buckingham: Open University Press).

Hearn, J. (1996) 'Is Masculinity Dead? A Critique of the Concept of Masculinity/ Masculinities' in M. Mac an Ghaill (ed.) *Understanding Masculinities* (Buckingham: Open University Press).

Heidensohn, F. (1985) *Women and Crime* (London: Macmillan).

Hendrick, H. (2006) 'Histories of Youth Crime and Justice', in B. Goldson and J. Muncie (eds) *Youth Crime and Justice* (London: Sage).

Hennessy, P. (1992) *Never Again: Britain 1945–51* (London: Jonathan Cape).

Henriques, U. R. Q. (1972) 'The Rise and Decline of the Separate System of Prison Discipline', *Past and Present*, 54, 61–93.

Highmore, A. (1822) *Philanthropia Metropolitana. A View of the Charitable Institutions Established in and Near London Chiefly During the Last Twelve Years* (London: Longman, Hurst, Rees, Orme & Brown).

HM Prison Service (2008) 'HMP Altcourse' [Online]: www.hmprisonservice. gov.uk/prisoninformation/locateaprison/prison.asp?id=225,15,2,15,225,0.

Hobhouse, S. and Brockway, A. F. (1922) *English Prisons To-day* (London: Longmans, Green & Co).

Hodgson, J. (2005) *French Criminal Justice* (Oxford: Hart).

Holland, H. S. and Carter, J. (1905) 'Commercial Morality', *Economic Review*, 16: 322–31.

Holmes, T. (1902) *Pictures and Problems from London Police Courts* (London: Arnold).

Holmes, T. (1908) *Known to the Police* (London: Thomas Nelson & Sons).

Holmes, T. (1912) *London's Underworld* (London: Dent).

Home Office (2003) *Prison Statistics England & Wales 2002* (London: TSO).

Horler, S. (1931) *Black Souls* (London: Jarrolds).

Horn, D. G. (2003) *The Criminal Body: Lombroso and the Anatomy of Deviance* (London: Routledge).

Horsley, J. (1887) *Jottings from Jail: Notes and Papers on Prison Matters* (London: T. Fisher Unwin).

Horsley, J. W. (1905) 'Crime and Gambling' in B. Seebohm-Rowntree (ed.) *Betting and Gambling: A National Evil* (London: Macmillan).

Horsley, J. W. (1913) *How Criminals Are Made And Prevented* (London: Fisher Unwin).

Houghton, W. E. (1957) *The Victorian Frame of Mind 1830-1870* (New Haven: Yale University Press).

Howe, A. (1994) *Punish and Critique: Towards a Feminist analysis of Penality* (London: Routledge).

Humphries, S. (1981) *Hooligans or Rebels? An Oral History of Working-Class Childhood and Youth, 1889–1939* (Oxford: Basil Blackwell).

Hunt, G., Mellor, J. and Turner, J. (1989) 'Wretched, Hatless and Miserably Clad: Women and the Inebriate Reformatories from 1900–1913', *British Journal of Sociology*, 40 (2): 244–70.

Hutter, B. and Williams, G. (1981) *Controlling Women* (London: Croom Helm).

Hutton, Rev. T. (1874) 'Causes and Prevention of Crime', *TNAPSS*: 311–13.

Hyland, J. (1994) *Yesterday's Answers: Development and Decline of Schools for Young Offenders* (London: Whiting & Birch).

Ignatieff, M. (1978) *A Just Measure of Pain – The Penitentiary in the Industrial Revolution* (London: Macmillan).

Ireland, R. W. (2007) *A Want of Order and Good Discipline: Rules, Discretion and the Victorian Prison* (Cardiff: University of Wales Press).

Jackson, B. S. (1988) *Law, Fact and Narrative Coherence* (Roby: Deborah Charles).

Jencks, C. (1993) *Heteropolis* (London: Academy Editions).

Jenkins, R. (2001) *Churchill* (London: Macmillan).

Jewkes, Y. (2002) *Captive Audience: Media, Masculinity and Power in Prisons* (Cullompton: Willan).

Jewkes, Y. (ed.) (2007) *Handbook on Prisons* (Cullompton: Willan).

Jewkes, Y. and Johnston, H. (eds) (2006) *Prison Readings: A Critical Introduction to Prison and Imprisonment* (Cullompton: Willan).

Jewkes, Y. and Johnston, H. (2007) 'The Evolution of Prison Architecture' in Y. Jewkes (ed.) *Handbook on Prisons* (Cullompton: Willan).

Jewkes, Y. and Johnston, H. (2008) ' *"Cavemen in an era of speed-of-light technology"': Historical and contemporary perspectives on communication within prisons'*, Unpublished Conference Paper, Delivered at Justice, Media and Public: Historical and Comparative Perspectives, Keele University, Feb 2008.

Johnston, H. (2004) *The transformations of imprisonment in a local context: a case-study of Shrewsbury in the nineteenth century*, Unpublished Ph.D. thesis, Keele University, UK.

Johnston, H (2006a) 'Working the Prison: Prison Officers in Nineteenth-Century Shrewsbury', *Prison Service Journal*, 168, 45–52.

Johnston, H. (2006b) '"Buried Alive": Representations of the Separate System in Victorian England' in P. Mason (ed.) *Captured by the Media: Prison discourse in popular culture* (Cullompton: Willan).

Johnston, H. (2008) 'Reclaiming the Criminal': The role and training of prison officers in England, 1877–1914, *Howard Journal of Criminal Justice*, 47 (3): 297–312.

Johnston, N. (2000) *Forms of Constraint – A History of Prison Architecture* (Chicago: University of Illinois Press).

Johnstone, G. (1996a) *Medical Concepts and Penal Policy* (London: Cavendish).

Johnstone, G. (1996b) 'From Vice to Disease? The Concepts of Dipsomania and Inebriety, 1860–1908', *Social and Legal Studies*, 5: 37–56.

Johnstone, G. J. and Ward, T. (forthcoming) *Law and Crime* (London: Sage).

Kelly, J. (1977) 'Did women have a Renaissance?' in R. Bridenthal and C. Koonz (eds) *Becoming Visible: Women in European History* (Boston: Houghton Mifflin).

Kennedy, H. (1993) *Eve Was Framed* (London: Vintage Books).

Kerr, N. (1880) *Inebriety: Its Etiology, Pathology, Treatment and Jurisprudence.* (London: H. K. Lewis).

King, P. (2006a) *Crime and the Law in England, 1750–1840* (Cambridge: Cambridge University Press).

King, P. (2006b) *Narratives of the Poor in Eighteenth-Century Britain – The Refuge for the Destitute* (London: Pickering & Chatto).

King, R. D. (1999) 'The rise and rise of supermax: an American solution in search of a problem?' *Punishment & Society* 1 (2): 163–186.

King, R. D. (2007) 'Imprisonment: some international comparisons and the need to revisit panopticism' in Y. Jewkes (ed.) *Handbook on Prisons* (Cullompton: Willan).

Laing, M. M. (1866) 'Finance, Frauds and Failures', *Temple Bar*, 17: 381–95.

Lancet (1919) 'The Psychopathic Criminal', *Lancet*, 1: 143–4, 432.

Lancet (1936) 'Delinquency as an Ailment', *Lancet*, 1: 1,082.

Lane, H. (1928) 'An Account of the Little Commonwealth at Evershot, Dorset', *Talks to Parents and Teachers* (London: George Allen & Unwin).

Langbein, J. H. (1977) *Torture and the Law of Proof: Europe and England in the Ancien Régime* (Chicago: University of Chicago Press).

Langbein, J. H. (2003) *The Origins of Adversarial Criminal Trial* (Oxford: Oxford University Press).

Lawes, L. E. (1932) *Twenty Thousand Years in Sing Sing* (London: Constable and Co Ltd).

Lee, J. (1885) *The Man They Could Not Hang: The Life Story of John Lee* (London: Arthur Pearson).

Lefebvre, H. (1974/5, 2003) 'The Other Parises' in S. Elden, E. Lebas and E. Kofman (eds) *Henri Lefebvre: Key Writings* (London: Continuum).

Lefebvre, H. (1991) *The Production of Space* (trans. D. Nicholson-Smith) (Oxford: Blackwell).

Leigh, J. (1941) *My Prison House* (London: Hutchinson & Co).

Lemke, T. (2002) 'Foucault, Governmentality and Critique' [online] www.thomaslemkeweb.de/publikationen/Foucault,%20Governmentality,%20and%20Critique%20IV–2.pdf.

Leps, M. (1992) *Apprehending the Criminal: The Production of Deviance in Nineteenth-Century Discourse* (Durham: Duke University Press).

Lettsom Elliot, H. (1869) 'What are the Principal Causes of Crime, considered from a Social Point of View?' *TNAPSS*: 324–37.

Levi, M. (1989) 'Fraudulent justice? Sentencing the business criminal' in P. Carlen and D. Cook (eds) *Paying for Crime* (Milton Keynes: Open University Press).

Linebaugh, P. (1975) 'The Tyburn Riot against the Surgeons' in D. Hay, P. Linebaugh, J. G. Rule, E. P. Thompson and C. Winslow (eds) *Albion's Fatal Tree: Crime and Society in Eighteenth-Century England* (London: Allen Lane).

Linebaugh, P. (1993) *The London Hanged: Crime and Civil Society in the Eighteenth Century* (London: Penguin).

Lloyd, A. (1995) *Doubly Deviant, Doubly Damned* (Harmondsworth: Penguin).

Lloyd Baker, T. B. (1889) *'War with Crime', Being a Selection of Reprinted Papers on Crime, Reformatories, etc, by the Late T. Barwick Lloyd-Baker, Esq.* (London: Longmans, Green, & Co).

Locker, J. P. (2004) *'This most pernicious species of crime': embezzlement in its public and private dimensions, c.1850–1930*, Unpublished PhD thesis, Keele University, UK.

Lynch, M. (2005) 'Supermax meets death row: legal struggles around the new punitiveness in the US' in J. Pratt, D. Brown, M. Brown, S. Hallsworth and W. Morrison (eds) *The New Punitiveness: Trends, Theories, Perspectives* (Cullompton: Willan).

Macartney, W. (1936) *Walls Have Mouths: A Record of Ten Years' Penal Servitude.* (London: Victor Gollancz).

MacLeod, R. (1967) 'The Edge of Hope: Social Policy and Chronic Alcoholism, 1870–1900', *Journal of the History of Medicine*, 22 (3): 215–45.

Mackay, R. D. (1995) *Mental Condition Defences in the Criminal Law* (Oxford: Oxford University Press).

Magarey, S. (1978) 'The Invention of Juvenile Delinquency in Early Nineteenth-century England', *Labour History* [Canberra], xxxiv, 11–27.

Magistrates Association and B.M.A. (1939) 'Medical Aspects of Crime' (report of a joint conference) *British Medical Journal* 2: 28–9.

Mahood, L. (1995) *Policing Gender, Class and Family: Britain, 1840–1940* (London: UCL Press).

Mannheim, H. (1939) *The Dilemma of Penal Reform* (London: George Allen & Unwin Ltd).

Manton, J. (1976) *Mary Carpenter and the Children of the Streets* (London: Heinemann).

Marwick, A. (1998) *The Sixties: Cultural Revolution in Britain, France, Italy and the United States, c.1958–1974* (Oxford: Oxford University Press).

Masterman, L (1964) 'Churchill: The Liberal Phase' *History Today*, 14 (11): 741–7 and 14 (12): 820–7.

Mathiesen, T. (1974) *The Politics of Abolition* (London: Robertson).

Maudsley, H. (1874) *Responsibility in Mental Disease* (London: Henry S. King).

May, M. (1973) 'Innocence and Experience: The Evolution of the Concept of Juvenile Delinquency in the Mid-Nineteenth Century', *Victorian Studies*, 17 (1), 7–29.

Mayer, J. A. (1983) 'Notes towards a Working Definition of Social Control in Historical Analysis' in S. Cohen and A. Scull (eds) *Social Control and the State* (Oxford: Martin Robertson).

Mayhew, H. (1861) *London Labour and the London Poor*, Volume 4 (London: Griffin).

Mayhew, H. and Binny, J. (1862) *The Criminal Prisons of London and Scenes of Prison Life* (London: Charles Griffin).

McConville, S. (1981) *A History of English Prison Administration Vol.1 1750–1877* (London: Routledge).

McConville, S. (1995) *English Local Prisons 1860–1900: Next Only to Death* (London: Routledge).

McConville, S. (1998) 'The Victorian Prison, 1865–1965' in N. Morris and D. J. Rothman (eds) *The Oxford History of the Prison – The Practice of Punishment in Western Society* (New York: Oxford University Press).

McCook Weir, J. (1885) *Prison Despotism: A Personal Narrative* (London: The National Publishing Co).

McGowen, R. (1983) 'The Image of Justice and Reform of the Criminal Law in Early Nineteenth Century England', *Buffalo Law Review*, 32: 89–125.

McGowen, R. (1986) 'A Powerful Sympathy: Terror, the Prison, and Humanitarian Reform in Early Nineteenth Century Britain', *Journal of British Studies*, 25: 312–34.

McGowen, R. (1990) 'Getting to Know the Criminal Class in Nineteenth-Century England', *Nineteenth Century Contexts*, 14, 1: 33–54.

McGowen, R. (1994) 'Civilising Punishment: The End of Public Execution in England', *Journal of British Studies*, 33: 257–82.

McGowen, R. (2000) 'Revisiting *The Hanging Tree*: Gatrell on Emotion and History', *British Journal of Criminology*, 40 (1): 1–13.

McNay, L. (1992) *Foucault and Feminism* (Cambridge: Polity Press).

Measor, C. P. (1861) *The Convict Service* (London: Robert Hardwicke).

Measor, C. P. (1864) *Criminal Correction* (London: William Macintosh).

Medico-Psychological Association (1895) Annual Meeting: Report of the Committee on Criminal Responsibility', *Journal of Mental Science* 41: 744–7.

Medico-Psychological Association (1896) 'Report of the Criminal Responsibility Committee', *Journal of Mental Science* 42: 863–6.

Mellor, J., Hunt, G., Turner, J. and Rees, L. (1986) 'Prayers and Piecework: Inebriate Reformatories in England at the End of the Nineteenth Century', *Drogalkohol*, 3: 92–206.

Melossi, D. and Pavarini, M. (1981) *The Prison and the Factory* (London: Macmillan).

Mercier, C. A. (1904) 'Recent Medico-Legal Cases', *Journal of Mental Science* 50: 588–95.

Mercier, C. A. (1905) *Criminal Responsibility* (Oxford: Clarendon).

Mills, S. (2003) *Michel Foucault* (London: Routledge).

Moran, R. (1981) *Knowing Right from Wrong: The Insanity Defence of Daniel McNaughtan* (London: Collier Macmillan).

Morier Evans, D. (1859) *Facts, Failures and Frauds: Revelations Financial, Mercantile, Criminal* (London: Groombridge & Sons).

Morris, R. J. (1979) *Class and Class Consciousness in the Industrial Revolution 1780–1850* (Basingstoke: Macmillan).

Morris, T. (1988) 'British Criminology: 1935–48', *British Journal of Criminology*, 28 (2): 150–64.

Morrissey, B. (2003) *When Women Kill: Questions of Agency and Subjectivity* (London: Routledge).

Morrison, B. (2005) *Ordering Disorderly Women: Female Drunkenness in England c. 1870–1920*, Unpublished Ph.D. thesis, Keele University, UK.

Morrison, W. D. (1891) *Crime and its Causes* (London: Swan Sonnenschien).

Mullins, C. (1948) *Fifteen Years' Hard Labour* (London: Gollancz).

Nash, M. D. (1987) *The Settler Handbook* (Cape Town: Chameleon Press).

Neill, A. S. (1973) *Neill! Neill! Orange peel! A Personal View of Ninety Years* (London: Weidenfeld & Nicolson).

Nellis, M. (1996) 'John Galsworthy's *Justice*', *British Journal of Criminology*, 36 (1): 61–84.

Nevill, W. (1903) *Penal Servitude* (London: William Heinemann).

Newsome, D. (1997) *The Victorian World Picture: Perceptions and Introspections in an Age of Change* (London: Murray).

Nicholl, D. (1897) *The Ghosts of Chelmsford Gaol* (Sheffield: Publisher Unknown).

Nicolson, D. (1874) 'The Morbid Psychology of Criminals, Part 4: Prison Discipline as a Test of Mind', *Journal of Mental Science*, 20: 167–85.

'No. 7' (1903) *Twenty Five Years in Seventeen Prisons: The life story of an ex-convict* (London: F. E. Robinson & Co).

Norrie, A. (2001) *Crime, Reason and History* (Second Edition) (London: Weidenfled & Nicolson).

Nye, R. (1984) *Crime, Madness and Politics in Modern France* (Princeton: Princeton University Press).

O' Brien, P. (1982) *The Promise of Punishment: Prisons in Nineteenth-Century France* (Princeton: Princeton University Press).

O'Donovan, K. (1985) *Sexual Divisions in Law* (London: Weidenfeld & Nicolson).

Offer, J. (2006) *An Intellectual History of British Society Policy: Idealism versus Non-Idealism* (Bristol: Policy Press).

One Who Has Endured It (1877) *Five Years Penal Servitude* (London: Richard Bentley).

One Who Has Suffered (1882) *Revelations of Prison Life* (London: Potter).

One Who Has Tried Them (1881) *Her Majesty's Prisons: Their Effects and Defects* (London: Sampson Low).

Oppenheim, J. (1991) *'Shattered Nerves': Doctors, Patients and Depression in Modern England* (New York: Oxford University Press).

Pallot, J. (2005) 'Russia's penal peripheries: space, place and penalty in Soviet and post- Soviet-Russia', *Transactions of the Institute of British Geographers*, 30: 98–112.

Panetta, R. (1986) 'The design and construction of Sing Sing prison, 1825–1828', *The Westchester Historian*, 62 (2): 35–55.

Parr, R. (1908) 'Alcoholism and Cruelty to Children', *British Journal of Inebriety*, 6 (2): 77–81.

Pashukanis, E. (1980) *Pashukanis* (London: Academic Press).

Paterson, A. (1911) *Across the Bridges or Life by the South London Riverside* (London: Edward Arnold).

Peddie, A. (1861) 'Dipsomania: A proper subject for legal provision', *TNAPSS*, 1862: 538–46.

Pelling, H. (1976) *A History of British Trade Unionism*, Third Edition (Harmondsworth: Penguin).

Pentonville from within (1902) *Pentonville Prison from within* (London: Greening and Co).

Penwarden, M. R. (1980) *'Juvenile Delinquency and its Treatment in Victorian London, with Special Reference to the Parkhurst Experiment'*, Unpublished MSc. Thesis, University of Wales, Swansea, UK.

Peterson, V.W. (1947) 'Why Honest People Steal', *Journal of Criminal Law and Criminology*, 38 (2): 94–103.

Piacentini, L. (2004) *Surviving Russian Prisons: punishment, economy and politics in transition* (Cullompton: Willan).

Pick, D. (1996) *Faces of Degeneration: A European Disorder, c.1848–c.1918* (Cambridge: Cambridge University Press).

Pinchbeck, I. and Hewitt, M. (1973) *Children in England Society, Volume II, From the Eighteenth Century to the Children Act 1948* (London: Routledge & Kegan Paul).

Piper, L. (1991) *Murder by Gaslight* (London: O'Mara).

Pitch, T. (1995) 'Feminist politics, crime law and order in Italy' in N. H. Rafter and F. Heidensohn (eds) *International Feminist Perspectives in Criminology* (Buckingham: Open University Press).

Phelan, J. (1940) *Jail Journey* (London: Secker & Warburg).

Platt, A. M. (1969) *The Child Savers: The Invention of Delinquency* (Chicago: University of Chicago Press).

Pratt, J. (1997) *Governing the Dangerous: Dangerousness, Law, and Social Change* (Sydney: Federation Press).

Pratt, J. (1999) 'Norbert Elias and the Civilized Prison', *British Journal of Sociology*, 50 (2): 271–96.

Pratt, J. (2002) *Punishment and Civilization: Penal Tolerance and Intolerance in Modern Society* (London: Sage).

Pratt, J. (2004) 'The acceptable prison: official discourse, truth and legitimacy in the nineteenth century', in G. Gilligan and J. Pratt (eds) *Crime, Truth and Justice: Official inquiry, discourse and knowledge* (Cullompton: Willan).

Pratt, J., Brown, D., Brown, M., Hallsworth, S. and Morrison, W. (eds) (2005) *The New Punitiveness: Trends, Theories, Perspectives* (Cullompton: Willan).

Pratt, J. (2006) 'The Dark Side of Paradise: Explaining New Zealand's History of High Imprisonment', *British Journal of Criminology*, 46 (4): 541–60.

Pratt, J. (2007) *Penal Populism* (Abingdon: Routledge).
Price, B. (1914) 'The Inebriate's Derelict Problem in Relation to Men', *British Journal of Inebriety*, 12 (2): 101–2.
Priestley, P. (1985) *Victorian Prison Lives: English Prison Biography, 1830–1914* (London: Methuen).
Priestley, P. (1989) *Jail Journeys: The English Prison Experience 1918–1990* (London: Routledge).
Prison Reform Trust (2008a) 'Prison population hits new all time high: 82,319' [Online]: www.prisonreformtrust.org.uk/index.asp?id=1.
Prison Reform Trust (2008b) 'Overcrowding' [Online]: www.prisonreformtrust. org.uk/subsection.asp?id=442.
Prison Reform Trust (2008c) 'Appalling conditions at Pentonville Prison' [Online]: www.prisonreformtrust.org.uk/subsection.asp?id=1087.
Quennell, P. (ed.) (1983) *London's Underworld* (extracts from the work of Henry Mayhew) (London: Bracken).
Radzinowicz, L. and Hood, R. (1990) *A History of English Criminal Law and its Administration from 1750, Volume 5: The Emergence of Penal Policy* (Oxford: Clarendon).
Rafter, N. H. (1983) 'Chastising the Unchaste: Social Control Functions of a Women's Reformatory, 1894–1931' in S. Cohen and A. Scull (eds) *Social Control and the State* (Oxford: Martin Robertson).
Rafter, N. H. (1985) *Partial Justice: Women in State Prisons 1800–1935* (Boston: Northeastern University Press).
Rafter, N. H. (1997) *Creating Born Criminals* (Urbana: University of Illinois Press).
"Red Collar Man" (1937) *Chokey* (London: Victor Gollancz).
Renton, A. W. (1890) 'The Legal Test of Lunacy', *Law Quarterly Review*, 317–19.
Rich, Lieut. Col. C. E. F. (1932) *Recollections of a Prison Governor* (London: Hurst & Blackett).
Richards, E. (2004) *Britannia's Children: Emigration from England, Scotland, Wales and Ireland since 1600* (London: Hambledon).
Rimmer, J. (1986) *Yesterday's Naughty Children: Training Ship, Girls' Reformatory and Farm School: A History of the Liverpool Reformatory Association founded in 1855* (Manchester: Richardson).
Riot, P. (1978) 'The Parallel Lives of Pierre Rivière' in M. Foucault (ed.) *I, Pierre Rivière, Having Slaughtered my Mother, my Sister and my Brother...* (Harmondsworth: Penguin).
Robb, G. (1992) *White-Collar Crime in Modern England: Financial Fraud and Business Morality 1845–1929* (Cambridge: Cambridge University Press).
Roberts, D. (1986) 'The Scandal at Birmingham Borough Gaol 1853: A Case for Penal Reform, *The Journal of Legal History*, 7, 315–40.
Rose, G. (1961) *The Struggle for Penal Reform: The Howard League and its Predecessors* (London: Stevens).
Rose, G. (1967) *Schools for Young Offenders* (London: Tavistock Publications).
Rose, N. (1985) *The Psychological Complex* (London: Routledge & Kegan Paul).
Rossa, J. (1872/1991) *Irish Rebels in English Prisons* (Ireland: Brandon).
Rothman, D. J. (1971) *The Discovery of the Asylum* (Boston: Little, Brown & Co).
Rothman, D. J. (1990) *The Discovery of the Asylum* (Second edition) (Boston: Little, Brown & Co).

Rotman, E. (1995) 'The Failure of Reform – United States, 1865–1965' in N. Morris and D. J. Rothman (eds) *The Oxford Handbook of the Prison* (Oxford: Oxford University Press).

Ruck, S. K. (1951) *Paterson on Prisons* (London: Muller).

Ruggles-Brise, E. (1921) *The English Prison System* (London: Macmillan & Co).

Rusche, G. and Kirchheimer, O. (1939) *Punishment and Social Structure* (New York: Columbia University Press).

Russell, C. E. B. (1910) *Young Gaol-Birds* (London: Macmillan).

Rutherford, A. (1984) *Prisons and the Process of Justice: The Reductionist Challenge* (London: Heinemann).

Sargant, W. (1967) *The Unquiet Mind* (London: Heinemann).

Saunders, J. (1986) 'Warwickshire Magistrates and Prison Reform, 1840–1875', *Midland History*, XI, 79–99.

Scott, J. (1990) *Domination and the Arts of Resistance: Hidden Transcripts* (New Haven: Yale University Press).

Scull, A. (1993) *The Most Solitary of Afflictions: Madness and Society in Britain, 1700–1900* (New Haven: Yale University Press).

Segal, L. (1990) *Slow Motion* (London: Virago).

Shapiro, B. J. (1991) *'Beyond Reasonable Doubt' and 'Probable Cause': Historical Perspectives on the Anglo-American Law of Evidence* (Berkeley: University of California Press).

Shapiro, B. J. (2000) *A Culture of Fact: England 1550–1720* (Ithaca: Cornell University Press).

Shore, H. (1999) *Artful Dodgers: Youth and Crime in Early Nineteenth Century London* (Woodbridge: Royal Historical Society).

Shore, H. (2002) 'Transportation, Penal Ideology and the Experience of Juvenile Offenders in England and Australia in the Early Nineteenth Century', *Crime, Histoire & Sociétés / Crime, History & Societies*, 6, 81–102.

Sim, J. (1990) *Medical Power in Prisons: The Prison Medical Service in England, 1774–1989* (Milton Keynes: Open University Press).

Simmons, E. J. (1974) *Memoirs of a Station Master* (Bath: Adams & Dart, originally 1879).

Simmons, H. G. (1978) 'Explaining Social Policy: the English Mental Deficiency Act of 1913', *Journal of Social History* 11: 388–403.

Slobogin, C. (1998) 'Psychiatric Evidence in Criminal Trials: to Junk or Not to Junk?' *William & Mary Law Review*, 40: 1–56.

Smalley, G. W. (1890) *London Letters*, Volume 2 (London: Macmillan).

Smart, C and Smart, B. (eds) (1978) 'An introduction' in *Women, Sexuality and Social Control* (London: Routledge & Kegan Paul).

Smart, C. (1995) *Law, Crime and Sexuality* (London: Sage).

Smith, D. (1982) 'The Demise of Transportation: Mid-Victorian Penal Policy', *Criminal Justice History* 3: 21–45.

Simon, J. (1995) 'They died with their boots on: the boot camp and the limits of modern penality', *Social Justice*, 22 (2): 25–48.

Simon, J. (2000) 'From Big House to the Warehouse: Rethinking Prisons and State Government in the 20th Century', *Punishment & Society*, 2 (2): 213–34.

Smith, M. (2001) 'Repetition and difference: Lefebvre, Le Corbusier and modernity's (im)moral landscape', *Ethics, Place and Environment*, 4 (1): 31–44.

Smith, M. H. (1922) 'The Medical Examination of Delinquents', *Journal of Mental Science*, 68: 254–62.

Smith, R. (1981) *Trial by Medicine* (Edinburgh: Edinburgh University Press).

Smith, R. (1985) 'Expertise and Causal Attribution in Deciding between Crime and Mental Disorder', *Social Studies of Science* 15: 67–98.

Smith, R. P. (1901) 'A Case of Epileptic Homicide', *Journal of Mental Science*, 42: 528–40.

Soja, E. (1996) *Thirdspace: Journeys to Los Angeles and other real-and-imagined places* (Oxford: Blackwell).

Souttar, R. (1904) *Alcohol: Its Place and Power in Legislation* (London: Hodder & Stoughton).

Sparks, R. (1961) *Burglar to the Nobility: The Autobiography of Ruby Sparks* (London: Secker & Warburg).

Spierenburg, P. (1984) *The Spectacle of Suffering* (Cambridge: Cambridge University Press).

Spierenburg, P. (1991) *The Prison Experience: Disciplinary institutions and their inmates in early modern Europe* (New Brunswick: Rutgers University Press).

Spierenburg, P. (2005) 'The Origins of the Prison' in C. Emsley (ed.) *The Persistent Prison* (London: Francis Boutle).

Springhall, J. (1986) *Coming of Age: Adolescence in Britain, 1860–1960* (Dublin: Gill & Macmillan).

Springhall, J. (1987) 'Building character in the British Boy: the attempt to extend Christian manliness to working-class adolescents, 1889–1914' in J. A. Mangan and J. Walvin (eds) *Manliness and Morality* (Manchester: Manchester University Press).

Stack, J. A. (1979) 'Deterrence and Reformation in Early Victorian Social Policy: The Case of Parkhurst Prison, 1838–1864', *Historical Reflections*, 6, 387–404.

Stack, J. A. (1994) 'Reformatory and Industrial Schools and the Decline of Child Imprisonment in Mid-Victorian England and Wales', *History of Education*, 23 (1) 59–73.

Stedman Jones, G. (1983) 'Class Expression versus Social Control? A Critique of Recent Trends in the Social History of "Leisure"' in S. Cohen and A. Scull (eds) *Social Control and the State* (Oxford: Martin Robertson).

Stephen, J. F. (1863) *A General View of the Criminal Law of England* (First edition) (London: Macmillan).

Stevens, R. (1979) *Law and Politics: the House of Lords as a Judicial Body, 1800–1976* (London: Weidenfeld & Nicolson).

Stockdale, E. (1976) 'The Rise of Joshua Jebb, 1837–1850', *British Journal of Criminology* 16 (2): 164–70.

Stockdale, E. (1977) *A Study of Bedford Prison, 1660–1877* (Chichester: Phillimore)

Strange, C. (2003) 'Masculinities, Intimate Femicide and the Death Penalty in Australia 1890–1920', *British Journal of Criminology*, 48, 310–39.

Stutfield, H. (1898) 'The Higher Rascality', *The National Review*, 31: 75–86.

Sudjic, D. (1993) *The 100 Mile City* (Orlando: Harcourt).

Sutherland, E. H. (1949) *White Collar Crime* (New York: Holt, Reinhart & Winston).

Sykes, G. M. (1958) *Society of Captives: A Study of a Maximum Security Prison* (Princeton: Princeton University Press).

Symons, J. C. (1855) 'On Juvenile Crime as it affects Commerce, and the best means of Repressing it', *Journal of the Society of Arts*, III.

Taruffo, M. (2003) 'Rethinking the Standards of Proof', *American Journal of Comparative Law* 51: 659–77.

Taylor, A. (1969) 'The Statesman' in A. Taylor, R. Rhodes-James, J. Plumb, B. Liddell-Hart and A. Storr (eds) *Churchill: Four Faces and the Man* (London: Allen Lane).

Ticket of Leave Man (1879) *Convict Life; or Revelations concerning Convicts and Convict Prisons* (London: Wyman & Sons).

Thomas, J. E. (1972) *The English Prison Officer since 1850: A Study in Conflict* (London: Routledge & Kegan Paul).

Thomas, J. E. (1978) '"A Good Man for Gaoler?" – Crisis, Discontent and the Prison staff' in J. C. Freeman (ed.) *Prisons, Past and Future* (London: Heinemann).

Thomas, J. E. and Pooley, R. (1980) *The Exploding Prison: Prison riots and the case of Hull* (London: Junction Books).

Thomson, M. (1998) *The Problem of Mental Deficiency: Eugenics, Democracy and Social Policy in Britain, c.1870–1959* (Oxford: Oxford University Press).

Tod, Miss. (1881) 'Prison Mission and Inebriates' Home', *The Englishwoman's Review*, 12, July: 247–52.

Tomlinson, H. M. (1978) "Prison Palaces': A Re-appraisal of Early Victorian Prisons, 1835–77', *Bulletin of the Institute of Historical Research* 51: 60–71.

Tomlinson, H. M. (1981) 'Penal Servitude 1846-1865: A System in Evolution' in V. Bailey (ed.) *Policing and Punishment in Nineteenth Century Britain* (London: Croom Helm).

Tooley, S. (1901) 'Lady Henry Somerset at Duxhurst: Restoring Woman's Ideal', *Sunday Strand*, 4: 9–25.

Tosh, J. (2004) 'Hegemonic Masculinity and the History of Gender' in S. Dudlink, K. Hagermann and J. Tosh (eds) *Masculinities in Politics and War* (Manchester: Manchester University Press).

Train, A. (1907) *The Prisoner at the Bar: Sidelights on the Administration of Criminal Justice* (London: Werner Laurie).

Valverde, M. (1998) *Diseases of the Will: Alcohol and the Dilemmas of Freedom* (Cambridge: Cambridge University Press).

Van Oss, S. F. (1898) 'The 'Limited-Company' Craze', *The Nineteenth Century*, 43: 731–44.

Vogler, R. (1990) 'Magistrates' Courts and the Struggle for Local Democracy, 1886–1986', in C. Sumner (ed.) *Censure, Politics and Criminal Justice* (Milton Keynes: Open University Press).

Vogler, R. (2005) *A World View of Criminal Procedure* (Aldershot: Ashgate).

Wacquant, L. (2001) 'Deadly symbiosis: when ghetto and prison meet and mesh', *Punishment and Society*, 3 (1): 95–134.

Wacquant, L. (2002) 'From slavery to mass incarceration – rethinking the 'race question' in the US', *New Left Review*, 13: 41–60.

Wacquant, L. (2005) 'The great leap backward: incarceration in America from Nixon to Clinton' in J. Pratt, D. Brown, M. Brown, S. Hallsworth, and W. Morrison (eds) *The New Punitiveness: Trends, Theories, Perspectives* (Cullompton: Willan).

Wagner, G. (1982) *Children of the Empire* (London: Weidenfeld & Nicolson).

Walker, N. (1968) *Crime and Insanity in England,* vol. 1. (Edinburgh: Edinburgh University Press).

Walker, N. and McCabe, S. (1973) *Crime and Insanity in England,* vol. 2. (Edinburgh: Edinburgh University Press).

Walmsley, R. (2006) *World Prison Population List* (Seventh Edition) (London: International Centre for Prison Studies).

Ward, T. (1996) *Psychiatry and Criminal Responsibility in England, 1843–1939,* Unpublished PhD thesis, De Montfort University, UK.

Ward, T. (1997) 'Law, Common Sense and the Authority of Science: Expert Witnesses and Criminal Insanity in England, ca. 1840–1940', *Social & Legal Studies,* 6 (3), 343–62.

Ward, T. (1998) 'Law's Truth, Lay Truth and Medical Science: Three Case Studies' in H. Reece (ed.) *Law and Science* (Oxford: Oxford University Press).

Ward, T. (1999) 'Psychiatric Evidence and Judicial Fact-Finding', *International Journal of Evidence & Proof* 3: 180–94.

Ward, T. (2001) 'Observers, Advisers or Authorities? Experts, Juries and Criminal Responsibility in Historical Perspective', *Journal of Forensic Psychiatry,* 12: 105–22.

Ward, T (2002) 'A Terrible Responsibility: Murder and the Insanity Defence in England, 1908–39', *International Journal of Law and Psychiatry,* 25 (4): 361–77.

Warren, A. (1987) 'Popular Manliness: Baden-Powell, Scouting and the Development of Manly Character' in J. A. Mangan and J. Walvin (eds) *Manliness and Morality* (Manchester: Manchester University Press).

Watson, J. (1896) 'Reformatory and Industrial Schools', *Journal of the Royal Statistical Society,* 59 (2) 162–81.

Watson, J. A. F. (1939) *Meet the Prisoner* (London: Jonathan Cape).

Watson, J. A. F. (1942) *The Child and the Magistrate* (London: Jonathan Cape).

Watson, S. (1988) *'The Moral Imbecile',* Unpublished Ph.D. thesis, University of Lancaster, UK.

Watson, S. (1994) 'Malingerers, the "Weak-minded" Criminal and the "Moral Imbecile": How the Prison Medical Officer became an Expert in Mental Deficiency, 1880–1930' in M. Clark and C. Crawford (eds) *Legal Medicine in History* (Cambridge: Cambridge University Press).

Webb, S. and B. (1963) *English Prisons under Local Government* (London: Frank Cass).

Weymans, W. (2004) 'Michel de Certeau and the limits of historical representation', *History and Theory,* 43: 161–78.

Whiting, J. R. S. (1975) *Prison Reform in Gloucestershire 1776–1820* (Chichester: Phillimore).

Wiener, M. (1990) *Reconstructing the Criminal: Culture, Law and Policy in England 1830–1914* (Cambridge: Cambridge University Press).

Wiener, M. (1995) 'The Health of Prisoners and the Two Faces of Benthamism' in R. Creese, W. F. Bynum and J. Bearn (eds) *The Health of Prisoners: Historical Essays* (Amsterdam and Atlanta, GA: Rodopi).

Wilcott, S. and Griffin, C. (1996) 'Men, Masculinity and the Challenge of Long-term Unemployment' in M. Mac an Ghaill (ed.) *Understanding Masculinities* (Buckingham: Open University Press).

Wilczynski, A. (1991) 'Images of Women Who Kill Their Infants: The Mad and the Bad', *Women and Criminal Justice,* 2 (2) 71–88.

Wilde, O. (1897) 'De Profundis', reprinted in O. Wilde (1999) *The Soul of Man and Prison Writings* (Oxford: Oxford University Press).

Wilde, O. (1898a) 'The Ballad of Reading Gaol', reprinted in O. Wilde (1999) *The Soul of Man and Prison Writings* (Oxford: Oxford University Press).

Wilde, O. (1898b) 'Wilde's second post-prison letter to the Daily Chronicle', reprinted in O. Wilde (1999) *The Soul of Man and Prison Writings* (Oxford: Oxford University Press).

Wills, A. (2005a) 'Delinquency, masculinity and citizenship 1950–1970', *Past and Present*, 187, 157–85.

Wills, A. (2005b) *Juvenile Delinquency, Residential Institutions, and the Permissive Shift, England 1950–1970*, Unpublished PhD thesis, University of Cambridge, UK.

Wills, W. D. (1964) *Homer Lane. A Biography* (London: George Allen & Unwin).

Wilson, D. (2006) 'Social Control' in E. McLaughlin and J. Muncie (eds) *The Sage Dictionary of Criminology* (London: Sage).

Wilson, G. B. (1940) *Alcohol and the Nation* (London: Nicholson & Watson Ltd).

Wilson, S. (2000) 'In Defence of Respectability: Financial Crime, the 'High Art' Criminal and the Language of the Courtroom 1850–1880' in I. Inkster, C. Griffin, J. Hill and J. Rowbotham (eds) *The Golden Age: Essays in British Social and Economic History, 1850–1870* (Aldershot: Ashgate).

Wilson, S. (2003) 'Moral Cancers: Fraud and Respectable Crime' in J. Rowbotham and K. Stevenson (eds) *Behaving Badly: Social Panic and Moral Outrage – Victorian and Modern Parallels* (Aldershot: Ashgate).

Wontner, T. (1831) *Old Bailey Experience: Criminal Jurisprudence and the Actual Working of our Penal Code of Laws: also an Essay on Prison Discipline, to which is added a History of the Crimes Committed by Offenders in the Present Day* (Unknown: London).

Worrall, A. (1990) *Offending Women* (London: Routledge).

Wright, T. (1997) *Out of Place: Homeless Mobilizations, Subcities, and Contested Landscapes* (Albany: State University of New York Press).

Young, J. (1999) *The Exclusive Society* (London: Sage).

Young, R. (1970) *Mind, Brain and Adaptation in the Nineteenth Century* (Oxford: Clarendon).

Zedner, L. (1991) *Women, Crime and Custody in Victorian England* (Oxford: Clarendon).

Index